STOCKBROKING TODAY

STOCKBROKING TODAY

J. DUNDAS HAMILTON

WITH A FOREWORD BY

HAROLD WINCOTT

MACMILLAN

First edition 1968
Reprinted 1971

Published by
MACMILLAN AND CO LTD
London and Basingstoke
Associated companies in New York Toronto
Dublin Melbourne Johannesburg and Madras

SBN 333 08551 5 (hard cover)

Printed in Great Britain by
REDWOOD PRESS LIMITED
Trowbridge & London

TO
F. W. R. D.

CONTENTS

CONTENTS

FOREWORD

THE shelves of my bookcase are full of books about The Stock Exchange. Almost all of them are descriptive, intended more for the layman than for the professional. Inevitably, therefore, they tend to be superficial rather than penetrating and constructive.

This book by my old friend Dundas Hamilton strikes a new and to my mind very topical note. Britain, plagued by a succession of no fewer than seven severe economic crises since 1945, is now in a mood to examine the structure of her industry and commerce more critically than ever before. The little Neddies are doing the job in industry; the Prices and Incomes Board has examined or is examining our building societies, our banks and our solicitors. Age-old practices and habits and structures are being questioned. This is often an uncomfortable business for those with preconceived ideas, but it can be salutary.

The great merit of Dundas Hamilton's book seems to me to be that here we have a detached and impartial survey and analysis of what is, as Mr. Hamilton himself points out, at one and the same time an industry and a profession. The Stock Exchange, which I have been observing and commenting upon now for nearly forty years, has, to its credit, never believed itself to be perfect, has always been engaged in a process of continuing reform. But it has always insisted that the reforms should come from within.

The Stock Exchange itself should therefore welcome Mr. Hamilton's ideas, for they are essentially practical and born of long experience of The Stock Exchange and stockbroking and the needs of the clients. But the community at large should welcome his ideas too. For without an efficient Stock Exchange and modern, sophisticated stockbrokers, the capital market on which British industry depends cannot do its proper job.

That capital market is, in fact, the envy of many of our competitors in Europe and elsewhere. If it is to maintain the lead it has established, it will have to take good account of the constructive suggestions in which Mr. Hamilton's book abounds.

HAROLD WINCOTT
Investors Chronicle and Stock Exchange Gazette

INTRODUCTION

WHEN I was first asked to write a book under the title *Stockbroking Today*, it seemed to me that three principal questions required to be answered:

What was the purpose of the book?
For whom was it to be written?
What, if any, were my own qualifications for undertaking the task?

The purpose was perfectly clear. Many books have been written about investment and about the operation of stock exchanges, both in the United Kingdom and throughout the world, but none about the actual day-to-day work in a stockbroker's office, and very little seems to have been published to erase the pre-war image of the typical stockbroker. In this book I have endeavoured to lift the veil a little and to show that the efficient stockbroker of today must first and foremost be a technician, expert in his trade or a specialist in part of it.

The readership is intended to cover almost all those interested in investment, but particularly the student who is considering stockbroking as a career. It is proposed in the future that new entrants to all Federated Stock Exchanges shall be required to pass an examination. This book is not intended to provide the answers to all the technical questions set out in the draft syllabus. It is designed, however, to give a background to the profession of stockbroking, bridging the gap between a purely technical manual and a general study of the subject.

Finally, my own qualifications for writing on this subject are lamentably few. Almost exactly twenty-one years ago I became a clerk in a small firm of stockbrokers, whose total numbers amounted to eight, equally divided between partners and staff. It was an excellent grounding, for everyone was forced to cover almost all the facets of the business. Five years later I left to join a medium-sized firm, which later amalgamated to become a much larger and more decentralised organisation. I have been fortunate, therefore, in gaining experience from firms of all sizes and recently from the particular problems of management which develop with growth in the size of an organisation.

I must emphasise, however, that the opinions I have expressed are entirely my own and must not be construed as defining the policy of my firm or the views of my partners.

Many friends have been kind enough to read the various drafts of the typescript and suggest amendments, in particular the officers of the Council of The Stock Exchange, London, including the Public Relations Department, the Quotations Department, and the House Administration Department; partners in firms of jobbers and chartered accountants; and those in charge of the special departments of my own firm. In addition the officials of the various overseas stock exchanges have kindly provided the information on which Appendices 7 to 23 are based. To all these I express my sincere thanks and appreciation for the help and advice which they have so generously given.

J. D. H.

July 1967

PART ONE

STOCKBROKING TODAY

I

THE INDUSTRY AND
THE PROFESSION

A STOCK EXCHANGE exists to provide a market-place where
borrowers who require capital can be satisfied by lenders who
require an outlet for their funds. The essential requirement is
that of liquidity, so that an owner of securities can turn them
freely and speedily into cash, and so that a potential investor
can equally freely and speedily become the owner of securities.

Stockbrokers in the United Kingdom perform three separate
functions. Initially, they make arrangements for the quotation
of the stock or shares of a company so that dealings can take
place in the market. Secondly, they act as agents in the buying
and selling of securities, since no outside investor can deal
through the medium of a stock exchange without using the
services of a stockbroker. And finally, they act as advisers
to their clients in the selection and administration of their
investments.

It is the last function, the service of the client, that turns
stockbroking from being purely an industry into a profession.
It is the position of trust in which they are placed, acting as
both agent and adviser, that limits their activities and oddly
enough throws them open to criticism from the people whose
interests they are endeavouring to protect.

But first it is important to look at the industry as one would
look at any other industry in the financial sector, such as
banking, hire-purchase or insurance.

Stockbroking in the United Kingdom is so dominated by the
size and importance of The Stock Exchange, London, that
many members of the public are unaware that any other
exchanges exist. In fact London is the heart of a vast stockbroking network with stock exchanges in twenty-one of the
major towns and cities, and about 100 firms of stockbrokers
in other provincial areas. Firms in London have connections

with their correspondents in the provinces by telephone or telex, and sometimes by direct teleprinter or telephone line, so that price movements in one centre are almost instantaneously reflected in other exchanges throughout the country.

In the same way the London Stock Exchange is only one in a much larger global network. Most people are familiar with the famous New York Stock Exchange on Wall Street, but this is only the largest of three stock exchanges in New York and sixteen stretching across the American continent to Honolulu, Los Angeles and San Francisco. At the end of 1966 there were eleven stock exchanges in Australia, six in Canada and nine in Japan. New stock exchanges are being formed as one country after another reaches a state of modern development. For example, the Lagos Stock Exchange was opened in Nigeria in 1961.

Stockbroking, therefore, is an international industry, and the importance of London as a financial centre is emphasised by the number of branch offices of overseas firms which are maintained there. No less than twenty firms of American stockbrokers and eleven Canadian firms maintain London offices. In 1963 the four leading Japanese firms opened branches in London.

Membership of a stock exchange in the United Kingdom differs materially from that in other countries. It is limited to the individual, who must apply each year for re-election. The activities of a stockbroking firm are carefully prescribed and virtually restricted to dealing in stocks and shares. In America, however, stockbrokers may operate in the commodity markets. In West Germany the great majority of stock exchange transactions are carried out by the banks, who are also members of the exchanges. And in other countries stockbrokers may engage in insurance and other activities.

To write in detail of the stockbroking community in all these centres would require not only a volume many times larger than this, but also a knowledge infinitely greater than my own. Some readers may, however, be interested in dealing in foreign securities. Purchases or sales can be carried out in London of almost any security quoted on a foreign exchange, but for those who like to know the operation of foreign exchanges in more detail, appendices have been added giving the basic information about all the principal overseas markets whose securities are quoted daily in the *Financial Times*.

Although the purpose of this book is to describe the functions and operation of a stockbroking business, rather than a stock exchange, some introduction is necessary to the systems operated in the various exchanges.

STOCK EXCHANGE SYSTEMS

Three basic systems are maintained in the world's stock exchanges: the call-over system, used in the majority of the smaller exchanges; the trading-post system, used in a number of centres including Wall Street, and in Sydney and Melbourne, which recently transferred from the call-over system; and the jobbing system, which is peculiar to the United Kingdom.

(a) CALL-OVER

At fixed times, normally once in the morning and once in the afternoon, the members of the stock exchange assemble around the chairman or other official and the list of securities quoted in that centre is read out, together with the price ruling at the time. As each security is called, brokers who have buying orders will bid for stocks or shares and those with selling orders will offer them. When a buyer and seller agree on a price suitable to both, a transaction is made. If the agreed price is different from the call-over price, the latter is adjusted at the time of the next call-over.

This system would imply that shares can only be bought and sold at the fixed times of the call-over during the day, but this is not so in practice. When a broker receives an order at another time of the day he approaches those other brokers who have shown interest at the time of the previous call-over, and transacts his business.

(b) TRADING-POST

Under this system a given point on the floor of the stock exchange is allocated as a meeting-place for transactions in certain specified securities. Brokers with business to carry out in these stocks and shares meet at the trading-post and conclude a satisfactory bargain between themselves. In the New York Stock Exchange nineteen trading-posts have an average of some seventy common stock issues each, and price indicators show the price of the last sale in each security.

If the ruling price in a security is much different from the price at which a broker has instructions to deal, or if there are no other brokers who wish to match his order with one in the opposite direction, it is obviously a waste of his time to stand around the trading-post waiting on the off-chance that he may be able to deal. Certain members, therefore, undertake this duty as 'specialists'. Each security has its own specialist and one specialist may deal in several securities. Specialists not only accept 'limit orders' (orders at fixed prices, as opposed to 'market orders' which must be executed at the best price possible at the time of dealing), but they also trade for their own account. In order to help maintain an orderly market to protect other brokers for whom the specialist may be operating on limit orders, his own trading is hedged around with a number of restrictions.

(c) JOBBING SYSTEM

The London Stock Exchange was founded on the jobbing system. The Stock Exchange operates as a market, very much like any other, whether in meat, fish or vegetables. The floor is divided roughly (and quite invisibly to the untrained eye) into a series of smaller markets — the gilt-edged market covering all British Government, Dominion and local authority issues; the oil market; the Kaffir market for the shares in South African gold-mining companies, etc. — and here the jobbers act as stall-holders. While the specialist in New York acts primarily as an assistant to the broker in keeping his limits under surveillance, and only acts more infrequently on his own account, the jobber always acts as a principal. Unlike the stall-holder in the vegetable market, however, who knows the identity of the growers and also of the buyers, the jobber never knows until the last moment whether a broker is going to sell shares to him or buy them from him. This factor, combined with the competition between several firms of jobbers dealing in the same securities, tends to keep the margin between selling and buying prices down to a minimum.

Each of the three systems described has its own peculiar merits and is suited to a particular financial centre. The call-over system is most suitable for the small stock exchange where the number of transactions is limited, since the activity would be insufficient to provide a reasonable livelihood for either the jobber or the specialist. The trading-post system is suitable for those centres where there is a limited number of securities and a relatively high degree of activity. The jobber is of particular value in matching substantial institutional orders with a large number of small orders in the opposite direction from other sources. As a result the leading British securities enjoy a freer market than many of their counterparts in New York. The system comes under fire from a number of sources, largely on the grounds that the expense of dealing is higher than in other centres where the trading-post system is operated, owing to the jobber's turn (the difference between the jobber's buying and selling prices), and that only a few jobbing firms are prepared to take a really substantial position and then only in a limited number of leading securities. It is not my intention to become involved in this controversy at this stage, but some possible ideas on the future system of the London Stock Exchange, giving a compromise between the jobbing and the trading-post systems, are included in Chapter 11.

FUNCTIONS OF A STOCKBROKER

The three functions of the stockbroker have already been mentioned: to arrange the quotation of stocks and shares; to act as an agent in buying and selling securities; and to act as adviser to his clients in the selection and management of their investments.

Quotations are primarily required by either Government or quasi-Government organisations or commercial enterprises. When these concerns wish to raise funds by means of new issues, the stockbroker's function lies in submitting the necessary documents for a quotation, in advising on the best price which can be obtained for the issue, and in arranging that funds are available to guarantee its subscription.

The second function is relatively simple, although it covers more than just the procedures of buying and selling stocks and shares. Where securities are quoted in more than one centre, for example, the broker may check the market in both exchanges to ensure that he deals to the best advantage of his client, in some cases cabling or telephoning his agents or branch office in an overseas centre.

Although stockbrokers' charges are almost entirely derived from commission on the purchase and sale of securities, by far the greater part of their time is devoted to the third function, the advisory services in the selection and administration of investments. Valuations of clients' portfolios, written reports, attendance at meetings and a wide range of services on the telephone are all provided free of charge. In the days before the Second World War, stockbroking was largely a matter of having the right connections and using a certain amount of common sense. But today a far more scientific approach is made to investment. The quality of a stockbroker's business is much more dependent on the service that he offers to his clients than on his social connections.

VARIETY OF BUSINESS

The public image of the stockbroker still lies somewhere between the top-hatted plutocrat who drives up each morning in his Rolls-Royce to make a few thousand pounds capital profit at the share casino and, particularly to those who have seen the first of The Stock Exchange's publicity films, *My Word is My Bond*, a gentleman in a rather shiny blue suit who works in a poky, old-fashioned office and advises a garage proprietor to invest his savings in oil shares. In fact it is as difficult to draw a picture of a typical stockbroker as it is of a typical doctor, who may be a G.P. or a specialist, an adviser on all matters of health or an expert in one narrow but intricate field.

One of the fascinations of the stockbroker's work lies in its variety. One minute he may be recommending investments for a pension fund, running into several hundreds of thousands of pounds, and the next he may be advising an elderly widow on the investment of under a hundred. One day he may be advising on the tactics of taking over another company, and the following day discussing the plans for a quotation of shares on the stock market. One month he may be visiting a textile mill in Yorkshire and the next an electronics factory in Japan. In the larger firms the duties of individual partners and executives are usually somewhat specialised, as will be seen in the following chapters, but in the smaller firms members are expected to be Jacks-of-all-trades. And even in the largest organisations the personal contact, and the confidence inspired in the client by the personality of a particular individual, make it difficult to decentralise all responsibilities completely. However much, in the interests of efficiency, the work of the firm is delegated between carefully devised departments, in the end it all depends on whether the individual in the firm and the client see eye to eye and like and respect each other.

The move towards a more scientific approach to investment has produced two changes in the structure of stockbroking firms: firstly, it has led to a degree of specialisation by those firms who are closely connected with certain industries; and secondly, in order to provide the expert service demanded by the institutional investors, the smaller and medium-sized firms are tending to amalgamate into larger units.

SPECIALISATION

Specialisation in the past has largely been confined to classes of security and types of business. For instance, the bulk of the institutional business in the gilt-edged market was traditionally carried out by only half a dozen firms, although this has now spread to about a dozen. The issue of stocks for water companies is almost entirely carried out by one firm of brokers, and another has for many years been renowned for its business in fixed-interest securities, particularly preference shares. In recent years, however, certain firms have developed a reputation in selected ordinary share markets — the steel market, breweries, insurance and investment trust shares being well-known examples. This degree of specialisation demands a high quality in the service which is offered to investors and, while there may be times of stagnation in the turnover in some shares (the steel industry in the past, for example, with its political overtones), the degree of business undertaken when the market is active more than outweighs its erratic nature.

SIZE OF FIRMS

Out of the 270 member firms in the list of 3,264 members of
The Stock Exchange, London, for the year ending 24 March
1967, 225 were brokers and 45 jobbers. Some indication of the
size of the firms is given by the number of partners, single-
partner firms no longer being permitted under the rules. Over
the past decade, in common with most other professions, the
trend has been towards fewer and larger firms.

The term 'partner' normally indicates an individual whose
remuneration is taken partly or solely from his share in the
profits of the business. In The Stock Exchange, however, it is
traditional for some partners to be fully profit-sharing, while
others may be remunerated by means of salary and/or commission. In a business where the personal contact between the
client and the broker is all-important, the client often has more
faith in the individual if he sees his name on the firm's writing-
paper. For this reason, as well as it being the just reward for
services rendered to the firm, non-profit-sharing partners may
be included in the partnership list. There is no indication as to
which of the partners share the profits and which do not,
although all are liable to an unlimited share of any loss which
may be incurred if the firm becomes a defaulter.

Until the passage of the Companies Act, 1967, a statutory
limitation of twenty partners prohibited very large partnerships. As a result, particularly in those firms who had partnerships nearing twenty, the names of associate members were often
included on the writing-paper, and this practice has continued.

No record of the total number of employees exists, but the
size of staffs varies from several hundred in the largest firms to
only half a dozen in the smallest. The individuals who are
permitted to enter the trading floor of The Stock Exchange
itself are listed, and the breakdown is in Table 1 below.

There are thus a total of 4,318 allowed on to the floor, with
an additional 541 having entry to the Settlement Room in the
basement.

Authorised clerks are employees of member firms who are
permitted to transact the business of buying and selling in the
market. Unauthorised clerks, who are distinguished by the fact
that the name badge of the firm which they wear is blue instead

TABLE 1

At 28 March 1967

	Brokers	*Jobbers*
Partners	1,731	327
Associate members[1]	908	193
Authorised clerks	432	107
Unauthorised clerks	383	133
Settlement clerks	441	100

[1] There were also 105 members not in active business.

of silver, are not permitted to transact business, and are only used by their firms for obtaining prices, conveying messages, answering calls, etc.

At the time of writing, no member firm on the London Stock Exchange is permitted to operate a branch office in the United Kingdom, unless this is more than twenty-five miles distant from the office of any existing member of a Federated Exchange, nor in the same town in which a member of the Provincial Brokers Stock Exchange operates, except for the purpose of administration only; for example, a number of firms have considered housing some administrative staff outside the square mile of the City of London, where rents and other expenses are becoming very high. Branch offices in overseas countries are permitted, but only a few firms have taken advantage of this facility. The possibility of amalgamations between members of the Provincial Brokers Stock Exchange and members of Federated Exchanges is discussed in Chapter 11.

MEMBERSHIP

All members of the London Stock Exchange are subject to the Rules and Regulations of The Stock Exchange, which are comprised in a book of some three hundred pages, covering over two hundred rules and fifty-seven appendices, and to all decisions of their elected Council. But over and above these printed rules and regulations, members are constrained to observe the strict etiquette and traditions of their profession.

This is probably best summed up in Rule 17 (1):

> The Council may censure or suspend any Member who in his conduct or business may act in a manner detrimental to

the interests of The Stock Exchange or unbecoming the character of a Member.

The most important rules governing membership are the following:

All Members must apply for re-election each year (Rule 21 (1)).
The Council has complete discretion in the power to re-elect a Member without dispute or challenge (Rule 21 (2)).
On application for admission or re-election a Member must state whether he proposes to act as Jobber or Broker (Rule 22 (1)), and may not act as both (Rules 86 and 87).
Members who wish to act as Principals or Employees in any business other than that of The Stock Exchange, or whose wife so wishes, must obtain the prior consent of the Council (Rule 30).

The full requirements for becoming a member are considered in Chapter 9.

CONDUCT OF BUSINESS

The conduct of business between members or between members and their clients is also strictly governed. In the former connection the most important rules are probably:

The Stock Exchange does not recognise in its dealings any other parties than its own Members: every bargain therefore, whether for account of the Member effecting it or for account of a Principal, must be fulfilled according to the Rules, Regulations and usages of The Stock Exchange (Rule 73).
A Member or Authorised Clerk may not accept instructions or adopt any procedure which would in any way or for any purpose override his duty to execute each transaction to the best advantage according to his judgement at the time of dealing (Rule 73A).
All disputes between Members not affecting the general interests of The Stock Exchange which arise out of Stock Exchange transactions or are connected with Stock Exchange business and including partnership disputes, shall be referred to the arbitration of a Member or Members of The Stock Exchange: and the Council will not take into consideration such disputes unless arbitrators cannot be found, or the arbitrators are unable to come to a decision (Rule 75 (1)).

And in the case of conduct between broker and client, the rule prohibiting advertising is of the greatest significance.

A Member of The Stock Exchange is not allowed to advertise for Stock Exchange business or for this purpose to issue circulars or business communications to persons other than his own Principals, except that a Member may with the prior consent of the Council issue on behalf of the Principal a circular to all shareholders of a company offering to acquire their shares provided that he shall not consider any shareholder so circularised as his Principal by reason of the issue of the circular (Rule 78).

The whole question of advertising and the definition of a principal is one that has been much discussed among brokers.

THE COUNCIL

The drafting and the enforcement of these rules is a matter for the Council, a body of thirty-six members, twelve of whom are elected each year for a three-year term of office.

The Council is elected by secret ballot (Rule 2) and from its members elects a chairman and two deputy-chairmen (Rule 4). They also appoint sub-committees, which currently cover the following subjects:

Property and Finance
Country Exchanges and Agents
Rules and Disputes
Members, Firms and Clerks
Firms' Accounts
Commissions
Objections to Marks
Public Relations
Quotations
Official Lists and Publications
Central Administrative Departments.

The power of the Council is absolute, as shown in Rule 12A, which states:

In all matters brought under the consideration of the Council, their decision whether expressed by a Resolution or otherwise shall be final and must be carried out forthwith by every Member concerned, provided that where a Resolution is required by the Rules to be confirmed such Resolution shall not be valid or put into force until confirmed.

As mentioned earlier, it is not the intention to discuss the operation of The Stock Exchange as such in this volume, but to concentrate on the work of the stockbroker. While members are expected to know the principal rules and regulations and to study the resolutions which emanate from the Council from time to time, in general terms the efficient operation of the Council and its secretariat is best reflected in the fact that the majority of members are only consciously aware of its existence when some major item of news (such as the rebuilding of The Stock Exchange) comes up for discussion, or when they have a personal problem on which advice from a member of the Council is sought.

THE ASSOCIATED EXCHANGES

Stock exchanges have been established in twenty-one of the leading towns and cities in the British Isles, as listed below in Table 2, although three, the Midlands and Western, Northern, and Scottish Stock Exchanges, are the amalgamation of several others.

TABLE 2

LIST OF ASSOCIATED STOCK EXCHANGES
(December 1966)

Belfast Stock Exchange
Cork Stock Exchange
Dublin Stock Exchange
Midlands and Western Stock
    Exchange   (This exchange was formed on 3 October 1966 by regionalisation, and the following exchanges joined: Birmingham, Bristol, Cardiff, Nottingham and Swansea.)

Northern Stock Exchange   (This exchange was formed on 2 August 1965 by regionalisation, and the following exchanges joined:

Scottish Stock Exchange

Bradford, Halifax, Huddersfield, Leeds, Liverpool, Manchester, Newcastle, Oldham and Sheffield.)
(This exchange was formed on 1 January 1964 by regionalisation, and the following exchanges joined:
Aberdeen, Dundee, Edinburgh and Glasgow.)

Note: In the Northern, and Scottish Stock Exchanges there are Country Brokers Associations forming a constituent part of each regional exchange.

All these exchanges are represented on the Council of Associated Stock Exchanges, which was originally formed in 1890. One other exchange, however, is not represented — the Provincial Brokers Stock Exchange (P.B.S.E.), which does not possess a trading floor of its own, since it was set up to co-ordinate the activities of stockbrokers in towns all over the country which did not possess the facilities of a stock exchange. In March 1967 there were no less than 205 members operating in 96 firms spread between 100 towns. The P.B.S.E. has by no means been backward in the standards which it has set for its members. In 1950 a guarantee fund was set up to safeguard clients against loss in the event of fraud, and a year later the Committee of the P.B.S.E. brought into effect a rule requiring every applicant for membership to pass a written examination to ensure that a high standard of investment knowledge was a qualification of membership.

For many years the country exchanges continued to operate under their own sovereignty, electing their own committees to govern their operations and applying their own rules and regulations, which, although based on those applied in London, varied in a number of ways. In 1964, however, the four Scottish stock exchanges at Aberdeen, Dundee, Glasgow and Edinburgh amalgamated into one exchange, although continuing to transact business in the four centres. As a result one Official List of Securities is published and all four exchanges operate under the same rules. They were followed by the formation of the Northern Stock Exchange in August 1965, and the Midlands and Western Stock Exchange in October 1966.

An endeavour to form a closer and more permanent system of collaboration between London, the Associated Exchanges and the Provincial Brokers led to the formation of a co-ordination committee in May 1962. Following interim reports on the progress made by this committee, all the exchanges signed a Prospectus of Federation in June 1965. Federation became a reality in July 1965, although many of the proposals contained in the prospectus (examination for members, etc.) will not come into force until a later date.

THE ASSOCIATION OF STOCK AND SHARE DEALERS

Under the provisions of the Prevention of Fraud (Investments) Act, 1958, all those carrying on the business of dealing in securities must operate under the authority of a principal's licence, issued under the regulations of the Board of Trade. Members of recognised stock exchanges and recognised associations of dealers in securities are specifically exempted in the Act, so that none of those mentioned in the previous paragraph requires a licence.

The largest recognised association of dealers in securities is the Association of Stock and Share Dealers, whose membership at May 1967 numbered about thirty-three, spread over some twenty-five to thirty towns. Members of the Association are often confused by the public with members of one of the recognised stock exchanges. The most obvious difference lies in the fact that members of the Association are permitted both to circularise individuals who are not already their clients and to advertise.

TRANSACTIONS OUTSIDE THE STOCK EXCHANGE

So much for the industry and the profession of stockbroking. Before turning to the detailed organisation of a stockbroking firm, one last point must be made clear. The law does not require that every sale and purchase of securities shall be made through the channels of a stockbroker or authorised dealer in securities. Fathers may transfer stocks and shares to their children, willing buyers and sellers may carry out transactions together, or a financial institution may undertake the normal functions of a stockbroker by placing shares with others with whom it has connections. In recent times the increasing quantity of securities by-passing the stock exchanges has given cause for some concern. The stringent regulations that are applied to protect the investor and promote a ready market have their reverse side in that they make a placing of large lines of securities more difficult and more expensive. Merchant banks, in particular, must find it difficult to resist the temptation of placing a large line of shares among their own connections at a greater profit to themselves or their clients than could be obtained had they carried out the transaction through a firm of stockbrokers. The remedy, however, lies largely in the hands of the stock exchanges. In a changing world they must be prepared to re-examine their traditional methods so that both the convenience of their clients and the cost of their services are under constant review.

ORGANISATION OF A STOCKBROKING FIRM

Stockbrokers are becoming more and more expert in the critical appreciation of management in those companies which they investigate. Rapidly increasing costs are making them more aware of the beams in their own eyes. For years the main drive in almost every firm of stockbrokers has been to increase the business, whether by broadening its connections or by expanding the business done with its existing clientele. Now that the advantages of size have created large organisations, the administrative problems have increased with them.

In the smaller firms, where all the partners may work in the same room, policy decisions can be taken at any time as a matter of course. With a staff of a dozen or twenty, an increase in the salary of one individual does not necessarily throw the whole wage structure out of line. But when the partnership exceeds twenty and the staff numbers several hundred, the administrative organisation approaches that of an industrial concern.

Each firm will have its own management structure and I can only speak with any authority about my own. We felt it important to cover the essential divisions which any concern, in any field of commercial operation, must cover —production, sales-and-service, finance, administration (including personnel) and research. The organisation chart shown in Fig. 1 includes also a management committee, which handles the day-to-day problems of the firm, reporting to the partnership at monthly meetings. It includes also the specialist departments dealing with fixed-interest, foreign securities and new issues.

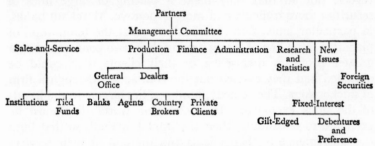

FIG. 1. Organisational Chart

The division of responsibilities between partners in some such organisation as that illustrated may seem unduly obvious, but partnerships which have grown up either out of mergers or out of gradual expansion tend to become haphazard in their administration. Unless some cut-and-dried organisational chart is drawn up, many jobs can be duplicated and others left undone. Many firms, for example, are quite unaware of the actual cost of a bargain. Others have no budget, either for capital or current expenditure, or monthly targets for trade. And priorities in research projects, which are requested by the Institutional Department or the Tied Funds Department, cannot easily be allocated unless some partner is responsible for the overall programme of the department.

The organisational chart also simplifies to some extent the problem of the private client who is an acquaintance of a partner or member of the firm. It is almost impossible to refuse to deal personally with a close friend or acquaintance, and yet much time and effort is probably wasted in almost every firm by partners whose talents would be more economically employed on their own specialised side of the business. No gynaecologist is expected by his friends to advise them on matters of general health, but every stockbroker, whatever his specialist activities, is expected to be a general practitioner as well. The chart puts the individual's responsibilities before him in black and white, and he is obviously doing a disservice to his partners if he does not introduce his friends to the partner in charge of the relevant department and leave him to serve them.

The organisational chart also provides a convenient guide for the division of this book into chapters. Since the firm is decentralised into departments, each one can be studied in some detail. Remembering always that the larger firms will probably be more decentralised than the smaller concerns and that a number will have specialist departments not mentioned here — short-term money dealing or overseas branch offices, for example — the greatest emphasis is placed on the first department, the sales-and-service to the client.

2

SALES-AND-SERVICE

To the majority of stockbrokers the concept of a salesman immediately conjures up the image of knocking on front doors or standing behind a counter. Foreign brokerage houses employ both these techniques, American bond salesmen travelling from house to house and Japanese firms setting up shop on railway stations and in department stores. In Great Britain the accent is applied much more on service, but the partners and senior executives of stockbroking firms are nevertheless the only sales outlet for the services which those firms have to offer. In the smaller firms members will also be involved in the production work of buying and selling securities and perhaps in office routines as well, but in the larger organisations there is a clear division of responsibilities.

The services which are offered depend partly upon the classification of the client and partly upon the wishes of the individual. It is convenient, therefore, to consider the sales-and-service organisation under the heading of the various types of client, and many firms have different departments for dealing with each type.

INSTITUTIONS

This is a fairly loose classification covering the leading financial organisations — about five hundred insurance companies, some three hundred investment trusts, the largest of the pension funds, over a hundred unit trusts and about fifty merchant banks. (For assets and share of the market, see Appendix 1.) The majority of these institutions utilise the services of a large number of stockbrokers and have investment departments fully capable of making their own decisions about the merits of any particular investment. The services they require are as follows:

(a) SPECIALISED INFORMATION

Where a firm of stockbrokers makes a particular study of an industry or a company, institutions will rely upon them for up-to-date and reliable information. A firm of stockbrokers which acts for a company in the raising of new capital and which keeps in touch with the management will be expected to provide informed opinion as to the company's progress. Those firms with strong connections in a single industry, which produce frequent studies of the prospects of the industry and the component companies, will tend to attract institutional business in this field. The sales force of a stockbroking firm has therefore a double task in handling institutional business in its own specialist companies and industries: it not only has to make out a case for a purchase or a sale, but it also has to provide an after-sales service, keeping the institution informed of the progress of the company for many years to come. A stockbroker may, in fact, receive higher praise from an investment manager for picking a loser and still keeping in touch, than for picking a winner and forgetting about it. On the whole the after-sales service of London stockbrokers is superior to that of their American counterparts, who tend to put greater effort into the sale and less effort into the service.

Each of the institutions mentioned requires a somewhat different approach. The insurance companies, with large funds accruing daily and future liabilities, tend to look towards income growth. They are somewhat more sophisticated than the majority of pension funds in spreading their interests into overseas securities. The pension funds, most of whom are able to reclaim all the income tax levied by the Inland Revenue and are not liable to capital-gains tax, normally take the view that the tax disadvantages of overseas securities outweigh the benefit of geographical spread of their portfolios. The investment trusts have a more difficult problem of investment, since, except for the relatively infrequent occasions when they raise additional funds by means of new issues, they have little new money available for investment, and a major purchase must be matched by the sale of an existing security. The same applies, but to a lesser extent, to unit trusts. Unit trusts on the whole have been growing fairly rapidly in recent years, the new units sold to the public more than outweighing the old units en-cashed. The last of the institutions, the merchant banks, operate a variety of funds which may include all those mentioned so far, together with charitable trusts, private trusts, company business and the funds of wealthy individuals.

(b) MARKET BIDS AND OFFERS

It is not always easy for the larger institutions to obtain shares in the quantities that they require, and they are thus the most likely buyers when substantial lines are offered on the market. Jobbers who have either bought a line of shares, or agreed to negotiate a purchase, approach one or more stockbrokers who they think are the most likely to find buyers. The offer is normally 'subject', meaning that the shares may not be avail-able at a later time since the offer may be made simultaneously to others. A 'firm' offer, on the other hand, indicates that the shares are offered only to the one party. In most firms of stock-brokers one individual in the Institutional Department has the responsibility of examining each offer to decide whether it is worth approaching the institutions with it or not. If it appears sufficiently attractive, calculations will then be made giving the various data that individual institutions require and the other members of the department will begin to ring the various insurance companies, pension funds and so on, offering the shares, either 'subject' or 'firm' as the case may be. An institu-tion which is given a 'subject' offer will realise that acceptance does not ensure that the shares have been bought, but that confirmation must be given after the deal has been completed with the jobber.

The competition between firms of brokers to obtain such offers from the market and to place the shares with their clients is such that speed in obtaining an answer is vitally important, since otherwise a competitor may have carried out the deal.

Those institutions which give rapid answers to offers, or conversely to bids of this nature, even if the reply is in the negative, will usually be among the first to receive this type of service. Those which require meetings of investment com-mittees before an answer can be given are less likely to be approached.

Many institutional investors will give serious consideration

only to offers which are 'in the office' of the broker who
approaches them. This term indicates that the broker is acting
for the seller, and is trying to place the shares with his own
connections.

(c) PLACINGS

The attractions to an institution of receiving an offer of shares
from a broker who is also acting for the seller are threefold.
Firstly, the origin of the shares is known. While the broker will
never divulge the identity of his client, he can give a general
indication of the reasons for the sale. It may be a deceased
estate, a family trust which already has an excessive proportion
in these shares, or simply another institution who may be taking
a profit. If the shares themselves are suspect, the broker will
not be prepared to offer them to his own clients, since he must
bear some responsibility for the future success of the investment.
Secondly, the offer is unlikely to have been hawked round the
market, which usually indicates that many other institutions
have examined it and found it unattractive. Finally, as the
broker is acting directly with the seller, if the institution feels
that the price is too high, a counter-bid a few pence lower can
be relayed directly to the seller.

From the stockbrokers' point of view the matching of buyer
and seller in his own office is also attractive. Under the rules
of the London Stock Exchange he is not allowed to sell shares
direct to his clients, without first offering them to the jobbers
in the market. This protects the seller against receiving less
from the stockbroker's own clients than he would if the shares
were offered freely elsewhere. Nor, if the jobbers are unable to
match either side of his bargain, is he permitted to pass the
shares directly between his clients, without obtaining written
consent from two firms of jobbers in that particular market.
Even if he has carried out these requirements he is then only
permitted to charge commission to the originator of the
business.

As a result a broker with a large order which he believes he
may be able to match will always approach a firm of jobbers
before starting the matching operation. He discusses with them
the terms of a 'put-through'. If the order is for the sale of a large
line of shares, he will arrange to sell the entire line to a jobber

and buy them back at a fractionally different price for the buyers. The broker then has the right (and the obligation) to charge commissions on both buying and selling transactions. The jobber receives the small 'turn' in the price differential and also has the right to demand that some of the shares be retained by him.

The larger the quantity in the original selling order compared with the normal number of shares in this company quoted in the market, the greater the discount that the seller may have to accept below the market price. In some cases a discount of as much as 10% may be fixed for a very substantial number of shares in difficult market conditions.

When the broker and jobber have agreed the number of shares wanted by the jobber and a fair price for both buyer and seller, this must be agreed by the originator of the business. The members of the Institutional Department are then free to telephone their connections offering them a participation in the placing.

On occasions the jobber will 'protect' the selling broker at a price a little below the placing price. If the placing operation is unsuccessful, therefore, the broker can still sell the shares in the market, the jobber having taken the risk that, with some of the likely institutions having already been covered, he can dispose of the holding in the normal course of jobbing over a period.

(d) MARKET PRICES AND OTHER INFORMATION

Many firms cement the good relations between themselves and their institutional connections by a regular service of prices, reports of dividend increases, budget news, etc. Too many telephone calls of this nature are naturally discouraged by the institutional investment managers, who have better uses for their time, but they require to be kept in touch with market movements and usually delegate this service to one or two firms, with whom they enjoy particularly close relations.

In recent years the advent of closed-circuit television has led to this medium being widely used in the City and now in Edinburgh. The investment manager has only to switch to the appropriate channel to see the movement in any particular market — gilt-edged, oils, industrials, etc. — and so obtain a 'feel' of the situation. In addition most firms rendering this service reserve at least one channel for up-to-date news, so that dividend announcements or other important matters can be covered. The opinion of most investment managers regarding their television services seems to be somewhat akin to their views on their wives — they rarely appreciate their value until they break down.

(e) COMPANY VISITS, CONFERENCES, ETC.

The importance of seeing a company in operation and of meeting the top management has become more apparent in recent years as the management of British companies has begun to be more broad-minded in its welcome to existing and potential institutional shareholders. Many firms of stockbrokers arrange parties of institutional clients to visit those companies with whom they enjoy particularly close relations or of whom they think particularly highly. Investment conferences, to which leading speakers are invited, and other facilities are also arranged by a number of firms.

(f) OTHER SERVICES

The allocation of underwriting or the placing of new issues, the publication of research material and service to institutions in fixed-interest and overseas securities are discussed in the relevant chapters under those headings.

TIED FUNDS

The institutions which have been discussed above are those which employ their own investment managers and which do not rely upon any single firm of stockbrokers to advise them. There are a number of funds, however, which rely entirely or in part upon one or more firms of stockbrokers, with perhaps an investment panel or sub-committee to decide overall policy. Among these are the local authority superannuation funds, the great number of charitable trusts, the universities and colleges, a large proportion of industrial pension funds and a vast number of private trust funds. Reference has been made to these as 'tied funds' because they do not utilise the competing services of a large number of stockbrokers, but rely upon the advice of only one or perhaps two.

The service which these funds require is very different from that of the institutions. Since no one is permanently employed full-time on investment matters, the day-to-day market situation is of little interest. Where a placing below the market would be of advantage to the fund, and the security fits well into its investment policy, the stockbroker will automatically reserve a participation, referring if necessary to one or more members of the investment panel or sub-committee. What these funds most require is either the absolute management of their investments or advice on their management. This is usually given in two ways.

(a) PERIODIC VALUATIONS AND REVIEWS

At regular intervals (normally half-yearly or annually) the portfolio of investments is valued and a review is prepared for the trustees. No standard pattern is followed, but it is normal procedure to prepare a summary of the portfolio as well as the valuation and recommendations for action.

(i) *Summary*

It is important to present an overall picture of the fund, divided into the various classes of investment, and to show the proportions both by cost and by current market values. A typical summary would divide the portfolio between fixed-interest holdings and equities. The fixed-interest might be divided into the following classes: British Government funds, corporation and county stocks, public boards, Commonwealth Government issues, foreign stocks and bonds, debentures and other loan stocks, and convertible loan issues.

In the case of ordinary shares, however, the portfolio is further broken down into industrial classifications. It is common practice to classify these under the same headings as the *Financial Times*-Actuaries Industrial Indices, to give a yardstick for comparison of performance. Some funds break down their total portfolio into industrial groups, lumping together the fixed-interest and the ordinary shares in each industry. A cardinal rule of investment in ordinary shares is to obtain a reasonable spread between different industries in order to ensure that a recession in any one sector of the economy does not prejudice the total portfolio. Fixed-interest securities, however, are not risk capital, and the objective of a balanced portfolio in this class of security must be to ensure that the spread of redemption dates is satisfactory. It would be quite misleading to summarise, for example, 5% of the total portfolio in breweries and 5% in stores, where the brewery section comprised only debentures and the stores section only ordinary shares.

Both values at cost (or book) and market will be shown. From the comparison of the two sets of figures it is possible to note which classes of security have shown appreciation or depreciation, and, of the ordinary shares, which industries have performed better than others. It is also useful to show the percentage of the portfolio (again both by book and market values) in each class of security and each industrial group.

Finally, it is usual to show the income, including a comparison of the average yield on the cost of each group and on the current market prices. The definition of yield is given in the following paragraphs.

(ii) *Valuation*

A valuation may be either a simple list of share holdings with market prices and values, or a full-scale review. In the latter case, the following may be shown for ordinary share holdings:

Amount or number of shares.
Description of stock or share.
Current middle market price.
Current value.
Book value.
Capital Gains Value (where appropriate).
Latest dividend.
Latest earnings on ordinary capital or dividend cover.
Income, based on the latest dividend paid.
Gross yield on current market price.
Gross yield on book price.
Price/earnings ratio.

Where comments are required on individual investments, these are normally given in the body of the report accompanying the valuation.

(iii) *Recommendations*

The gilt-edged and other fixed-interest holdings would probably be discussed with the relevant departments for advice in regard to necessary action, and consideration of the factors affecting changes in these holdings or investment criteria for new holdings will be deferred until later chapters. In the case of British ordinary shares, however, the department dealing with tied trusts will usually be responsible for recommending the action to be taken. In the case of static funds, trusts and charities with no new money available for investment, the addition of a new holding to the portfolio can only be made at the expense of all or part of an existing holding. Pension and superannuation funds, on the other hand, with regular new money for investment, will require constant recommendations of additions to their portfolios.

Five figures are normally quoted as basic information in the recommendation of an investment or a sale: price, dividend, earnings on ordinary capital, dividend yield and price/earnings ratio.

(1) *Price.* The price of an ordinary share, by itself, has no real significance in assessing whether or not the share is correctly valued. Moreover, investors should not let themselves be led into the trap of comparing the market price with the nominal value. There is normally no greater risk in buying a 5s. ordinary share at 95s. than a £1 share at 20s. The price of the share is only significant in relation to the rate of dividend declared and possibly, with some reservations, the previous price record of the share.

(2) *Dividend.* Most dividends are declared and shown in the Press as a percentage of the nominal value of the share. It is important, therefore, to show the nominal value so that the return on the investment can be easily calculated.

(3) *Earnings.* The earnings on the ordinary capital, expressed as a percentage of the nominal value, gives an indication of the 'dividend cover'. Some investors prefer this figure to be given as a factor of the dividend. In the case of a company earning 25% on its ordinary capital and paying 10%, the cover would be 2½ times. An indication is therefore given of the extent to which earnings could fall without uncovering the dividend

payment, or, taking a more optimistic view, the scope for improvement of the dividend if the directors decided to be somewhat more generous in their distribution.

(4) *Yield.* The yield on an ordinary share is the percentage ratio of the latest declared annual dividend to the current price. Where a dividend is declared as a percentage of the nominal value of the share, this must be reduced to monetary terms before the ratio can be determined. The figure for yield represents one of the basic premises upon which the investing public decides whether a share is too high in price, too low, or correctly valued.

The comparison is often made between the income yield obtainable on a fixed-interest security and that on an ordinary share, and care must be taken not to confuse the two figures. In the case of a fixed-interest security, such as War Loan $3\frac{1}{2}\%$ standing at a price of 60, an investment of £100 would provide a return (neglecting the expenses involved in investing) of $3 \cdot 5 \times 100/60 = £5$ 16s. 6d. per annum. The yield on War Loan $3\frac{1}{2}\%$ at this price is therefore referred to as £5 16s. 6d., and this sum will be received as interest by the investor for as long as the stock or the investor is in existence.

The income which will be derived from a holding of an ordinary share, on the other hand, cannot be assessed in advance. In the first year of holding the share an investment of £100 will produce an income identical with the yield, provided that the dividend paid is the same as that of the previous year. The reason for buying ordinary shares, however, is in the anticipation of improved profits and with them increased dividends. The comparison between the actual income 'yield' on a fixed-interest security and the 'dividend/price ratio' of an ordinary share should therefore be avoided.

The 'yield' on an ordinary share is best used as a yardstick to estimate the public's opinion of the prospects of the share.

(5) *Price/Earnings Ratio.* The ratio of the price to the earnings (P/E ratio) indicates the value of the share in terms of latest published earnings, irrespective of dividend. A P/E ratio of 10 would indicate that an investor would be paying a price equal to ten times the last year's earnings. This figure may be used to compare different shares in the same industrial group to determine their relative values.

(6) *Remarks*. Many firms of stockbrokers, in preparing lists
of recommendations, attach either one of the statistical cards
prepared by the statistical service companies, or one of their own
statistical sheets. In cases where trustees prefer a précis of the
company's activities without too much additional paper, a short
paragraph may be attached to the list of recommendations.

(b) ATTENDANCE AT MEETINGS

One of the partners or senior executives from the Tied Funds
Department will usually attend a meeting of the trustees to
discuss the report and comment upon the recommendations for
action. This maintains the personal contact between the stockbroker and his client and provides the trustees with the opportunity of obtaining additional information and enlargement
upon any of the points made in the report.

From the stockbroker's point of view the tied fund has the
advantage of continuity provided that he maintains a satisfactory service. Where he is fully responsible for investment
advice it is obviously in his interest that the fund should show
a better-than-average performance, since the stockbroker's
business can only grow on personal recommendation.

Between meetings the portfolios of the 'tied funds' will be
examined, particularly when the investment policy pursued by
the firm indicates the sale of an existing security or a switch from
one security to another. The system of keeping records of clients'
holdings under the headings of both the clients' names and
under the title of the security automatically ensures that each
portfolio is considered in such circumstances.

Advice will also be required concerning 'rights' issues of
ordinary shares, where action must be taken either to subscribe
for the shares allocated or to sell them. Very often funds consider that all 'rights' issues should be accepted in order to avoid
reducing the stake in the company concerned. In fact the terms
of rights issues will be studied carefully by members of the Tied
Funds Department to assess whether a better destination
cannot be found for the available money.

Similarly, the terms of take-over bids or other matters
affecting the rights of shareholders must be examined and the
trustees advised of any recommendations.

BRANCH BANKS

The widespread network of branches throughout the country enables the banks to provide a unique service to investors, and the majority of small business comes to the stockbroker through this source. Banks are able to advertise for stock exchange business, and the relationship of trust and respect that the local branch manager enjoys with many of his customers assists in giving them confidence when dealing with investment matters. In the past the clearing banks have preferred not to take any responsibility for advice regarding investment, but have simply handed on to their client the opinion of a firm of stockbrokers. In recent years, however, one or two have opened new departments concerned with advising and managing investment portfolios.

The department dealing with bank business is therefore largely occupied with producing short summary reviews in answer to enquiries from branch banks. The head offices of the banks are usually omitted from this department since, operating either for the bank itself, particularly in the gilt-edged market, or for the employees' superannuation and pension funds, they are normally included under the heading of institutions.

Banks operate on various systems when placing orders with stockbrokers. Some allocate a specific branch to a firm of stockbrokers, so that the branch manager deals direct with his counterpart in the Banks Department of the firm. Others bring all their orders from their branches to one of their City offices and allocate the orders among firms of stockbrokers from the centre. In many cases the amount of business allocated to a firm will depend, not only on the service which the firm offers to the bank, but also on the balances which lie to the credit of the firm's account. The central allocation system makes it simpler to adjust the business allocated on this basis, but may cause some lack of personal contact between branch manager and broker. All accredited banks are entitled to a return of one-quarter of the stockbroker's commission for business which they introduce.

AGENTS

The principal agents directing business to stockbrokers are solicitors, accountants and, a small but growing body, investment counsellors.

(a) SOLICITORS

The majority of work for solicitors concerns either trusts or deceased estates. Following the Trustee Investments Act, 1961, the department dealing with these clients has been required to divide portfolios into Narrower and Wider Ranges, and, where appropriate, allocate securities to the Special Range. The effect of this Act, in its simplest terms, has been to permit trusts whose investment powers were limited under the 1925 Trustee Act virtually to Government securities and little else, to invest up to one-half of their assets in certain ordinary shares, with the balance in a somewhat broader selection of fixed-interest securities. The service to those trusts introduced by firms of solicitors is likely to be similar to that offered to a firm's own tied funds.

In the case of deceased estates the stockbrokers are first required to produce a valuation of the quoted securities for probate purposes. The prices for such valuations are taken as 'a quarter up' on the lower of the two quotations published in the Stock Exchange Official List on the date of death. Normally this price is accepted by the Estate Duty Office without question. In special circumstances (such as the death of a holder with a very large number of shares in one company for which the jobbers in the market would not have been prepared to bid the normal price), the stockbrokers may be asked to put forward a case to the Estate Duty Office for reducing the probate price.

The Agents Department may also be asked to advise on securities which should be sold to provide the moneys required for duty and also to prepare lists of securities for division between a number of beneficiaries, so that the interests of each are safeguarded.

(b) ACCOUNTANTS

Firms of accountants often act as managers for investment trust companies, which would be included among the institutions. They are also often asked to advise on the portfolios of the trusts and companies whose audits they undertake and on the holdings of their private clients. The service which they require from their stockbrokers varies widely from one firm of accountants to another, but in the main is similar to that offered to the broker's own trusts or private clients.

(c) INVESTMENT COUNSELLORS

Some firms of investment counsellors have been in existence for many years, but following the American pattern the numbers have increased very considerably recently. The larger merchant banks have only been prepared to manage an investment port-folio if its value was of the order of £100,000, and the pre-occupation of some firms of stockbrokers with institutional business left a void in the direct management of portfolios of £10,000 to £80,000. Private clients with this size of fortune have felt (often with justice) that the larger firms of stockbrokers have taken too conservative a view of their affairs. Investments have been made in a wide spread of leading securities and the only advice they have received is to stay put.

The investment counsellor has thrived on a more dynamic approach. He has been prepared to recommend both switching out of existing securities and taking an interest in the smaller and less well-known concerns. The client has the feeling at least that he is being looked after, whether the investment changes are successful or not. It is often difficult to judge which policy would have been the most advantageous to the client, but there is little doubt that the majority of investment counsellors today are highly experienced in investment work and that they have the advantage of being served by a number of different firms of stockbrokers, obtaining information from each on the subject in which they are most expert.

From the stockbroker's viewpoint, although the investment counsellor appears to be doing the stockbroker's job and charging a fee for it, his work is largely complementary. Some stockbrokers, with clients requiring a particular service which they are either not prepared or not competent to give, have recommended investment counsellors to these individuals.

It is normal then for the investment counsellor to place orders
for these clients back through the originating broker.

All the agents listed above, besides being entitled to charge a
fee to their clients, are also entitled to a fifth share of the broker's
commission on transactions carried out, provided that their
names are included on a Stock Exchange Register of Agents.
This list is renewed annually, agents applying for re-election,
sponsored by a member firm of stockbrokers and paying a
yearly fee of 10 guineas.

(d) COUNTRY BROKERS

Among the agents on the Register, the country brokers have
been left to the last, since they fulfil an almost identical role to
the London broker but in the provinces. Commission on transactions by London brokers for country brokers is on a set scale,
approximately at one-half the rate of full commission charged
by a London broker to his clients. The largest firms of country
brokers have their own research organisations and, apart from
specialising in the stocks of those companies operating in their
vicinity, may have a substantial institutional connection in
other fields. They have the advantage that they are not normally
tied to one firm in London (although probably the bulk of their
day-to-day business may be transacted by one or two firms),
and they have at their disposal the research departments and
expertise of all their other stockbroker connections.

London firms specialising in country business provide a wide
range of services, including direct telephone and teleprinter
communication, and occasionally the preparation of reviews on
the letterheads of their smaller country connections.

Where the principal market in a share is in London, and the
amount for investment is relatively small, country brokers will
usually ask that the contract for the transaction be rendered
'net'. The London stockbroker applies his own commission to
the price at which he has dealt, adding it to a purchase or sub-
tracting it from a sale. The country broker will then insert this
net price in the contract note which he sends to his client,
charging commission at the normal minimum scale. This results
in the client of the country broker paying a commission of
approximately one and a half times the normal level. In view

of the heavy expenses of telephone and other charges and the small average size of such country bargains, this additional charge is by no means unfair.

Where orders from a country broker are large, the two firms will share the commission between them, each taking approximately half. This applies particularly to institutional business carried out through country brokers.

PRIVATE CLIENTS

The service given to private clients depends very largely on the requirements of the client and the type of firm which is handling the business. With the investment firms, handling primarily institutional business, the client is treated rather like a 'tied fund'. His portfolio is valued and reviewed at regular intervals, participations in attractive placings are taken if they suit the requirements of his list, and from time to time he is advised on sales and switches.

(a) VALUATIONS

The introduction of long-term capital-gains tax in the Finance Act, 1965, has caused an immense increase in the work of the Valuation Department. Not only must the value of each holding at 6 April 1965 be recorded, but also, where known, the cost of the original purchase with adjustment for intermediate sales and purchases. One of the inevitable problems in this connection concerns 'rights' and 'capitalisation' issues. In general it is assumed that a client will have taken up rights and capitalisation issues offered to him unless the sale has been carried out through the stockbrokers. Many clients, however, instruct their banks to sell such issues or assign them to their children or, in the case of rights, allow them to lapse without informing their stockbrokers. Much time is wasted in the Private Clients Department attempting to agree the list of securities on the firm's records with that of the client's bank, where they are normally held.

Some clients hold the view that, because the amounts they have for investment are relatively small, they are bothering their stockbroker when they require advice or ask for a meeting. The economics of investment for the various categories of client are discussed later, but quite apart from whether or not a client's business is remunerative to the firm, almost all stockbrokers feel they have a duty to the public to give their advice and act for even the smallest clients. In fact the amount of personal trouble and worry that is caused to the stockbroker is almost in inverse proportion to the wealth of the client. The institutional investor, sophisticated in these matters, appreciates that stockbrokers inevitably make mistakes either in the selection of an investment or in the timing of a purchase or sale. With their wide spread of interests they can afford to take some rough with the smooth. To an individual, however, with a small capital and therefore a narrow spread of investment, a substantial fall in the price of only one or two securities can cause considerable worry. The member of the Private Clients Department is likely to spend more sleepless nights worrying over his clients' holdings than any of those engaged in the Institutional Department.

(b) STOCKBROKERS' UNIT TRUSTS

In order to cut down the mass of small orders which a large number of private clients brings with it, some stockbrokers operate unit trusts within their own firms. The costs of operation can be reduced compared with unit trusts run by recognised management firms, but a unit trust does not always satisfy the requirements of the client. Many of them like to follow the prices of their shares in the daily Press and some like to feel that they are supporting their own investments when they purchase goods or utilise the services of companies whose shares they hold. Investment trusts and unit trusts have the advantage of giving an investor with a relatively small amount of capital a wider spread of interest than he could otherwise obtain, and a compromise is probably the best solution, a fair proportion of a small investor's holdings being held in investment trusts or unit trusts, with direct investment in other securities to suit his particular requirements.

(c) REQUIREMENTS OF PRIVATE CLIENTS

Individuals who have not previously transacted business with stockbrokers are inclined to approach the problem of investment in much the same light as shopping for Christmas. They write to say that they have money available and can they please have some recommendations. If advice is to be given on a sound basis, the stockbroker will require to know much more about the background of the client and exactly what it is hoped to achieve from the investment.

In particular the stockbroker will want to know:

(i) *The Income Position*

If the client is a heavy surtax-payer already, it would obviously be unwise to recommend an investment that is primarily an income-producer. Alternatively, if the client pays income tax at a lower figure than the standard rate, investments must be considered where a full reclaim of tax may be made from the Revenue.

(ii) *Cash Requirements*

It is important to consider whether the client may require to realise all or part of the investment to pay some known liability (such as the purchase of a car or school fees) in the relatively near future. If such is the case, investments should be selected which are easily marketable and possibly where the capital, in money terms, is relatively secure.

(iii) *Children or Other Beneficiaries*

In the case of elderly clients it may be appropriate to know the ages and income positions of children or other beneficiaries under their wills. An elderly person, with no close next-of-kin and with little income, may be better advised to purchase an annuity than to buy stock exchange securities. A high surtax-payer, who wishes to provide for his grandchildren, may be well advised to form trusts and part with some capital.

(iv) *The Existing Portfolio*

Finally, the stockbroker will want to know what shares the client holds already. Although, for example, shares in the oil industry may look attractive at the time, it would obviously be inadvisable to recommend them to a client who already holds a high proportion of his portfolio in this industry.

(v) *The Objective of the Investment*

Having taken into account the client's own financial position, the immediate requirements for liquid funds and the existing investments, the stockbroker is now in a position to discuss with the client the objective of the investment that is to be made. At the same time, he may recommend alterations to the existing portfolio in the light of this knowledge.

In some cases the choice of investment lies largely between the alternatives of a security producing the maximum income and one which it is hoped will produce the maximum capital appreciation. But in many cases the client hopes to achieve something of each. There is a general misunderstanding that, because stockbrokers work in the City and are close to the market, they must have inside information about the affairs of companies and the likely effect of this information upon the price of the shares. If this were true, most stockbrokers would gladly divorce themselves from any concern with their clients' affairs and be content to make substantial fortunes for themselves using their own funds. Unfortunately it is almost inevitable that the only time when stockbrokers have reliable inside information is when they are concerned in some operation on behalf of a company and then, of course, they are unable either to reveal it to their clients or to act upon it.

SOURCES OF INFORMATION

One of the tasks facing the stockbroker, particularly the non-specialist partners handling private client affairs, is the enormous quantity of reading matter which it is necessary to consume in order to keep up to date. He is expected to be an expert on all the 4,500 companies quoted on the London market, as well as having a fairly detailed knowledge of at least the U.S.A., Canada and Australia. The sources of information can be divided into five: the ticker-tapes and direct computer services; the press; the statistical services; the jobbers; and the firm's own Research and Statistical Department. The partners and executives operating in the sales-and-service departments are expected, therefore, to have a general knowledge obtained from the first four of these sources, and only to make enquiries of the research side of the business on the more detailed or abstruse points.

(a) THE TICKER-TAPES

Two ticker-tape services are currently in operation, one provided by Reuters and the other by the Exchange Telegraph Co. The former tends to specialise more in general and international items of news, and the latter in company news and stock-exchange prices. But both offer a valuable service of immediate information concerning company announcements, Budget summaries, etc., relayed direct to the subscriber's office.

Direct computer services are provided by SCAN (Stock-market Computer Answering Network) and by Centre File. SCAN is inclined primarily towards analytical data — price/earnings ratios and yields at various prices, profitability ratios and trends, together with fixed-interest calculations of a wide range of U.K. and foreign securities. Centre File was set up primarily as a central accounting organisation for subscribing members to carry out general office production routines, with portfolio valuation and direct access to company information as a secondary facility.

(b) THE PRESS

(i) *Daily Newspapers*

The *Financial Times* is obligatory reading for all stockbrokers and maintains an exceptionally high quality of reporting. Its range is considerable, so that it takes the student some time to be able to find his way about in the paper and find out the section which contains the information he requires.

Of the more serious daily papers, *The Times*, the *Daily Telegraph* and the *Guardian* all have substantial City coverage, the first two having special business supplements, although the investment impact of editorial comment in the *Daily Mail* and the *Daily Express* is probably greater, owing to their wider readership. Stockbrokers tend to skip through a number of daily newspapers to ensure that they do not miss some report or comment which might affect the prices of shares in which their clients are particularly interested.

(ii) *Weekly Publications*

Apart from the City comment in the national Sunday papers, such as the *Sunday Times*, with its special business supplement, the *Sunday Telegraph*, the *Observer* and the *Sunday Express*, one weekly periodical is almost entirely devoted to investment matters, namely the *Investors Chronicle*, now amalgamated with the *Stock Exchange Gazette*. This publication gives a range of general and specific investment reviews and is widely used for reference purposes. Another periodical widely read for more general economic and political coverage is *The Economist*. The intermittent reports of the Economist Intelligence Unit on specific industries or fields of interest are highly regarded, but more likely to be utilised by the research departments than by the sales-and-service organisations.

(c) STATISTICAL SERVICES

Two companies produce statistical sheets covering industry and company information — Moodies Services Ltd. and the Exchange Telegraph Co. Ltd. Stockbrokers often send their clients copies of these cards with recommendations, since they show a record of the company's progress, together with any up-to-date information that has been published, and replacement cards can easily and inexpensively be obtained from the statistical companies.

Both systems have their advantages. The Exchange Telegraph reproduces the entire card when any new piece of information is added, so that it is only necessary to send one piece of paper to the client. Moodies Services supply a large card, with rather more information than is contained on the Exchange Telegraph card, and a smaller card containing the latest news. The Exchange Telegraph produces specialist services dealing with statistics and with Australian and European securities, while Moodies publishes an abridged service in loose-leaf form for quick reference, together with industrial and economic reviews on a regular basis.

One of the problems of having an easily available book of reference to take to meetings when enquiries may be made about shares not listed for discussion has been solved by *Moodies Investment Handbook*, containing information and statistics covering a range of some nine hundred leading U.K. companies.

The two services operate to complement each other, and many firms of stockbrokers subscribe to both.

(*d*) THE JOBBERS

For the small firms, particularly those who are unable to afford their own research or statistical offices, the jobbers form a useful centre of information. Many of the jobbing firms maintain their own research sections and take pains to investigate the companies in whose shares they deal. In addition, where stockbrokers publish reviews of industries or companies, they often send copies to the jobbers dealing in those shares. 'The market' therefore becomes particularly well informed about a company, and their opinion can be obtained by any broker who cares to ask.

In addition the jobbers indicate the public's reaction to information and the public's forecast of the prospects. If a client asks, 'What dividend does the market expect will be paid?', the jobbers will provide the answer. If that dividend is declared, and results are in line with anticipation, then it is unlikely that the price of the shares will move.

In the past some cynics have given their view that jobbers will give a 'market opinion' which happens to suit their own books. If they want to sell shares, the opinion will be favourable; if they want to buy them, unfavourable. In practice, this rarely occurs. With fierce competition between different jobbing firms, the jobber depends for his livelihood upon the goodwill of the brokers with whom he deals. He must, therefore, be at pains to be as impartial as possible in giving information of this sort, but will adjust his quotation of the shares to suit his own book.

(*e*) RESEARCH AND STATISTICAL DEPARTMENT

The work of this department is considered in detail in Chapter 4.

SPECULATIVE BUSINESS

The great bulk of stock-exchange transactions can be classified as investment business, since the institutions, charities, trusts and private investors who are looking for a relatively long-term home for their funds predominate. It would be idle to deny that speculative business also plays its part, although the amount of speculation is far less than the headlines in the daily Press would indicate. The speculator, in fact, can be a useful aid to the market, and the introduction of the new capital-gains taxes in the Finance Act, 1965 had a marked effect upon the freedom of trading. The absence of the professional speculator has caused wider price movements with greatly reduced turnover. When some crisis developed in the past, due to bad domestic or international news, and sellers forced down the price of stocks, it was usually the professional speculators who decided that the fall had gone far enough and whose buying steadied the market.

Those stockbroking firms which specialise in private-client business may also accord to the speculator additional services in carrying out closing bargains, arranging contangos, dealing in options or transacting business on margin.

(a) CLOSING TRANSACTIONS

Settlement for transactions in the great majority of the securities on the London market is made on a fortnightly accounting basis (see Chapter 3). As a result a security purchased during the account period may be sold later in the same account without the necessity of payment. Similarly a security sold during the account can be bought back at a later date without the necessity of delivering the stock. In either case the client pays or receives the difference between the cost of the purchase and the proceeds of the sale.

Transactions on this basis attract smaller expenses than normal investment transactions. While commission on the 'opening' bargain is charged at the normal rate, the 'closing' bargain attracts no commission and the charge to cover Government transfer stamp duty will be refunded, since the security will never be registered in the name of the client.

Transactions 'for the account' usually indicate that the client has insufficient ready cash to take up the shares he has purchased or may not actually possess the shares he has sold. As a result stockbrokers whose business is primarily concerned with investment rather than speculation may indicate to their clients after one or two closing transactions that this is not the type of business that they like to undertake.

(b) CONTANGOS

The account period of a fortnight (or three weeks where Bank holidays are involved in the period) is a relatively short time for a stock to move sufficiently to cover the expenses of the 'opening' transaction and produce a worth-while profit. In order to offer the facility to clients of prolonging the period, some stockbrokers will try and 'carry over' the transaction into the next account by means of a 'contango'. In order to effect this operation, a jobber or another broker must be found who wishes to 'carry over' the stock in the opposite direction. The client who has bought shares (the giver) will give a rate of interest for the privilege of not paying for them until the following settlement, the 'taker' accepting a rate for delaying the delivery of the security. The date when these transactions are matched is Contango Day, three days before Settlement Day, so that, if a carry-over is not possible, the client has time to close the bargain before dealings end for that account.

A client's request to 'carry over' a transaction again indicates that either he does not have the ready money to pay for his stock, or the stock to deliver, and many firms of stockbrokers will not accept 'carry-over' instructions.

(c) MARGIN TRADING

Financial facilities are also offered by some firms in the form of 'margin' trading. The broker may accept a fractional payment of the total cost of a purchase (usually not less than 20%) and finance the balance from his own resources. Should the price of the share fall sufficiently to endanger the broker's advance, the client is required to put up further capital or the shares can be sold at the broker's discretion. The amount of trading on margin is extremely small in the London Stock Exchange, with the result that no fixed margin limits are laid down by the Council. In Japan, for example, where it is calculated that about a quarter of the transactions on the Tokyo market are on margin account, margin transactions can only be undertaken in specified securities, and the proportion of the cost to be put up either in cash or in collateral is strictly governed.

(*d*) OPTIONS

In every commodity market, whether wool or metal or foreign exchange, opportunity is given to insure against fluctuations in price by 'forward' dealing. By this means a premium can be paid to cover the risk involved in delivering or receiving the commodity at a future date. The stock market is no exception. The insurance premium is termed 'option money' and the option is the right, usually over a period of three months, to buy a given security or to sell it at a fixed price. The individual who gives the option money is called the 'giver', and the other party, usually a firm of brokers rather than jobbers specialising in this field, is the 'taker'. Those who believe a share may rise in price take out 'call' options, which give the right to buy at the fixed or 'striking price' at any time in the three-month period. Those who take the opposite view take out 'put' options, giving the right to sell at the striking price during the period. The option, whether for a put or a call, is quoted at the same price, but the striking price may be slightly different. It is also possible to take out a 'double option', or 'put and call', giving the right either to sell or buy during the period. The cost of the double option is exactly twice that of the single option, but the striking price is the same for both.

An option enables the holder to benefit from any substantial fluctuation in the price of a volatile stock, with the outlay of a limited amount of capital and a known loss should the option not be exercised.

The 'striking price' of a call option is the offered price of the share in the market at the time of dealing, plus an allowance for half the *ad valorem* stamp duty and the cost of contango interest during the period of the option. For a three-month option, at current rates, the striking price would be about 2% above the offered price of the share. For a 'put' option, the striking price would be the bid price in the market at the time of dealing, plus an allowance for the contango interest, say $1\frac{1}{2}\%$ below the bid price for a three-month option. In the case of double options the striking price is usually the middle market price at the time of dealing.

During the period of the option the 'giver' has two courses open to him if the transaction shows a profit which he wishes to secure. If the option is for the 'call' he can either:

(i) close the transaction with the 'taker' of the option by selling the shares to him; or

(ii) sell the shares in the market in the ordinary way, carrying them over, if necessary, until the option expires.

For a 'put' option the alternatives are exactly the same, with the exception that the shares will be bought rather than sold.

If the option has not been closed at the end of the period, the giver has to 'declare' it (state whether or not he intends to exercise it) on Declaration Day, the Thursday before the Making-Up Day of the account (see Table 3, pp. 58–59) in which the option expires. If a profit can be taken, or at worst some part of the loss saved, the stockbroker will exercise the option on behalf of his client, otherwise it will be allowed to lapse.

The holder of an option is entitled to all rights, dividends, etc., that accrue during the period of the option. Dividends and rights are settled in cash, but capitalisation issues in shares.

The expenses of taking out an option are not much different from those applied in buying and selling shares in the ordinary way. Commission is charged at the same rate as though the 'giver' had carried out the transaction at the striking price, and contract stamp is charged at half the normal rate. The other half of the contract stamp is payable at the time of exercising the option.

(e) BULLS AND BEARS

It may be appropriate at this point to define the terms 'bull' and 'bear', which are well known in stock exchange parlance. Anyone who has purchased shares in the anticipation of a rise is termed a 'bull', while anyone who has sold shares in the anticipation of a fall is termed a 'bear'. A 'stale bull' or a 'stale bear' is someone whose initial judgement was at fault and who finds that the price of the stock has gone in the opposite direction, leaving him with a loss. An 'uncovered bear' is a seller of a security who does not possess it but is hopeful of buying it back at a profit, while a 'covered bear' is a seller who can deliver the security if required. The term 'bear covering', which may often be seen in the Press to explain a sharp rise in price, indicates that a number of earlier sellers were buying back their stock. Finally, the adjectives 'bullish' or 'bearish' are widely used to indicate optimism or pessimism in regard to future movements of prices.

CONCLUSION

The change which has taken place in stockbroking since the Second World War lies primarily in the emergence of the institutions, particularly the insurance companies, pension funds and unit trusts as a powerful influence in the markets for ordinary shares. The numbers of very rich private clients have simultaneously fallen, owing to the heavy impost of death duties. The combination of these two factors has caused a requirement for a much higher degree of technical skill in stockbroking and a far smaller dependence on private connections. In this day and age, however charming a stockbroker is as an individual, he will not achieve the really important business unless he provides a first-class technical service. The first leg of this service lies in an efficient system of production of all the accounting and other paperwork which makes up the transfer of securities from seller to buyer.

3

PRODUCTION

IN a service industry such as stockbroking, the production side of the business is almost entirely concerned with paper. In common with most professional partnerships in any walk of life, stockbrokers have neglected their general offices and devoted much more time and effort to improving their sales-and-service facilities and their research departments. Often the entire work of the general office is left in the care of the office manager, with at best the part-time direction of one of the partners who looks on it as an unremunerative chore. This attitude of mind has had two effects: firstly, it has resulted in an antiquated system of accounting and delivery of securities, since until recently there has been no concerted effort by member firms of The Stock Exchange to improve it; secondly, there is a marked lack of uniformity between the various firms in the systems operated in their own offices, which makes any major advance difficult to achieve.

Economies in production may, in fact, be the key to much of the future growth in stockbroking. Most firms find little difficulty in increasing their total business from year to year, but few of them have succeeded in maintaining the same profit margins on turnover to show an equally sharp increase in profits. The rise in wages and salaries, the increased rents on modern offices and the rise in prices of raw materials (printing and stationery in particular) have been unusually marked in the City of London. More and more firms, therefore, are paying increasing attention to new production and organisation methods.

The simplest method of describing the somewhat complex procedures that are carried out in the execution of an order to buy or sell shares is to follow the route taken by such an order from the moment it is received by letter or telephone from the client to the time that he in turn receives either a cheque in payment for the stock sold or his certificate showing his entitlement to the stock purchased.

In order to illustrate the examples chosen, a number of names will be mentioned and it may simplify matters if a code is used which will indicate their application:

All *clients'* names will begin with　　C.
　„ *jobbers'*　　　„　　　„　　„　　J.
　„ *brokers'*　　　„　　　„　　„　　B.
　„ *shares'*　　　„　　　„　　„　　S.

Provincial brokers will have the names of well-known towns and cities in the provinces, beginning with letters other than the four above.

Three principal departments are involved:

(*a*) the dealers in The Stock Exchange who actually make the 'bargain';
(*b*) the accounting sections who settle the money side of the transaction;
(*c*) the transfer sections who physically handle the deeds transferring the title between buyer and seller.

It should be appreciated here that the various sections mentioned may only exist in the larger firms and, in those with smaller staffs, one individual may carry out the work of several different sections.

STOCKS AND SHARES

Under current company law all shares must have a par or nominal value. If a company has an authorised ordinary capital of £1 million divided among 1 million ordinary shares, each share will have a par or nominal value of £1. Had there been 4 million shares, each share would have a nominal value of 5s.

In the distant past all risk capital (preference and ordinary capital) was quoted as shares, and these were individually numbered. The recording of the numbers of each share transferred became unduly burdensome to company registrars and, as a result, many companies altered their ordinary capital to ordinary stock. The quotation then applied to 'stock units' rather than shares. Subsequently the law was altered to permit transfer of unnumbered shares.

Since the term 'share' is more widely understood by members of the public, in the examples which follow this word will be used throughout, to avoid the constant repetition of 'stock or share'.

It should be noted that loan capital, which will be discussed more fully in later chapters, is always quoted as 'stock' since the owner does not possess a share in the concern, only a participation in a loan to it.

Let us suppose that a client, Mr. Charles Cuthbertson, wishes to sell 500 Smith's Potato Crisps Ltd. 5s. ordinary shares and to reinvest the proceeds in the purchase of Shell Transport & Trading Co. Ltd. registered ordinary 5s. shares. His instructions may be given verbally on the telephone, or may be addressed either to an individual or to the firm by way of correspondence, cable or telegram. In any event the instructions will be passed, first of all, to the Order Department.

ORDER DEPARTMENT

This department may be located in the stockbroker's office situated outside the confines of The Stock Exchange itself, or in his 'dealing box' adjoining the trading floor. The name 'box' adequately describes the room, which is usually a small kiosk, containing a number of telephones direct to the firm's switchboard and to important clients, and in some cases telex machines or teleprinters for direct contact with provincial exchanges and other centres throughout the world. The box is a convenient centre into which all orders are passed for execution in The Stock Exchange and from which information is passed to the sales-and-service departments operating from the main office or, in some cases, to clients direct.

Owing to the limited accommodation in the present Stock Exchange building, not all firms are able to possess boxes, but this situation should be greatly improved when the rebuilding is completed. Firms who do not have boxes normally telephone their instructions direct to their dealing staffs through the private telephones on the trading floor, or a number receive instructions direct from the clients through telephones situated in rooms immediately adjoining the floor itself.

DEALING STAFF

Three categories of individual make up the dealing staff: members of The Stock Exchange, who enjoy all the normal rights and privileges of membership, but who may or may not be partners of the firm; authorised clerks, who are employees of the firm, authorised to deal in securities, but who do not share any financial responsibility; and unauthorised clerks (or 'Blue Buttons'), who are permitted on to the floor but are not author-ised to buy or sell securities. Members and authorised clerks are difficult to distinguish from each other at a distance, each wearing a silver badge in the buttonhole or along the top of the breast pocket, inscribed with the name of the firm. On closer examination it will be seen that the badges of authorised clerks are also surrounded with a black line. In the case of the unauthorised clerks the badge is coloured blue, indicating to the jobbers that the individual may not actually deal in securities.

One of the dealers will receive from the order room the details of Mr. Cuthbertson's order, and will immediately enter the market to carry it out. Speed is important, particularly in times of great activity, since prices can change materially in a matter of minutes.

At the time of writing, the London Stock Exchange is in the process of rebuilding and the location of the various markets on the new trading floor is not yet finalised. It is as well therefore to describe the old trading floor as it existed for many years. The market (or 'the House', as it is called) was irregularly shaped, like a rather badly constructed coffin, with a large dome over the feet of the corpse and a smaller one over its chest. The roof was supported by columns, around which bench seats were placed, and the walls were lined with that green-tinged marble the colour of ripe Gorgonzola. The firms of jobbers are grouped into ill-defined markets (see Fig. 2), so that all dealings in Government securities take place in the gilt-edged market (which was appropriately located at the head of the corpse), while those of commercial and industrial enterprises are carried out in the middle of the floor (about the heart and stomach). Each firm of jobbers has its own designated position or pitch in each market in which it operates. Almost all have

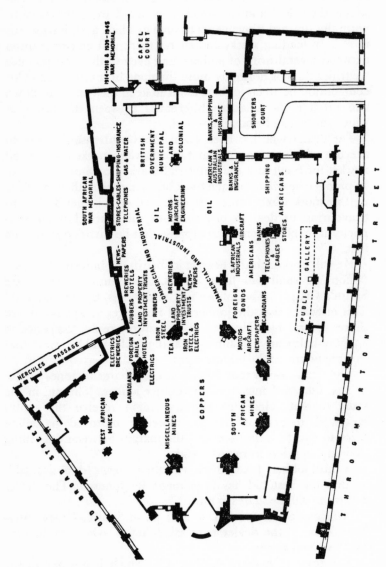

FIG. 2

on display a board showing the principal stocks or shares in which they deal and on which they mark price movements, normally upward movements in blue or black and downwards in red. In leading stocks and shares there will be competition between several firms of jobbers, and even in the least popular securities there is normally more than one firm interested. This competition between jobbers tends to keep their margins down and provide the smallest differential between the prices at which shares can be bought or sold.

The dealer who has been given Mr. Cuthbertson's order to execute will have to deal in two separate markets — the oil market for Shell and the industrial market for Smith's Crisps. In practice he will approach the jobbers in each of these markets in the most direct order, irrespective of whether he is endeavouring to deal in one share or the other, but for simplicity in explanation let us suppose that he carries out the sale first.

He will approach the nearest jobber in the industrial market (whom we shall call Jones & Co.) and enquire: 'What are Smith's Crisps?' The jobber will reply: '24s. 6d. to 25s. 1½d.' This indicates that the jobber will *buy* shares at 24s. 6d. or *sell* shares at 25s. 1½d. He may in fact simply reply, 'Sixpence to a penny-halfpenny', assuming that the dealer will be aware that the 'big figure' in the middle is 25s.

The dealer notes that he can sell his shares to Jones & Co. at 24s. 6d., and moves on to another jobber, Johnson, in the same market. Here his enquiry might receive the reply: '24s. 7½d. to 25s. 3d.' He has therefore improved his selling price to 24s. 7½d. and reduced the margin between the selling and buying prices from 7½d. to 6d.

A third jobber, Jakes, might call them '24s. 4½d. to 25s. 3d.', so that the best bid has been made by Johnson. The dealer returns to sell the shares to him.

'You made me 24s. 7½d. to 25s. 3d. in Smith's Crisps. Anything closer?' the dealer may ask Johnson, who may in turn ask: 'Are you many?'

The price in a share such as this, which is not one of the largest companies, may hold good in two to three thousand shares — in Shell considerably more — and the jobber will obviously be more prepared to improve his price if the number of shares is relatively small, or the transaction suits the position he holds in the shares.

'I'm only five hundred,' the dealer will reply, and it is important to note that at this stage the jobber does not know whether the broker wants to sell shares or to buy them. Johnson looks at his book to ascertain his position in the shares, since he is trading as a principal, buying from some brokers and selling to others.

'I'll make you 24s. 7½d. to 25s. 1½d.,' he might reply.

He has not improved on the bid, but he has shown his position to the broker (he would prefer to sell shares at 25s. 1½d. than to buy them at 24s. 7½d. — hence his movement of the offer price downwards), and the broker is morally bound to deal with him.

'Thank you,' says the dealer, 'I'll sell you five hundred at 24s. 7½d.'

Both dealer and jobber note this transaction in their own dealing books and the dealer moves on to check the price in Shell among two or three jobbers and to reinvest the sum of about £600 raised by the sale of Smith's Crisps. At length he finds the cheapest offer of Shell is made by Joseph & Co., and he enters the two deals in his dealing book.

This example answers one or two questions which are always asked about transactions on The Stock Exchange. Firstly, the jobber is not in a position to raise his price when a buyer approaches him or to lower it when a seller makes enquiries, because he never knows until the moment of concluding the deal whether the broker is a buyer or seller of the shares. Secondly, it illustrates the relatively narrow margin on which jobbers operate in the popular shares. To be quoted a 3d. price in Shell from the start (a margin of less than 1%) is by no means unusual, while in other higher-priced shares the margin may fall to considerably less. It must also be remembered that jobbers are taking considerable risks when they deal in large numbers of shares in volatile markets. One of the largest firms of jobbers in the industrial market has averaged a profit of ⅜d. per share in recent years.

It will be noted that prices move in multiples of 1½d. Over the years this system has been evolved to enable the jobber to move his prices conveniently as buyers or sellers predominate.

In gilt-edged and other loan capital, where prices are quoted per £100 nominal, the variation is in fractions of £1 — $\frac{1}{2}, \frac{1}{4}, \frac{1}{8}$, $\frac{1}{16}, \frac{1}{32}$ and $\frac{1}{64}$.

The quotation of a Government stock standing at 80 might therefore be $79\frac{7}{8}$–$80\frac{1}{8}$. Similarly in the higher-priced shares, quotations are in fractions of £1, such as £$6\frac{1}{8}$–£$6\frac{1}{4}$ (122s. 6d.–125s.). In the lower-priced shares the variations are in the same fractions, but of a shilling — $\frac{1}{2}$ = 6d., $\frac{1}{4}$ = 3d., $\frac{1}{8}$ = $1\frac{1}{2}$d., $\frac{1}{16}$ = $\frac{3}{4}$d. In the very low-priced shares, under about 5s., where there is considerable activity, prices will be quoted in changes of $\frac{1}{4}$d. or occasionally $\frac{1}{8}$d.

Thirdly, it illustrates the motto of The Stock Exchange — 'Dictum Meum Pactum' ('My word is my bond') — for neither the broker nor the jobber signs any contract on the deal, their respective words being sufficient evidence that a bargain has been transacted.

And finally, it times the change of ownership of the shares. From the moment that the dealer said to the jobber, 'I sell you five hundred Smith's Crisps at 24s. $7\frac{1}{2}$d.', as far as The Stock Exchange is concerned Mr. Cuthbertson ceased to be the owner of the Smith's Crisps shares. And from the time he said to Jones & Co., 'I buy Shell', Mr. Cuthbertson became the owner of these shares. If, one minute later, a take-over bid had been announced for Smith's Crisps that caused the shares to rise suddenly by 10s., the firm of stockbrokers is responsible for delivering five hundred shares for the payment of only 24s. $7\frac{1}{2}$d. a share. When stockbrokers act for a client they are entirely responsible for completing his transactions, to the extent of all the financial resources of all the individual partners. As a result they are understandably cautious in checking the credit-worthiness of new clients.

Having concluded the transaction, the dealer will report back to the order room so that, where instructed, the client can be informed on the telephone of the prices at which the sale and purchase were effected. The details of the two bargains will also be transmitted to the general office for the preparation of the relevant documents.

LIMIT ORDERS

In the simple example quoted, the client merely instructed his broker to sell one security and purchase another. On many occasions, however, the client will fix a price at which he wishes the transaction to be carried out, and reference is made to such an order as a 'limit'. Every firm of brokers maintains a Limit Book in which such orders are entered, and it is often the duty of one dealer to keep a constant check throughout the day on all the limits which are nearing completion. Where no specific time-limit is set, clients are circularised at regular intervals to enquire whether their limit instructions still hold good.

Some reinvestment orders may also be fixed at limit prices, so that the purchase may only be carried out if the sale can be effected, or vice versa. Such orders are referred to as 'contingent'.

MARKING

The dealing staff has an additional duty to perform concerning each transaction carried out during the day, which is known as 'marking the bargain'. Slips are provided in the House with columns for the name of the stock or share, the price, the date, the name of the firm of brokers and any special remarks. The marks are reproduced daily in the Stock Exchange Daily Official List and also in the *Financial Times*. They provide figures against which a client can check that his own transaction has not been carried out at an unduly high or low price.

The total number of marks is also used as an indicator of the activity in markets, although it is only an approximate guide. The marking slip does not contain the number of shares transacted, so that a single mark can represent one share or 100,000 shares. Marking, although normal, is only compulsory in the following special cases.

(i) *Bargains between Non-Members*

It has already been explained that brokers in London are not permitted under the rules to match buying and selling orders in their own offices, without first offering the business to the jobbers in the market. If the jobber can carry out one side of the transaction, either bidding or offering, then the broker must

deal with him and disregard the matching order. Where the
jobbers are unable to compete on either side of the transaction,
the broker may carry out the deal, charging commission only
to the client initiating the business, and the marking slip must
be signed by two firms of jobbers agreeing to the business as
'between non-members'. A special symbol is attached to the
mark in the list the next day.

(ii) *Bargains at Special Prices*

A broker may have an order in a very large line of shares, often
valued at some hundreds of thousands of pounds, and a jobber
may either supply these shares or buy them, as the case may be,
at a price outside the normal quotation. Alternatively the
broker may carry out a 'put-through', as described in the
previous chapter, again at a price outside the normal quotation.
In either case the mark will bear a symbol denoting a bargain
at a special price in the lists.

'Put through' business is a source of some contention both
inside and outside The Stock Exchange. The fractional difference in price mentioned earlier as the jobber's profit is normally
one-half of the standard stockbroker's commission rate ($\frac{1}{2} \times$
$1\frac{1}{4}\%$), although it may be a smaller figure when the size of the
transaction is very large. The broker who carries out the
business, because he has in effect made two transactions, selling
for his original client and buying for his other clients, is entitled
to charge commissions on both sides of the transaction and
welcomes this opportunity. This situation has resulted in a
number of large transactions being made outside The Stock
Exchange altogether. A merchant bank, for example, with a
large line of shares to place and with friendly relations among
the likely buyers in the shape of insurance companies, pension
funds and other investment institutions, is able to offer a line of
shares at a price exclusive of either the broker's commissions
or the jobber's turn.

Some brokers feel that, while the jobber should obviously receive some reward because it is on his quotation of price that the
'put-through' is based, a rate of half the commission is too high
and that this is one reason why more and more business is by-
passing The Stock Exchange. The leading jobbers, on the other
hand, who would be prepared to risk taking a substantial line

of shares in the hopes of gradually selling them over a period
with the possibility of a higher profit because of the enhanced
risk, find that these opportunities become increasingly scarce.

It should also be remembered that the jobber carries a
residual risk if the broker becomes a defaulter. Failures of
broking firms in the past have made this point unpleasantly
clear.

A bargain may be carried out at a special price for an
entirely different reason. Where the number of shares that a
broker has to sell (not to buy) is so small that the work of taking
delivery of the shares makes the transaction unremunerative to
the jobber, he may bid a price a few pence lower to compensate for this. This mark will bear the same symbol in the
lists as a 'put-through' at a special price.

(iii) *Previous Day's Bargains*

The marking board closes at 2.15 p.m. each day, while The
Stock Exchange itself remains open until 3.30 p.m. and dealing
between jobbers and brokers continues on the telephone until 5.30
p.m. or later. As a result the bargains carried out towards the
end of the day are omitted from the lists published the following
morning and will be shown with a symbol denoting 'previous
day's business' one day later.

MARKET BOOK

In most firms the entries from the dealers' own books are
transcribed into a consolidated list termed the Market Book.
This gives a record of all bargains transacted and will be used
later in the day to check against the contract notes in order to
ensure that none has been completed incorrectly or omitted.

ACCOUNTING PERIODS

Before explaining the preparation of a contract note, however,
a word should be said about Stock Exchange accounting
periods.

In the U.S., Canada, Japan and a number of other overseas
stock exchanges, shares sold or purchased on one day must be
delivered or paid for four or five business days later. The delays
inherent in our transfer system (now largely eliminated by

the Transfer Act of 1963), the requirements of the jobbing system and certain concessions in the rules on commissions have caused the London Stock Exchange to divide the year into twenty-two accounting periods. The majority of these are fortnightly periods, with three-weekly accounts covering the Easter, Whitsun and August Bank Holidays, and Christmas periods. Taking one of the normal fortnightly accounts, any shares purchased in the two business weeks from, say, Monday 1st to Friday 12th must be paid for by Tuesday 23rd (see Table 3 below). Similarly, a client who sells shares in this period, provided that he has delivered his securities and signed the necessary transfer forms, will be paid on the 23rd. It follows that anyone who buys shares and sells them again within the period of the account does not require to pay for them at all, and is not liable for the 1% *ad valorem* stamp duty levied on the purchases, and anyone who sells shares early in the account and buys them back again later does not require to deliver them. The fortnightly accounting system therefore encourages some degree of short-term speculation, although this has been considerably reduced by the capital gains tax.

TABLE 3

ACCOUNTING DATES

Day of the week	Description	Date in Example	Details
1st Week			
		October	
Monday	First day of end-October account	1st	First day for dealing in normal way for transactions to be settled on October 23rd. Securities usually declared 'ex dividend'.
Tuesday		2nd	
Wednesday		3rd	
Thursday		4th	
Friday		5th	

Day of the week	Description	Date in Example	Details
2nd Week			
Monday		8th	
Tuesday		9th	
Wednesday		10th	
Thursday		11th	First day on which forward dealings for next account may be made ('new time' bargains).
Friday	Last day of end-October account	12th	Last day of dealing in normal way for settlement on October 23rd.
3rd week			
Monday	Contango Day	15th	'Making-up' prices published.
Tuesday	Making-Up Day	16th	
Wednesday	Ticket Day	17th	3 p.m. last time for issuing tickets.
Thursday	First intermediate day	18th	
Friday	Second intermediate day	19th	
4th Week			
Monday	Third intermediate day	22nd	
Tuesday	Account Day	23rd	Date of settlement of all transactions in end-October account.

CASH TRANSACTIONS

While the majority of dealings in the stocks and shares of companies are settled at the end of each account, there are two exceptions — gilt-edged securities and almost all new issues.

The gilt-edged market covers securities issued by the central Government, Dominion and colonial Governments, local authorities and certain public boards. Transactions in these securities are normally settled on a cash basis, delivery and payment being made the following day.

New issues, both of companies coming to the market for the first time and capitalisation or rights issues of established companies, are normally transferred on allotment letters or renounceable certificates. In either case the seller signs the reverse of the document of title, renouncing his right to the stock or shares, and delivery without the payment of stamp duty can be effected by the purchaser for a limited period. In effect, therefore, new issues transferred in this way have many of the attributes of bearer documents and are considered in more detail in a later paragraph (see p. 100).

GENERAL PROCEDURE FOR THE DELIVERY OF SECURITIES

At the end of each accounting period, when hundreds of thousands of shares have changed hands through the medium of the jobbing system, there is a mammoth job of matching buyers against sellers. In addition to this a broker, who may have bought many thousands of the same shares for different clients, has the task of identifying which shares belong to whom as they are delivered.

At the end of the account, therefore, the broker produces a slip of paper for each purchase, entitled a ticket. This bears the details of the purchase (number of shares, price, consideration and stamp duty payable), together with a reference number (ticket number) from which the broker can identify the buyer of the shares. Before the Stock Transfer Act, 1963, it used also to bear the name into which the shares should be registered, and although this practice is no longer compulsory, a number of brokers continue to include the name, since it gives an easier method of identification than the ticket number alone and can be used as an additional check if the ticket number becomes altered in copying.

The tickets are sent to the jobber from whom the shares were purchased. He now has the task of matching these against the brokers from whom he has bought shares. In The London Stock Exchange there is no penalty for 'odd lots' as there is in New

York. In other words, a seller can get the same price for 233 shares that he could obtain for 200, whereas in New York, since certificates are made out in round numbers of hundreds and tens, the small odd number of shares will not command such a high price. The jobber may match a buyer of 1,000 shares against sellers of 500, 220, 150 and the last 130 out of another seller of, say, 357. The ticket for the 1,000 shares therefore has to be split into the requisite amounts to make up the total, and these split tickets are despatched by the jobber to the brokers who acted for the four different sellers.

This system would work perfectly if, during an account, the total number of shares sold in a given company exactly matched the total number purchased. In practice, of course, this situation rarely occurs. The function of the jobber is to make a market and, as a result, at the end of an account he almost always finds himself either 'long' of shares (having bought more than he has sold) or 'short' (having sold more than he owns). Where he is long of shares the remedy is simple, for he receives the shares himself and pays for them. Jobbers have a special reduction of the normal 1% *ad valorem* stamp duty on shares which are held in their names for less than two months in order to assist them to keep a free market.

Where the jobber has sold short of shares, however, the situation is obviously more complicated. The normal remedy is simply to postpone delivery of the shares until the following account, or sometimes over an even longer period. Where certain rights are attached to shares purchased but not delivered (i.e. dividends, capitalisation issues, etc.), the jobber is responsible for making these good at the time of delivery.

Where the jobber has exactly matched sellers and buyers, he is no longer concerned in the delivery of the shares. He has passed to each of his sellers a ticket showing the buying broker and the price the buying broker paid, and it is up to them to get together and settle direct.

Under the simplest of systems, the selling broker would only have to pin the ticket to the documents of transfer and, on Account Day, deliver them to the buying broker and receive payment.

If the selling broker and the buying broker settled the payment between themselves, how then does the jobber receive his remuneration? The answer is also simple. On the ticket was marked the price which the *buyer* had paid for the shares. This may be quite different from the price at which the seller sold his shares, because the two transactions could have taken place a fortnight apart during the account. Nevertheless the buying broker would have paid the seller the price at which he dealt with the jobber. As far as he is concerned, therefore, his account with the jobber on this particular transaction is square. The seller, on the other hand, dealt with the jobber at one price and has received a cheque for something different. This difference is therefore credited or debited to the account of the jobber.

SETTLEMENT OFFICE

Sorting out the 'shapes' in a jobber's office to match buyers and sellers most economically is a skilled job and one which lends itself to the use of sophisticated equipment. In the shares of the leading companies as many as eight jobbers may be dealing, and it would be more economical to pool the results of all these firms so that shares bought from Jackson might be married against shares sold by Judd.

Taking this system to its ultimate conclusion, a clearing-house could be set up in The Stock Exchange which took note of all the transactions by every member firm and matched the buyers and sellers in the most economical manner. In fact the Settlement Office undertakes this task for the leading securities in which there is a reasonable turnover, representing about one-third of the total daily transactions.

Each day member firms submit to the Settlement Office a list of their transactions in clearing stocks. At the end of the account the Settlement Office issues to each firm of brokers a list of the 'shapes' of the securities sold by them and the names of the brokers to whom each number of shares should be delivered. At the same time a list of the 'shapes' making up each of their purchases is given to buying brokers, showing the names of the brokers who will be delivering the securities, to whom they should issue their tickets.

MAKING-UP PRICE

A complication arises in clearing stocks, for the same jobber may not have dealt with both the buyer and the seller. If therefore the buyer paid the seller the price shown on the ticket, the seller would not know to whom the difference between this price and his selling price should be credited or debited. To overcome this, the Settlement Office publishes a 'making-up price', at which all transactions in a particular clearing stock are settled. This price is marked on the ticket and the purchasing broker pays the selling broker the value of the shares based on this price. Any difference between this price and the price at which the seller dealt will therefore be credited or debited to the jobber's account. Similarly, the buying broker's account with the jobber will now show a credit or a debit based on the difference between the making-up price and the price at which the purchase was made.

CENTRAL STOCK PAYMENT

Under the simple system described, each selling broker would receive a cheque from each buying broker (or jobber) for each piece of stock delivered, and would pay cheques to each buying broker (or jobber) for all stock received. The Central Stock Payment Office of the Stock Exchange co-ordinates all these payments so that each member firm receives only one cheque for all stock delivered and pays only one cheque for all stock received.

The physical delivery of tickets and the securities themselves (with the exception of gilt-edged and some bearer securities) is also centralised, so that messengers are not constantly walking round the City between member firms.

CONTRACT DEPARTMENT

Returning to the example of Mr. Cuthbertson's sale and purchase, the details of the two transactions were transmitted by the order room to the Contract Department. Different firms of brokers use different forms of transmission, some collecting written slips at intervals from the House, some using telephone reporting or direct transmission on teleprinter or facsimile machines. The destination of these reports, however, is the Contract Department, and all of them will bear the same essential information — the name of the client, the number of shares bought or sold, the description of the share, the price,

SOLD THIS 10 JAN 1966 **FOR** 18 JAN 1966 **SETTLEMENT BY THE ORDER OF** C. CUTHBERTSON, ESQ.

CONTRACT No. 23714

(A) AMOUNT	(B) SECURITY	(C) PRICE	(D) CONSIDERATION		(E) SUNDRIES		(G) GOVERNMENT CONTRACT STAMP	COMMISSION (H)				(I) NET AMOUNT	
					PARTICULARS	AMOUNT		RATE	AMOUNT				
500	SMITH'S POTATO CRISPS LTD. 5/- SHARES.	24/7½	615	12	6			4 0	1¼%	7	13	11	607 14	7

Subject to the Rules, Regulations & Customs of the London Stock Exchange.

BOUGHT THIS 10 JAN 1966 **FOR** 18 JAN 1966 **SETTLEMENT BY THE ORDER OF** C. CUTHBERTSON, ESQ.

CONTRACT No. 23594

(A) AMOUNT	(B) SECURITY	(C) PRICE	(D) CONSIDERATION	(E) GOVERNMENT TRANSFER STAMP	(F) COMPANY'S REGISTRATION FEE	(G) GOVERNMENT CONTRACT STAMP	COMMISSION (H)			(I) TOTAL AMOUNT	
							RATE	AMOUNT			
330	SHELL TRANSPORT & TRADING CO. LTD., 5/- ORDINARY SHARES.	36/-	594 0 0	6 0 0		4 0	1¼%	6 18 6		607 2	6

Subject to the Rules, Regulations & Customs of the London Stock Exchange.

FIGS. 3 and 4. Contract Note Details

and the name of the firm of jobbers with whom the transaction was carried out. The report will also contain other relevant instructions — in the example quoted, that the Shell shares purchased are a reinvestment of the proceeds of the sale of Smith's Crisps.

The Contract Department prepares the invoices for the business carried out. These invoices, termed contract notes, are signed by the firm of brokers and in law are binding upon them. The sale and purchase contract notes to illustrate our example are shown in Figs. 3 and 4.

The following information is included:

Dates. The date of the transaction and the settlement date by which payment must be made for shares purchased or on which payment should be received for shares sold.

Amount (A). The number of shares.

Description (B). The full description of the share.

Price (C). The price at which the transaction was executed.

Consideration (D). Column A × column C.

The following three figures in the case of a sale and four in the case of a purchase represent the expenses of the transaction.

Ad Valorem Stamp Duty (E). An *ad valorem* duty of 1 % is payable on the *purchase* of all U.K. registered stocks and shares, other than the majority of gilt-edged securities, and is shown in Table 4 below. New shares and shares transferable as bearer documents are exempt.

TABLE 4

U.K. TRANSFER STAMP DUTY

(Finance Act, 1963, effective from 1 August 1963)

Any registered stocks and shares (subject to stamp £ s. d.
duty) where the amount or value of the consideration
for the sale does not exceed £1 5s.   3

Exceeds:			£	s.	d.
£1 5s. but does not exceed	£2 10s.				6
£2 10s. ,, ,,	£3 15s.				9
£3 15s. ,, ,,	£5			1	
£5 ,, ,,	£10			2	
£10 ,, ,,	£15			3	

TABLE 4 CONTINUED

Exceeds:

£15	but does not exceed	£20		4
£20	„	„	£35	5
£35	„	„	£60	10
£60	„	„	£80	15
£80	„	„	£100	1
£100	„	„	£125	1 5
£125	„	„	£150	1 10
£150	„	„	£175	1 15
£175	„	„	£200	2
£200	„	„	£225	2 5
£225	„	„	£250	2 10
£250	„	„	£275	2 15
£275	„	„	£300	3

£300 — for every £50 and also for any fractional part
of £50 10

The duties on transfers not on sale and not by way of voluntary disposition are liable to the fixed duty of 10s.

Transfers in favour of a charitable body or charitable trust are stamped at the normal rate, i.e. at 1%.

Registration Fee (F). A registration fee of 2s. 6d. per transfer deed is payable to many companies, although a number have recently cancelled this payment. South African shares and certain other overseas securities attract a higher payment. Where a contract note represents a single transaction with one firm of jobbers it is usual to charge only 2s. 6d. for registration,` but where more than one bargain may have been undertaken to obtain the total number of shares, several registration fees may be charged.

Contract Stamp (G). A stamp is affixed to both sale and purchase contract notes based on the value of the consideration, as shown in Table 5 below:

TABLE 5

Up to	£5				nil
Over	£5	but does not exceed		£100	1s.
„	£100	„	„	£500	2s.
„	£500	„	„	£1,000	4s.
„	£1,000	„	„	£1,500	6s.
„	£1,500	„	„	£2,500	8s.

TABLE 5 CONTINUED

Over	£2,500	but does not exceed		£5,000	12s.
,,	£5,000	,,	,,	£7,500	16s.
,,	£7,500	,,	,,	£10,000	20s.
,,	£10,000	,,	,,	£12,500	24s.
,,	£12,500	,,	,,	£15,000	28s.
,,	£15,000	,,	,,	£17,500	32s.
,,	£17,500	,,	,,	£20,000	36s.
,,	£20,000 and over				40s.

Commission (H). The full details of commission rates are shown in Appendix 2. The minimum rate is almost invariably applied by all firms of stockbrokers and it will be noted that the smallest commission which can be charged on a transaction in ordinary shares is £2 (other than those 'at discretion', where quite often no commission is charged at all, or transactions under £100 in value). The paperwork involved in a typical transaction, which is described later in this chapter, illustrates the uneconomical nature of small business.

Concessions. A number of concessions are available, the most important being for bargains over £5,000, over £25,000, and closing transactions. In addition reduced commission may be charged on orders of over £50,000 in gilt-edged securities.

Over £5,000. Where the consideration on a transaction in one security for the same client exceeds £5,000, commission may be charged *on the excess* at a rate of not less than half the minimum.

Over £25,000. Where the consideration on a transaction exceeds £25,000, commission may be charged at half the minimum rate throughout. Where the consideration is less than £25,000, commission of not more than half the rate on the full amount of £25,000 need be charged. In effect, since commission is normally charged at the full rate on the first £5,000 and at half-rate thereafter, any bargain where the consideration lies between £20,000 and £25,000 is carried out at the rate of commission applicable to £20,000.

Continuation. Where an order is given exceeding £5,000 and, for one reason or another (shortage of stock or price movement), cannot be completed immediately, the concessions may be applied for a period of three calendar months after the date of the original transaction.

Closing. A transaction opened during one account period and closed for the same client during the account need attract commission only on the original purchase or sale. In the case of bargains for cash settlement (such as gilt-edged), the closing bargain may be carried out free of commission within a period of twenty-eight days.

Agent's Commission. Orders executed on the instructions of a recognised bank, other than for principals of the bank, attract a refund of commission of one-quarter. Firms and individuals on the list of authorised agents (solicitors, accountants and others specialising in investment) may obtain a refund of one-fifth of the commission on orders for their clients.

Employees of the firm of stockbrokers are also entitled to a share of the commission on business which they have introduced, at the discretion of the firm, normally up to a maximum of a half-share for individuals who are members of The Stock Exchange. Other employees, providing they are on the Register of Attachés and Clerks, may receive up to one-third of the commission. Where a return of commission is given to banks or other agents outside the firm, a note to this effect must be shown on the contract note.

Total (I). In the case of the sold contract note the expenses in columns E to H are deducted from the consideration in column D and the total proceeds to which the client is entitled entered in the final column. In the case of a purchase the expenses are added to the consideration to produce a total cost.

In the example it will be noted that it was impossible to re-invest exactly the proceeds of the sale, so that Mr. Cuthbertson will have a small credit balance of 12s. 1d. at the settlement date.

The contract notes are checked. The contract stamps are affixed and they are then signed by one of the partners of the firm. Since the contracts are binding, care is taken to see that no mistakes occur at this stage, and the contract notes are des-patched to the client.

Before proceeding further, a word of warning should perhaps be given to the reader. The object of the remainder of this chapter is to show the logical steps which are taken in both the accounting procedures and the delivery of the documents of title. The exact steps taken are a mystery even to some members of The Stock Exchange themselves, but unfortunately they make fairly dry and unpalatable reading. The reader who prefers the more entertaining work of the Research Department and other specialist sections is advised to skip lightly on to Chapter 4.

BOUGHT AND SOLD CONTRACT JOURNALS

Separate books of account are kept for purchase and sale transactions. The first of these are the Contract Journals. Each journal is, in effect, a list of all the contract notes, columnised so that totals may be obtained of all the items in columns D to I.

These journals form the first entry in the accounting system, and we shall follow through each posting to the various ledgers as the accounting system is described. The journals also give an immediate indication of the business carried out. It is common practice for one of the partners to examine these journals each morning to keep a check on the firm's business. From this he can assess whether the total commissions appear to be satisfactory, whether any particular client (or occasionally even a member of the staff) is engaged in speculative transactions, whether each department is keeping up to its target and so on.

The journal sheets are columnised and all the sub-totals should agree across the page. When the daily postings to the other ledgers have been completed, their totals should agree with the totals for the individual columns of the respective journals.

CHECKING THE BARGAIN

It will be recalled that, at the time of making each bargain with the jobber, no written contract was signed but the transaction was made by word of mouth between the jobber and broker. Dealers of both parties wear the names of their firms on metal strips either clipped through their buttonholes or along the tops of their breast pockets. In the confusion of great activity in markets, mistakes can be made by either side, both in identifying the person with whom the deal has been made and in entering the correct details in the dealing book. Also, particularly in the case of a reinvestment, the exact number of shares bought or sold cannot be known until the contract details have been calculated. In the example quoted earlier the dealer would have bought 'about 300 Shell' after calculating in his head the approximate proceeds of the sale of Smith's Crisps.

Each morning clerks from the brokers' and jobbers' offices meet in the Settlement Room beneath the floor of The Stock Exchange and check the bargains of the previous day. This gives an opportunity for brokers to give jobbers the exact details of their 'about' bargains and to correct any other occasional errors that may have occurred.

The question is often asked as to what happens if either the jobber or the broker repudiates the bargain. With the many thousands of bargains each day there are occasionally cases where one or other side has no record of a bargain (after checking with all the other likely firms who might have dealt, on the assumption that the dealer booked the bargain to the wrong firm); where both sides appear to have either sold the shares or bought them; or where the number of shares or price does not agree. Normally, if the error is not obviously the fault of one party, any resulting loss is divided between the jobber and the broker. On very rare occasions, where the dispute cannot be resolved amicably between the member firms, it is referred to the arbitration of one or more members.

Checking lists are prepared in a variety of ways, one system being a carbon copy of part of the contract set. It is important that the checking list should be sorted into jobber order, so that the clerk can check all his bargains with a given jobber at the same time, and also that the name of the client does not appear on the checking slip, so that his identity is not inadvertently revealed to other brokers.

CLIENTS' LEDGERS

A specimen sheet from a machine posting system for Clients' Ledgers is illustrated in Fig. 5, showing the two bargains taken in our example. In the case of the purchase bargain all the items shown in the columns of the contract note (Fig. 4) are debits to the client's account. While these items are going to be credited individually to other accounts in order to provide the balancing entries required, it is obviously unnecessary to list them individually in the client's account. The total amount (column I) is therefore posted in the debit column.

A similar procedure is adopted for the sale bargain, but in this case net proceeds are posted to the credit of the client, while the relevant expenses involved (column G and H) are credited to the Stamp and Commission Accounts. Again, by posting the net proceeds to the client's credit, the same effect is achieved as posting the consideration to his credit and the individual expenses to his debit. The client's account now shows a small balance in favour of Mr. Cuthbertson, being the difference between the proceeds of the sale and the amount reinvested.

Unless other instructions are given by the client, a cheque for this amount would normally be posted to him on Settlement Day.

THE LIST BOOK

It is necessary to keep a record of the transactions not only under the names of the clients, which can be found from the Clients' Ledger, but also under the heading of the share. A List Book of all transactions is kept, classified under the names of the shares, for the passing of names. The List Book is also used for checking claims for dividends and rights and capitalisation issues.

Two shares have been selected for the example quoted, one of which is a clearing stock and one a non-clearing stock, so that the clearing-house system can be examined.

The List Book provides a record in alphabetical order of transactions carried out in each stock. Some firms may keep separate List Books for clearing and non-clearing stocks, and as the books will be in constant use during the period of the passing of names, separate volumes are probably kept for various groups of letters of the alphabet.

Fig. 6 illustrates the purchase bargain in our example. It will be seen that this is only one of many throughout the account. In this case Mr. Cuthbertson is listed as the buyer and Joseph & Co., the jobber, as the seller.

The same procedure is carried out in the case of the sale bargain, shown in Fig. 7. Here the jobber's name, Johnson, appears in the buyer's column and the client's in the seller's column.

The four columns on the right-hand side of the List Book are left blank, but will be completed during the three intermediate days.

PAYMENTS TO

DIVIDENDS TO

CLIENT.

LLOYDS BANK LTD.,
LITTLE WREN,
CAMBRIDGE.

C. CUTHBERTSON.
76, SNOWY LANE,
BASHFORD.

CARD NUMBER   1.

FOR SETTLEMENT   18 JAN 1966.

DATE	BOUGHT	SOLD	SECURITY	PRICE	DEBIT	CREDIT	BALANCE	NUMBER OR FOLIO	REMARKS	OLD BALANCE
10 JAN 66	330		SHELL TRANSPORT & TRADING CO. LTD. ORD	36/-	£607. 2. 6					12. 1CR
		500	SMITH'S POTATO CRISPS LTD. ORD.	24/7½		£607.14. 7	12. 1CR	23594		
18 JAN 66			TO CHEQUE		12. 1		0CR	23714		

FIG. 5. Clients' Ledger Extract

MAKE - UP PRICE   38/-   SHELL TRANSPORT & TRADING ORDINARY.

Bargain Date	Amount	Buyer	Price	Contract Number	Seller	Amount	Amount	From	Price	Passed to
10 JAN 66	330	C. CUTHBERTSON.	36/-	23594	JOSEPH & CO	330	330		36/-	C. H. TRACE.
"	300	Wigan & Co.	36/-	23596	Joseph & Co.	300	300		36/3	"
11 Jan 66	500	Mrs Clegg.	38/-	23598	Jones & Co.	500				
12 Jan 66	1000	Mr Crabb.	39/-	23599	Jenkins & Co	1000	1000	23599	39/-	Miss Chase.
18 Jan 66	1000	Joseph & Co.	38/6	23604	Miss Chase.	1000	1000	C. H. Trace	39/-	C. H. Trace.
20 Jan 66	500	Jones & Co.	39/-	23608	Mrs Clegg.	500	Closing			

SMITH'S POTATO CRISPS 5/- ORDINARY.

Date	Amount	Buyer	Price	Contract Number	Seller	Amount	Amount	From	Price	Passed to
10 JAN 66	500	JOHNSON & CO.	24/7½	23714	C. CUTHBERTSON.	500	300	JOHNSON	24/9	C. CUTHBERTSON
							120	"	25/1½	"
							80	"	25/6	"

FIGS. 6 and 7. List Book Extracts

TICKET No. **2 3 5 9 4**

ALL NEW SHARES, DIVIDENDS AND OTHER RIGHTS ARE HEREBY CLAIMED

DATE OF BARGAIN   10 JAN 1966   SETTLEMENT   18 JAN 1966

JOBBER	AMOUNT	SECURITY	PRICE	CONSIDERATION		GOVERNMENT TRANSFER STAMP	
JOSEPH & CO.	330	SHELL TRANSPORT & TRADING CO. LTD., 5/- ORDINARY SHARES.	36/-	594	0 0	6	0 0
			STAMP M U	6	0 0		
			38/-	627	0 0		
			TOTAL	633	0 0		

A. BROKER & Co.
THROGMORTON STREET, E.C.2   PAY 999

GIVEN TO   C. H.

FIG. 8. Ticket

BOUGHT BARGAINS

NAMES DEPARTMENT

At this stage it is desirable to trace through the procedures for the purchase and the sale transactions separately, since they are somewhat different. A ticket is prepared for every purchase (see Fig. 8) which bears much of the information of the original contract note. This ticket shows in addition the name of the jobber and also the code number of the firm of brokers. The code number must be printed clearly on all tickets and transfer forms to enable the Settlement Office to sort these items rapidly and simply into their correct destinations.

Where the security is a clearing stock, as in our example, the jobbers fix a making-up price, based on the price ruling at the close of business on the last day of the account. The list of making-up prices is available at 10.30 a.m. on Contango Day (see Table 3).

The making-up price is inserted in the space provided on the ticket and a new consideration is calculated based on this price. As already mentioned, the buying broker will pay this new consideration to the selling broker when the stock is delivered, making good any difference to the jobber.

As the tickets are passed out to the Central Stock Payment Office, they are ticked off in the List Book, the amount, the price and the jobber's name being completed in the last four columns until the List Book contains the entries shown in Fig. 6. The second column is left blank, since this is used only for sold tickets.

At first sight it may seem a waste of time and effort to insert the price at which the ticket is made out and the name of the jobber yet once more in the List Book. The reasons behind these entries will be seen in the succeeding entries in Fig. 6.

Wigan & Co., who purchased 300 shares at 36s., are country brokers and it will be recalled that it is permitted to 'net' the bargain in this case. In other words the London broker, having dealt with the jobber at 36s., renders a contract note to the broker in the provinces without charging commission, but adds his commission on to the price of the share (in this case 3d.). The ticket will therefore bear the price of 36s. 3d. The form of transfer will contain a consideration based on this figure and will attract *ad valorem* stamp duty levied at this consideration.

In this case, therefore, the final column but one will have the net price of 36s. 3d. shown in it, while the price column in the centre of the List Book sheet will be shown at 36s.

The name of the jobber is added because this shows that the ticket has actually left the broker's office. The next two entries in Fig. 6 show the purchase by Mrs. Clegg of 500 shares on the 11th of the month and the sale of the same shares before the end of the account. If the tickets were allowed to leave the office of the broker, in due course 500 shares would be delivered for Mrs. Clegg, which she had already sold. Not only would the broker have to pay for the shares on delivery and would not be able to recoup the money until sale documents had been signed by Mrs. Clegg, but the *ad valorem* stamp duty would be forfeit. The entry in the final columns therefore gives proof that the ticket has been held back in the office, since the bargain has been 'closed' by a later sale.

In the subsequent entries it will be seen that two other clients have dealt in the same number of shares in opposite directions, Mr. Crabb having bought 1,000 shares and Miss Chase having sold 1,000. In this event, when the numbers match and there is no possible loss of *ad valorem* stamp duty to the brokers, it is simpler to leave these two bargains out of the settlement and 'cross' them within the broker's own office. No ticket is passed out of the office, but is delivered across to the Sold section of the Names Department to be matched internally.

NON-CLEARING STOCK

The only difference that concerns the Names Department when a non-clearing stock is purchased is that the ticket itself is delivered to the jobber with whom the transaction was carried out (normally through his box in the Settlement Room).

Tickets should be issued before 3 p.m. on Ticket Day (see Table 3), except for clearing stocks, for which an additional business day is allowed.

SPLITTING THE TICKET

(i) *Clearing Stocks*

When Mr. Cuthbertson reinvested the proceeds of his sale in Shell, he bought 330 shares. It is very unlikely that a seller of exactly this number of shares will be found to match his purchase. The returns which are made to the Settlement Office each day are processed on their electronic equipment in order to provide the best possible match. On the first intermediate day the Settlement Office issues to each firm a list showing the 'shapes' for each of their purchases and the firms to whom the names should be sent. In the example chosen the shapes might well be 280 shares due from one broker and 50 from another.

The buying brokers therefore pass their tickets direct to the selling brokers by placing them in the relevant 'boxes' in the Settlement Room.

(ii) *Non-Clearing Stocks*

For the purchase of a non-clearing stock a slightly different procedure is adopted. On Ticket Day the tickets for all purchases are placed in the jobbers' boxes in the Settlement Room. It is then the jobbers' task to match up the buyers and sellers in the most economic fashion. In many cases they can simply pass a buying broker's ticket direct to the selling broker. In other cases they may have to split a buyer's ticket between several sellers, and this involves preparing duplicate tickets with the appropriate number of shares on each. A large buying order may be satisfied on occasions by dozens or even hundreds of small sellers.

A broker may have bought and sold the same shares for a client during the account, but carried out the purchase through one firm of jobbers and the sale through another. In the case of clearing stocks this all evens out during the clearing procedures. In non-clearing stocks, however, the broker will owe a ticket to the jobber from whom he made the purchase and expect to receive one from the jobber to whom he sold the shares. When he receives this ticket, he records the price and number of shares, and merely marks the back of the ticket with the firm of jobbers to whom he owes it and passes it on. A single ticket may therefore pass through a number of different hands before it finds its ultimate destination. The list of names on the back of a ticket is called 'the trace'.

LOSS OF STAMP AND FEE ON SPLITS

It will be recalled that, on considerations over £300, the *ad valorem* stamp duty moves in steps of 10s. (Table 4) for every

END JAN 1966

JOSEPH & CO.

1 SHELL TRANSPORT & TRADING ORD.

2 LONDON PRUDENTIAL INVESTMENT TRUST ORD.

3 Cols 3 - 9 cover other securities in which Joseph & Co deal.

4

5

6

7

8

9

TOTAL DEBIT	DATE	DEBIT	PRICE	DETAILS	1	2	3	4	5	6	7	8	9
1925. 0. 0	18 JAN 66	1925. 0. 0	38/6	B 23064	1000								
		627. 0. 0	38/-	T 23594	330								
		570. 0. 0	38/-	T 23596	300								
3547. 0. 0		425. 0. 0	8/6	T 26897		1000							

TOTAL CREDIT	DATE	CREDIT	PRICE	DETAILS	1	2	3	4	5	6	7	8	9
		594. 0. 0	36/-	B 23594	330								
1559. 0. 0	10 JAN 66	540. 0. 0	36/-	B 23596	300								
3459. 0. 0		425. 0. 0	8/6	B 26897		1000							
3547. 0. 0		1900. 0. 0	38/-	T 23604	1000								
		88. 0. 0	RECD	Diff.ce.cheque									

FIG. 9. Jobbers' Account Extract (Bought Bargain)

£50 or part of £50 of the consideration. In the example quoted, where the ticket for 330 Shell has been split into one for 280 and one for 50, the considerations on the transfers at the purchase price of 36s. will amount to £504 and £90 respectively. The first will therefore attract *ad valorem* duty of £5 10s. and the second £1. It is no fault of Mr. Cuthbertson that his purchase has been delivered in two pieces and he has only been charged £6 on his contract note. Someone, therefore, has to make good the extra 10s.

In the case of clearing stocks the total number of shares that pass through the clearing is calculated and each jobber is charged a proportionate share of the loss on stamps. In the case of non-clearing stocks the jobber bears the loss directly.

In addition there is a small loss involved where a company still charges a fee (normally 2s. 6d.) for the registration of each transfer. These losses are again borne by the jobbers.

JOBBERS' LEDGERS

The ledger used for the maintenance of jobbers' accounts is one of the more complicated books in a stockbroker's office. Fig. 9 illustrates a specimen sheet from the account of the jobber from whom Mr. Cuthbertson's Shell were purchased. Jobbers' accounts are settled on Account Days, and the accounting periods, being for the most part fortnightly, are known as 'mid-October account' or 'end-October account', etc. The accounting period is shown in the top left-hand corner of the sheet and the jobber's name in the top right-hand corner.

Firms of jobbers may deal in many different securities. The largest firm in the industrial market deals in no less than 3,000 different stocks and shares. The spaces marked 1 to 9 are used as headings for the columns appearing immediately beneath and numbered in a similar fashion. The heading for Shell and the entries underlined in column 1 refer to the example which has been followed.

When the Clients' Ledger was posted with Mr. Cuthbertson's purchase, it was stated that the *debit* for the consideration, the Government stamp, company's registration fee, contract stamp and commission would be matched with *credit* entries in other ledgers. The debit entry for the consideration of £594 is matched by a credit entry in the Jobbers' Ledger of the same

CONTRACT No. 23594

BOUGHT THIS 10 JAN 1966   FOR 18 JAN 1966   SETTLEMENT BY THE ORDER OF   C. CUTHBERTSON, ESQ.

JOBBER	AMOUNT	SECURITY	PRICE	CONSIDERATION	GOVERNMENT TRANSFER STAMP	COMPANY'S REGISTRATION FEE	GOVERNMENT CONTRACT STAMP	COMMISSION RATE	COMMISSION AMOUNT	TOTAL AMOUNT
JOSEPH & CO.	330	SHELL TRANSPORT & TRADING CO. LTD., 5/- ORDINARY SHARES.	36/-	594 0 0	6 0 0		4 0	1¼%	6 18 6	607 2 6
			STAMP M U 38/-	6 0 0 627 0 0						
			TOTAL	633 0 0						

	DEBIT. (A)	CREDIT. (B)	BALANCE. (C)	DETAILS. (D)
	537. 10. 0	627. 0. 0	633. 0. 0 CR.	STAMP
	96. 0. 0	6. 0. 0	10. 0 0	280 - BEAR & CO.
		10. 0	10. 0	50 - BULL & CO.
				SPLITS

GIVEN TO

FIG. 10. Bought Ticket Account

amount. Column 1 gives the number of shares. The 'details' column shows the contract number, which serves as an identifying number to trace the transaction through to its conclusion. The 'price' column shows the price at which the transaction was carried out with the jobber. The shares were bought from the jobber at a price of 36s. and therefore the jobber has a *credit* of £594 with the broker.

Once the making-up price has been published, the broker knows what price he is going to pay for shares that are delivered to him. In fact he will pay 38s. a share — a higher price than that at which he dealt with the jobber, and therefore the jobber will owe him the difference.

Once the tickets have been despatched to the Settlement Office, the clerks operating the Jobbers' Ledgers are able to post the *debit* item. In the same columns at the top half of the sheet they post the number of shares, the same identifying ticket number, the making-up price and the total debit. On this particular transaction the jobber will therefore owe the broker the difference between £594 and £627, or the sum of £33.

Where the purchase is in a non-clearing stock (see ticket T. 26897), the posting of the *credit* in the bottom half of the ledger will be carried out as before on the day after the bargain has been made. The posting of the *debit* will again be made shortly after Ticket Day, and this time the same price in most cases will be used in both credit and debit so that the difference will be nil.

Where the stockbroker made a purchase of 300 Shell at 36s. for Wigan & Co., a firm of provincial brokers (ticket B. 23596), the contract was submitted at a 'net' price of 36s. 3d. The jobber is *credited* with the consideration at the price of dealing (36s.), but is *debited* with the amount shown on the ticket — i.e. the making-up price of 38s. and the different consideration of £570, which is the price at which the buying broker will pay for the shares from the selling broker.

So far the example of the jobber's account illustrated shows only purchases made by the broker. The jobber's account for sale transactions will be considered when the sale example is followed through. In practice, of course, both purchase and sale transactions are entered on the jobber's accounts as they occur or as the documents come to hand, an overall debit or credit being shown by the difference between the total debit and total credit columns.

TICKET ACCOUNT

The overall position of the jobber has now been clarified in regard to the purchase transaction in our example, but it is important to follow through each individual purchase and ensure that the correct payment has been made.

The selling brokers are involved in the delivery of the Shell shares, one for 280 shares and the other for 50. Each will receive a split ticket bearing the identifying ticket number and showing the amount due (the number of shares × the making-up price). In addition, stamps in payment of the *ad valorem* duty, to be paid by the buyer, will have been affixed to the transfers by the selling brokers who will require additional payment to cover their outlay. As the stock arrives in the broker's office on Settlement Day, it is checked to see that it is in good order (described later), the split tickets are recalculated to ensure that no mistake has been made in the splitting, and one cheque, representing the total of all stock received, is paid to the Central Stock Payment Office. Twenty-four hours later a reconciliation statement is received from that Office and any discrepancies adjusted.

The *debit* entry of £627 in the Jobber's Ledger must be matched by a *credit* entry, and this credit opens up the Ticket Account (Fig. 10, column B). In column B a *credit* of the stamp duty matches the *debit* of the stamp from the Clients' Ledger. The two figures are added together to make the total credit in column C.

As one of the selling stockbrokers, Bear & Co., delivers shares, a cheque is paid for the securities and a *debit* for the amount due (the making-up value plus the *ad valorem* stamp duty) is entered in the debit column. The number of shares and the broker's name is also shown to identify the delivery. A second entry is made as the other selling broker, Bull & Co., delivers the balance of 50 shares. The total of debits on the Ticket Account would now balance with the total of credits, but for the small difference in the *ad valorem* stamp duty of 10s. as a result of splitting the name ticket into two amounts. This amount is posted to the credit of the ticket and will then be balanced by a debit to the Clearing-House Splits Account. In the case of a non-clearing stock the debit would be posted on the jobber's account.

DELIVERY OF BOUGHT SECURITIES

The delivery of the stock and its payment concludes the most straightforward part of the accounting procedures, although there are still a few more entries to be made and one or two complications which can arise. Following the example of the purchase of Shell on to its conclusion, therefore, it is worth turning to the departments dealing with the physical delivery of the security.

When Bear & Co. delivered the 280 shares, it may well have been the entire amount sold by their client, and the delivery would probably consist of three pieces of paper, pinned together. The first, the split ticket bearing the identifying number (usually referred to as the ticket number) is almost a duplicate of the original ticket illustrated earlier in Fig. 8.

The form of transfer (Fig. 11) is a standard form which must contain the name and address of the seller, the consideration (based on the 'ticket price', *not* the 'making-up' price), the *ad valorem* stamp duty, which is impressed on the document by the Stamp Office, and the number of shares with a full description. This original form of transfer is also signed by the seller. A space is left at (*a*) for the full name and address of the buyer to be inserted.

The third piece of paper is the share certificate. This in itself is of no value, since it is only a form of receipt showing that in the example quoted, Dr. Christopher Cantor is the owner of 280 Shell Transport & Trading Co. Ltd. ordinary shares of 5s. each. Combined with the form of transfer duly completed, however, these documents are considered 'good delivery'.

The stock will have been delivered by Bear & Co. to the Central Stock Payment Office, sorted there into the correct destination, and collected by the buying broker's messengers after 11.30 a.m. daily, or between 3 and 5 p.m. on the Monday before Account Day. Whenever the stock is brought into the broker's office, it is examined to ensure that it is in order. In

999

£5. 10. 0.
STAMP
DUTY
IMPRESSED
HERE

	(Above this line for Registrars only)	
		Certificate lodged with the Registrar
Consideration Money £ 504--------		(For completion by the Registrar/Stock Exchange)

Full name of Undertaking.	SHELL TRANSPORT & TRADING COMPANY LIMITED	
Full description of Security.	ORDINARY SHARES OF 5/- EACH FULLY PAID	

Number or amount of Shares, Stock or other Security and, in figures column only, number and denomination of units, if any.	Words	Figures
	TWO HUNDRED AND EIGHTY	- 280 -
		units of

Name(s) of registered holder(s) should be given in full: the address should be given where there is only one holder.

If the transfer is not made by the registered holder(s) insert also the name(s) and capacity (e.g., Executor(s)) of the person(s) making the transfer.

In the name(s) of

DR. CHRISTOPHER CANTOR,
2, WAYSIDE CLOSE,
FINCHINGSTEAD,
SUSSEX.

I/We hereby transfer the above security out of the name(s) aforesaid to the person(s) named below *or to the several persons named in Parts 2 of Brokers Transfer Forms relating to the above security:*

Delete words in italics except for stock exchange transactions.

Stamp of Selling Broker(s) or, for transactions whic not stock exchange transactions, of Agent(s), li acting for the Transferor(s)

Signature(s) of transferor(s)

1. *Christopher Cantor*

2. ....

3. ....

4. ....

Bodies corporate should execute under their common seal.

Date...

Full name(s) and full postal address(es) (including County or, if applicable, Postal District number) of the person(s) to whom the security is transferred.

Please state title, if any, or whether Mr., Mrs. or Miss.

Please complete in typewriting or in Block Capitals.

(a)

NAME AND ADDRESS OF BUYER TO BE COMPLETED IN THIS SPACE BY BUYING BROKER.

I/we request that such entries be made in the register as are necessary to give effect to this transfer.

Stamp of Buying Broker(s) (if any)	Stamp or name and address of person lodging this form (of other than the Buying Broker(s))

FIG. 11. Form of Transfer

particular the certificate will be examined with the transfer to ensure that they match, the consideration on the transfer will be checked against the consideration at the ticket price, and the stamps impressed on the transfer will be checked to ensure that the right amount has been applied. A further check with regard to the rights of the new owner of the stock to dividend payments or other benefits is also made and is considered in more detail on pp. 94–8.

The remaining shares are delivered via Bull & Co., and this may well be only a part of the total sale made by their client. The documents are likely to be only two in number, the split ticket and a broker's form of transfer. Just as the buying broker's ticket was split by the Settlement Office or the jobber, so the transfer form can be split by the selling broker. Instead of the seller of the shares having to sign all the transfers required by the various new owners of his shares, he signs only one for the total number sold and the others are prepared and stamped by the broker to guarantee that they represent part of the original. In the same way it is unlikely that Sir Charles Colinworth, who sold more than 50 Shell shares, will have a certificate for exactly 50. The broker's forms of transfer, splitting up his total holding, are therefore sent either to the Shell registrar's office or to the Certification Office of The Stock Exchange, where they are marked as 'certified'. The preparation of transfers and the certification of securities by the selling broker will be considered in more detail when the selling order is followed in our example. When the delivery of the 50 Shell shares is received from Bull & Co., the stock is examined and paid for.

BOUGHT TRANSFER DEPARTMENT

During the period of the account in which the Shell purchase occurred, the Bought Transfer Department, who will handle the securities as they are delivered, has been given details of the purchase. A record sheet is prepared (Fig. 12) to follow the various stages which the stock will undergo until it finally reaches the client in the form of a certificate. This record may be yet one more carbon copy of the original purchase contract note.

First of all the clerks in the department will refer to the

CONTRACT NO. 2 3 5 9 4

BOUGHT THIS 10 JAN 1966   **FOR** 18 JAN 1966   **SETTLEMENT BY THE ORDER OF**   C. CUTHBERTSON, ESQ.,

JOBBER	AMOUNT	SECURITY	PRICE	CONSIDERATION	GOVERNMENT TRANSFER STAMP	COMPANY'S REGISTRATION FEE	GOVERNMENT CONTRACT STAMP	COMMISSION RATE	COMMISSION AMOUNT	TOTAL AMOUNT
JOSEPH & CO.	330	SHELL TRANSPORT & TRADING CO. LTD., 5/- ORDINARY SHARES.	36/-	594 0 0	6 0 0		4 0	1¼%	6 18 6	607 2 6

(A) CHARLES CUTHBERTSON,
76, SNOWY LANE,
BASHFORD.

(B) CERT SENT TO:
LLOYDS BANK LTD.,
LITTLE WREN, CAMBRIDGE.

DATE DELIVERED (C)	AMOUNT (D)	DELIVERED BY (E)	TRANSFEROR (F)	CERT. NO. OR CERT. (G)
18 JAN 66	280	BEAR & CO.	DR. C. CANTOR	CERT NO 7284
19 JAN 66	50	BULL & CO.	SIR C. COLINWORTH	CERTD.

DATE LODGED (H)	AMOUNT (I)	TRANS. RECEIPT DATED (J)	CERT. NO. (K)	DATE SENT (L)
21 JAN 66	330	25 JAN 66	6281	11 FEB 66

Fig. 12. Bought Delivery Record

Clients' Register and mark on the record sheet the particulars shown at A and B. Mr. Cuthbertson's full name and the address at which he wishes his shares registered must be inserted at A. This name and address may be different from the client's usual postal address. He may prefer the address of his bank, for example, if he is likely to be away from home from time to time. He may not wish his identity disclosed to someone who looks through the records of shareholders, which can be examined at Companies House, and may prefer the shares to be placed in the name of a nominee company. All these details should be available from the Clients' Register. Details of the address to which the certificate should be sent and any particular instructions regarding the payment of dividends are entered at B. In the example quoted the client prefers that dividends should be paid directly into his bank account. A form of request must therefore be sent to the client for signature, instructing the registrar of the company where to pay all dividends.

As the stock is delivered, columns C to G are completed. On 18 January, 280 shares were delivered by Bear & Co. and the seller (or transferor) was Dr. C. Cantor. A certificate accompanied the transfer form. On 19 January the balance of 50 shares was delivered by Bull & Co., the seller being Sir C. Colinworth, and the transfer was certified.

The delivery of the 330 shares is now complete. The two transfers are therefore completed with the full name and address of Mr. Cuthbertson from the details on the delivery record. These two documents, together with the certificate for the 280 shares, are attached to the delivery record and passed to the Registration Department.

REGISTRATION DEPARTMENT

It is now the job of this department to turn the transfers received into a certificate and to ensure that this is received by the client safely. The documents are recorded in a Registration Fee Book and then despatched to the registrar of the company concerned (in this case Shell), the date of despatch being marked in column H. In due course the majority of companies will return a transfer receipt, acknowledging the transfers and giving a date when the certificate will be available. This date

ACCOUNT

END JAN 1966

JOBBER

JOHNSON & CO.

1	Cols 1 & 3 - 9 cover other securities in which Johnson & Co deal.
2	SMITH'S POTATO CRISPS ORD.	3
4		5		6
7		8		9

Debit

1	DETAILS	PRICE	DEBIT	DATE	TOTAL DEBIT	2	3	4	5	6	7	8	9	#
	S. 23714	24/7½	615. 12. 6	10 JAN 66	615. 12. 6	500								1
	Diffce cheque	PAID	8. 7. 6	18 JAN 66	624. 0. 0									2
														3

Credit

1	DETAILS	PRICE	CREDIT	DATE	TOTAL CREDIT	2	3	4	5	6	7	8	9	#
	T 23714	24/9	371. 5. 0			300								31
	T 23714	25/1½	150. 15. 0			120								32
	T 23714	25/6	102. 0. 0		624. 0. 0CR	80								33
														34–48

FIG. 13. Jobbers' Account Extract (Sold Bargain)

is entered into a diary so that the receipt may be sent off on the correct day. In due course the transfer receipt is exchanged for the certificate. The Registration Department clerk turns up the delivery record for instructions as to the despatch of the certificate. Mr. Cuthbertson likes them sent to his bank. The number of the certificate and the date of despatch is completed in the delivery record and the transaction is now complete.

SOLD BARGAINS

NAMES DEPARTMENT

In the example chosen, Smith's Crisps has been selected as a non-clearing stock. On Ticket Day the jobber (Johnson) receives from the buying brokers tickets for their various purchases. Where possible he matches these exactly against orders from selling brokers, but in the example it is supposed that three buyers are required to match Mr. Cuthbertson's sale. These buying brokers and the prices on their tickets are:

Blakehouse & Co.	300 shares	24s. 9d.
Bryant & Bryant	120 shares	25s. 1½d.
Benjamin & Son	80 shares	25s. 6d.

The tickets received from these buying brokers may have had to be split by the jobber or may be the originals. They are placed by the jobber in the selling broker's box in the Settlement Room and collected by the selling broker's settlement room clerk in due course.

Once in the office the names are sorted by the Names Department so that each name or batch of names matches a certain sale (identified by the contract number), and where there is more than one ticket they are pinned together. The final four columns of the List Book are then completed (Fig. 7), showing the numbers of shares on each ticket, and the ticket price. The calculation of the considerations on the tickets are then checked and they are passed to the Jobbers' Ledger Department.

JOBBERS' LEDGERS

It will be recalled that the *credit* entry of the consideration posted to the Clients' Ledger (Fig. 5) — £607 14s. 7d., being £615 12s. 6d. credit less debit of £7 17s. 11d. — must be balanced by similar *debit* entries elsewhere. On the day after the bargain has been made, therefore, a debit entry is created to open the Jobbers' Ledger in regard to this particular transaction (Fig. 13). As the tickets arrive, the considerations calculated at the ticket price are posted as credits to the jobber's account (Fig. 13).

Once again the number of shares, the identifying ticket number and the ticket price are listed, and the total of all credits in the jobber's account is shown in the final column.

On this particular transaction, therefore, the jobber receives the difference between the consideration at which Mr. Cuthbertson's shares were sold and the considerations which will be paid in due course by the three buying brokers.

TICKET ACCOUNT

The considerations shown on the three tickets, posted as a *credit* to the Jobbers' Ledger, must be balanced by a *debit* elsewhere. The three entries open the Ticket Account (Fig. 14, column B) as the first debit entries. The entries are usually shown individually, for identification purposes should enquiries arise later, and the total is given in the column of balances (column D).

In due course the transfer forms will be prepared for delivery and it is the duty of the selling broker to ensure that the correct *ad valorem* stamp duty is affixed. These duties are listed with the identifying ticket numbers of the bargains to which they refer, and in due course are posted as *debits* to the Ticket Account.

DELIVERY OF SOLD SECURITIES

Finally, the securities will be delivered and a cheque received from the Central Stock Payment Office representing payments from the buying brokers, Blakehouse, Bryant and Benjamin. The amounts in each case will be equal to the consideration, calculated at the ticket price, and the *ad valorem* stamp duty. These figures are posted to the *credit* of the Ticket Account, which should now balance exactly.

SOLD TRANSFER DEPARTMENT

When the letter enclosing the sale contract is sent to the client, a sale transfer form will be included for Mr. Cuthbertson to sign

CONTRACT NO. 23714

SOLD THIS 10 JAN 1966 **FOR** 18 JAN 1966 **SETTLEMENT BY THE ORDER OF** C. CUTHBERTSON, ESQ.

JOBBER	AMOUNT	SECURITY	PRICE	CONSIDERATION	SUNDRIES PARTICULARS	AMOUNT	GOVERNMENT CONTRACT STAMP	COMMISSION RATE	AMOUNT	TOTAL AMOUNT
JOHNSON & CO.	500	SMITH'S POTATO CRISPS LTD. 5/- SHARES.	24/7½	615 12 6			4 0	1¼%	7 13 11	607 14 7

DETAILS (A)	DEBIT (B)	CREDIT (C)	BALANCE (D)
	371. 5. 0		
STAMP	4. 0. 0		
	150. 15. 0		
STAMP	1. 15. 0		
	102. 0. 0		
STAMP	1. 5. 0		
18 JAN 66.			
CASH - BLAKEHOUSE		375. 5. 0	631. 0. 0
CASH - BRYANT		152. 10. 0	
CASH - BENJAMIN		103. 5. 0	0

NAMES RECEIVED

NO.	M/U	PRICE	POSTED JOBBERS CREDIT	AMOUNT
300		24/9		371. 5. 0
150		25/1½		150. 15. 0
80		25/6		102. 0. 0

FIG. 14. Sold Ticket Account

CONTRACT NO. 2 3714

SOLD THIS 10 JAN 1966 FOR 18 JAN 1966 SETTLEMENT BY THE ORDER OF C. CUTHBERTSON, ESQ.

JOBBER	AMOUNT	SECURITY	PRICE	CONSIDERATION			GOVERNMENT CONTRACT STAMP	COMMISSION RATE	AMOUNT			TOTAL AMOUNT		
JOHNSON & CO.	500	SMITH'S POTATO CRISPS LTD. 5/- SHARES.	24/7½	615	12	6	4 0	1¼%	7	13	11	607	14	7

	BUYERS' TICKET NO.	NUMBER OF SHARES	TICKET PRICE	TRANSFEREE	WHO PAYS	PARTICULARS	AMOUNT	CERT. NO. OR CERTD.	DATE DELIVERED
	XX1	300	24/9		BLAKEHOUSE			CERTD	18 JAN 66
A	762	120	25/1½		BRYANT			CERTD	DO
B	616	80	25/6		BENJAMIN			CERTD	DO
C									
D									
E									

FIG. 15. Sold Delivery Record

and return with the certificate for the shares sold. The transfer form is completed only in respect of the columns showing the number of shares in both words and figures and his name and address.

Most clients, if they are wise, keep their share certificates in a bank. To save them trouble a delivery order may be enclosed, instructing the bank to deliver the relevant certificates to the broker. This will be signed by Mr. Cuthbertson and sent on to the bank.

On receipt of the share certificate, the Sold Transfer Department will mark it with the sold ticket number for identification, before filing it in a suitable place to await delivery in due course.

When Mr. Cuthbertson returns his sold transfer, duly signed, it is married up with his certificate, coming from his bank. The Ledger Department is informed that the securities sold have been received with all the documents in order and the client may be paid on Account Day.

The transfer and certificate are then filed to await the receipt of the tickets from the buying brokers. In the example taken, three tickets will be received from Messrs. Blakehouse, Bryant & Bryant, and Benjamin. It is therefore necessary to split the transfer deed, which is carried out by preparing three 'broker's transfer forms', one for 300 at 24s. 9d. per share for Blakehouse, one for 120 at 25s. 1½d. per share for Bryant & Bryant, and one for 80 at 25s. 6d. per share for Benjamin. At the same time the reverse of the original transfer form is completed, showing the breakdown of sales. If Mr. Cuthbertson only sold a part of his total holding of Smith's Crisps and his certificate was for 800 shares, a balance of 300 will be due to him in due course.

STAMPING

The three 'broker's transfers' must now be stamped with the *ad valorem* duty in each case. The amount is marked in pencil on the left-hand side of each transfer and they are sent to the Inland Revenue Stamp Office for the requisite stamps to be affixed to the transfers. For this purpose the Stamp Office issues special forms not unlike the paying-in books issued by banks, a duplicate copy of which will be kept in the office for posting the individual stamps to the *credit* of the Stamp Account.

CERTIFICATION

The certificate representing the underlying shares sold must also be 'split', and this operation can be carried out either at the office of the company's registrars or the Certification Office of The Stock Exchange. Since the Certification Office is within easy reach of all brokers' offices, most of the certification work is carried out there.

The three broker's transfer forms, properly stamped, and the original form, duly signed by the client, are sent to the Certification Office, together with the certificate. If the documents are in order the office will certify the three broker's transfers accordingly, return these to the broker, and despatch the original transfer and certificate to the company's registrar.

In the selling broker's office, the Sold Transfer Department pins the buying broker's tickets to the transfer forms, which are now ready for delivery.

The Central Stock Payment Office provides a two-part set for stock delivery. The top sheet forms the record of delivery for retention in the broker's office; the second copy a similar record for the department.

In addition, selling brokers will keep a record of all deliveries in bargain order (Fig. 15) for reference purposes.

PAYMENT OF THE CLIENT

A client who is in credit will be sent a statement of account on Account Day. In the case of Mr. Cuthbertson a cheque for the small balance of 12s. 1d. will be enclosed. Clients in debit will be sent a statement a week before Account Day to enable them to pay their accounts by that date.

BALANCE CERTIFICATE

Mr. Cuthbertson is still due the balance of 300 shares out of the total certificate for 800 Smith's Crisps. The receipt received from the registrar of the company at the time of certification is held by the Registration Department until the due date for exchange into a certificate. It is then sent, according to the instructions on the client's record card, to his bank for safe keeping.

DIVIDEND DEPARTMENT

The examples selected have dealt only with a straightforward sale and purchase of securities. The stockbroker has an additional duty to ensure that his client is protected in regard to all dividends and other rights which may be attached to the securities bought or sold. On the first day of each account, Contango Day for the previous account, stocks and shares whose dividend announcements have been declared recently are quoted 'ex dividend' (xd). A buyer of these stocks or shares after this date is not entitled to the dividend or interest payment, although this may not be made for some weeks to come, unless the transaction is made under special provisions.

A list of 'ex dividend' securities is published in *The Stock Exchange Weekly Official Intelligence* which also contains information regarding the amount of the dividend, the date of the closing of the company's transfer books and the date of payment of the dividend. The transfer books are closed to enable the registrar of the company to pay the dividend to shareholders on record at the closing date. The 'ex dividend' date is normally selected so that it is virtually impossible for someone to buy shares which are not entitled to the dividend and register the transfer with the company before the books are closed. Any delay in delivery or of registration may, however, mean that a purchaser of shares is not registered in time to receive the dividend, although he is entitled to it.

Little difficulty would arise if all securities were delivered on Account Day, for the buying broker would know that all deliveries on a given date in a particular stock were entitled to the dividend, while a fortnight later all deliveries of this stock must have been purchased 'ex dividend'. The inevitable delays in delivery — a large number of trustees, all of whom are required to sign the sale transfer form; the seller on holiday abroad; or the jobber having sold short — while much improved by the Stock Transfer Act, 1963, make it imperative to scrutinise each delivery in order to protect the buyer's interests.

Where the transfer books of the company concerned have closed and the buyer is entitled to the dividend, the Dividend Department will make an immediate claim on the selling broker, in duplicate through the Central Stock Payment

SHELL TRANSPORT & TRADING ORDINARY.

BOOKS CLOSE	PAID	X.D.	RATE	TAX
10 FEB 66	28 FEB 66	31 JAN 66	-. 6d.	8/3d.

Amount	Claimed By.	Date.	Other Reference.	Ticket Number.	DEBIT.	Amount.	Claimed From.	Date.	Other Reference.	Ticket Number.	CREDIT.
..330	C. CUTHBERTSON	10 Jan 66	. .	23594	4. 16. 11	..330	JOSEPH & CO.	....	. .	23594	4. 16. 11
..300	Wigan & Co.	"	. .	23596	4. 8. 1	300	Joseph & Co.		..1234	23596	
..1000	Mr Crabb.	12 Jan 66	-23604	23599	14. 13. 9	..1000	Miss Chase.	18 Jan 66	-23604	23599	14. 13. 9

Fig. 16. Dividend Account Extract

Office. Settlement of this claim must then be made within
fourteen days.

In many cases, although the transfer books have not actually
closed by the date of delivery, insufficient time is available to
register the shares in the new holder's name before that date.
A claim is therefore made to the selling broker, which must be
settled within twenty-eight days. In the event of delays in settlement, recourse may be had to the Central Stock Payment Office.

The number of dividend claims, although greatly improved
compared with pre-1963 days, is still quite considerable.
Nothing is more infuriating to a client, who has filed his return
of income for the previous year, than to receive a claim for a
dividend paid many weeks previously. It is always difficult
to persuade the client that the selling broker has no control
over the registration of the stock in the name of the new buyer.
This action lies entirely in the hands of the buying broker and,
while in the opinion of The Stock Exchange nine months is a
maximum reasonable delay in claiming a dividend between
members, in law a client may claim back dividends over a
period of seven years.

BOUGHT BARGAINS

Before the delivery of the security, the Dividend Department
will examine the list of securities due to be received and open
accounts in the Dividend Ledger for those where the books will
be closed before the stock is due. On the assumption that the
Shell purchased in our earlier example fell into this category,
the entry in the Dividend Ledger would be as shown in Fig. 16.

At the head of the page the title of the stock is given with
details taken from *The Stock Exchange Weekly Official Intelligence*.
In the *debit* columns on the left-hand side the number of shares,
the client, the date of the bargain and the identifying ticket
number are recorded, together with the amount of dividend
due. At the same time the matching *credits* are posted to the
accounts of the clients concerned.

When securities are delivered, the Dividend and Transfer
Departments are usually responsible for checking that they
are 'good delivery'. They must confirm that either the correct
certificate is attached, or that the transfer form is certified;
that the stamp duty is correct; that the stock is correctly

described on the transfer form; and that either the original form is signed by the seller or a broker's form contains the broker's stamp. If the date on the ticket, which is pinned to the transfer form, indicates that the security was purchased in the previous account, *The Stock Exchange Weekly Official Intelligence* is examined to ensure that no dividend claims are involved. If the date indicates an earlier purchase, the daily Official List must be studied.

Referring to the example, *The Stock Exchange Weekly Official Intelligence* will indicate that the transfer books have closed, so that the seller, although not entitled to the dividend, will receive it from the company. The Dividend Department therefore calculates the amount of the dividend due, and prepares the dividend claim which is sent to the selling broker in duplicate through the Central Stock Payment Office. The *debit* entries in the Dividend Ledger will then be completed as shown in Fig. 16, and the first three columns of the *credit* entry may be made, leaving only the amount in the last column to be completed when the selling broker pays the claim.

SOLD BARGAINS

Much the same procedures are carried out for ensuring that prompt claims are made on clients who have sold securities for dividends to which they are not entitled.

Buying brokers' dividend claims are checked to ensure that the seller has in fact received the dividend. The claim is entered as a *debit* of the Dividend Account, and opens the matching *credit* of the buying broker's account. The balancing entry to the *credit* of the Dividend Account and the *debit* of the client's account follow, and the transaction is completed with the receipt of the client's cheque and the despatch of the firm's cheque to the buying broker.

DIVIDENDS ON AMERICAN AND OTHER FOREIGN SECURITIES

This somewhat specialised function of the Dividend Department is considered in Chapter 8.

RIGHTS DEPARTMENT

In just the same way that the Dividend Department ensures that clients do not miss dividends to which they are entitled or do not retain them if others are entitled to them, so the Rights Department plays the same role in regard to rights and capitalisation issues.

Whenever a company announces a rights or capitalisation issue, the relevant dates are published in *The Stock Exchange Weekly Official Intelligence*, issued each Monday. The Rights Department prepares a list of companies, recording the date when the share will be quoted 'ex rights' or 'ex cap.', the dates when the company's books close, the last date of renunciation and, in the case of rights issues, the dates of payment of the calls. Unlike the procedure in the payment of dividends, shares are not quoted 'ex rights' and 'ex cap.' on the first day of a new account, but on the day after the allotment letter or other document of title is posted to shareholders. In many cases an additional check will be made by a member of the Rights Department visiting the Quotations Department of The Stock Exchange daily to note those shares which are being quoted 'ex' on that day.

The Rights Department then examines the List Books to locate the bargains carried out in these securities over a number of past accounts. The 'open positions' are examined, a record made of shares which have been bought and which are not yet delivered by the selling brokers, or deliveries which cannot be registered before the books of the company close. Claims for the rights are then made on the selling brokers or clients.

The books kept in the Department are very similar to those kept by the Dividend Department.

When the documents have been received, either from selling brokers due to clients or from clients due to other buying brokers, they are held in the Rights Department until the total for each bargain is complete. Split tickets will mean a number of pieces to make up the whole, and the sale of part of a holding by a client may mean that only part of his allotment of new shares is required by the buyer. When the total of the new shares is completed for each bargain, they are handed over to the Bearer Department.

BEARER DEPARTMENT

All securities which are transferable by bearer or semi-bearer document pass through this department. Three types of share fall into this classification.

(a) ALLOTMENT LETTERS AND RENOUNCEABLE CERTIFICATES OF STOCKS AND SHARES IN U.K. COMPANIES

The majority of new issues, both original quotations and issues by companies already quoted, are carried out by means of allotment letters or renounceable certificates. In both cases the company pays stamp duty at the time of the issue, and for a period of several weeks (or months in some cases) transfer is free of stamp duty. The original allottee is only required to sign the appropriate part of the document, renouncing his right to the underlying security, and it is then delivered from hand to hand like a piece of currency.

Allotment letters differ from renounceable certificates in one major respect. The former must be exchanged for a definitive certificate at a stated date, while the latter also acts as the certificate itself. In the following paragraphs, to avoid repetition, both documents will be referred to as allotment letters.

All purchases and sales of new shares on allotment letters are made for cash settlement. A bargain carried out on one day, therefore, may be settled by delivery and payment the next. The settlement for this type of security is carried out in a similar fashion to registered stock through the Central Stock Payment Office.

Allotment letters are delivered on a three-part 'tag' set (two white copies, one pink), showing the name and number of the delivering broker, the date of the bargain, the stock and the amount of money due. The selling broker keeps the bottom copy, pins the top two to the allotment letter and sends the securities to the Central Stock Payment Office. They in turn keep one copy and send on the other, together with the stock, to the jobber.

The jobber, in turn, pins on a new 'tag' set for each allotment letter due for delivery to buying brokers and returns the security through the Central Stock Payment Office.

The Central Stock Payment Office sorts the debits and credits on the tag sets and prepares a statement of balances owed by or due to all the jobbers and brokers concerned. Each stockbroker's balance should agree with the total of the white tags (stock sold) and the pink tags (stock bought) in the Bearer Department.

The Bearer Department will hold the allotment letters for purchases until the full delivery is complete and will also hold up registration of new shares until the last possible date. A client may decide to sell the new security at the last moment and, should the allotment letters have been sent to the company for registration, the broker will have to deliver the security on a form of transfer, losing the *ad valorem* stamp duty of 1 %.

One other important function of the Bearer Department is the paying of calls on rights or other new issues. Where payment is due on a fixed date, the Bearer Department will again wait until the last moment before paying, if the value of the rights appears to be in doubt. There is no point in paying a call on a security which may fall below the value of the call immediately afterwards.

The Bearer Department is also responsible, in some offices, for acquiring application forms for new issues and seeing that these are completed for clients and despatched to the issuing bankers, with cheques, before the closing date.

(b) BEARER BONDS

The shares of a number of international companies and many foreign loans are transferable in bearer form. These documents contain a series of coupons attached, which entitle the owner to dividend or other distributions. On delivery they must be carefully checked to ensure that the bond has not been damaged, that it has been stamped, and that the coupons are intact. A record is made of all the bonds received and the number of each one. Under Exchange Control Regulations, bearer securities must be held in safe keeping by an authorised depositary, such as a bank, and not by an individual. The Bearer Department will therefore despatch the completed delivery to the client's bank.

Bearer bonds are not good delivery unless they bear *ad valorem* stamp duty at the appropriate rate. This may have been paid twenty years ago, when the rate was considerably lower than today, but bonds not already stamped bear the following duty:

Bearer with coupons attached* 2% of market value per bond.
Inland bearer (British
securities such as Shell and
British-American Tobacco)   3% of market value per bond.

(c) AMERICAN AND CANADIAN SECURITIES

American and Canadian securities are often loosely called bearer stocks, although in fact each one carries the name of a stockholder, registered in the company's books. They are very similar to the renounceable certificates mentioned earlier in discussing new issues by British companies. Certificates for American and Canadian securities are prepared in round amounts of hundreds, tens and units, and are renounceable by signing the reverse of the document.

Dealings in both bearer and semi-bearer securities are normally for account settlement. The Bearer Department will keep a book of 'Stock In and Stock Out', entering the exact details of the security, the name in which it is registered and the firm who has delivered it or to whom it must be delivered for record purposes.

Deliveries of stock in overseas markets are considered at the end of Chapter 8.

GILT-EDGED TRANSFER DEPARTMENT

The last department to be reviewed in the general office concerns the transfer of Government securities. In gilt-edged transactions the jobbing system operates at its best. Because the Government is the largest individual owner of gilt-edged and because of the excellent management of the Government debt by the Bank of England, a free market is maintained in almost all Government issues. Jobbers can therefore deal in substantial quantities without the fear of being unable either to supply or get rid of the stock. The banks will lend a high proportion of the capital required when stock is taken on jobbers' books, and the

* Under the provisions of the Finance Act, 1967, Bearer instruments relating to stock expressed in the currency of a territory outside the Scheduled Territories need not be stamped, if delivery takes place after 1 August 1967.

Government Broker is always ready to assist in maintaining an orderly market.

As a result the jobber in the gilt-edged market acts not as a post office between brokers in the delivery of securities, but as a principal. Virtually all gilt-edged stock is delivered out of jobbers' nominees or is put into them. Transfers are exempt from stamp duty, so that little cost is attached.

Gilt-edged transactions are for cash settlement. The day after a purchase transaction, therefore, the Gilt-Edged Department passes the name of the buyer direct to the jobber. On the same day the stock is delivered and paid for. The lack of delay in such transactions means that claims for interest payments are rare and the paperwork involved reduced to a minimum.

In many offices the Gilt-Edged Transfer Department acts as a miniature of the entire Transfer Office. Names are passed, transfers prepared, deliveries checked, dividend mandates prepared, stock sent for registration and certificates despatched to clients, all by only one or two individuals.

One of the problems faced by Gilt-Edged Transfer Departments is the size of individual bargains, running sometimes into several million pounds. Since payment is made against delivery, there must be no delay in obtaining payment from the client. Where institutions are concerned, payment is usually made by a bank against the delivery of the security. In the case of tied trusts, however, with substantial funds, a switch may be made on occasion from securities settled on Account Day into gilt-edged due for payment the following day. A careful check must be kept to ensure that the firm is not out of money overnight or for longer periods.

CONCLUSION

The operation of the production side of a stockbroker's office is the least understood division of the business. It is to be hoped that the introduction of electronic data-processing machinery and the gradual centralisation of accounting as part of the Stock Exchange Central Services will simplify many of the procedures in the future.

4

RESEARCH AND
STATISTICS

THE greater emphasis placed on technical investigation for investment has resulted in the rapid growth of research and statistical departments during the last decade. The terms 'research' and 'statistics' are fairly loosely applied and as easily confused as 'research' and 'development' in industrial concerns. In some firms the Statistical Department's materials consist of nothing more than the published statistical services, and operations are largely confined to producing brief reports on companies and reviewing the lists of private clients. In others a highly qualified staff of actuaries, economists, accountants and statisticians may be employed, possibly using their own computer.

The objectives of the department, however it is composed, must be threefold: to provide evidence on which the firm's investment policy may be based; to investigate securities, either individually or by some other classification, providing a service both to the members of the firm and to clients on the investment merits of these securities; and to develop new methods of investigation, so that additional techniques are available for assessing these investment merits.

EVIDENCE FOR INVESTMENT POLICY

As firms of stockbrokers grow larger and the links in the chain of communication between partners become more extended, there is an inevitable tendency towards individuals stating their own personal investment ideas. It is important that the firm should have a definite investment policy and that all clients should receive broadly similar advice. The Research Department must provide the evidence to support, and even on which to formulate, policy from time to time. Research will be required into both the global and national economic outlook. The work of the department may vary from a simple study of published statistics, with an attempt to identify the trend-indicators, to a full-scale construction of a complicated model of the national economy.

From time to time suggestions are made that the mass of effort which is poured into research and statistical studies could well be pooled in some common research organisation. On the face of it this proposal seems sound enough. Work in any one broker's office is almost certainly being duplicated elsewhere, but the broker maintains his connections, in particular his institutional connections, by the service he is able to offer, and must therefore compete on knowledge. The most important service is the presentation of his investment recommendations in a form which shows that he is either better informed, or has been able to reach more effective conclusions, than his competitors. The operation of the Research Department is vitally important as a source of information and evidence to the sales-and-service departments.

Only the activities of the Research Department in connection with ordinary shares are considered here, the investigation of fixed-interest or overseas securities being considered under the headings of the relevant departments.

The science of investment analysis can be divided into two separate but overlapping functions:

1. The selection of investments.
2. The timing of a purchase or sale.

The problems of selecting an investment and timing the action on it are interrelated in that, however good the management or prospects of a company, its shares are almost certain to fall in price in sympathy with a general market recession. Conversely the shares of a small company, in which dealings are relatively rare, may hold up against a general downward trend because either the market is never tested or the restricted marketability makes it almost impossible to deal. A study of the high and low points printed on the back page of the *Financial Times* shows that, in any given year, the low price of many leading shares will be as much as a third below their highs, although the *FT*-Actuaries Share Index may only have varied by 10%. In the short term, therefore, timing can be said to be even more important than selection.

For pension and superannuation funds, with very long-term liabilities and with new money available for investment for many years to come, it is comforting to think that a fluctuation of even as much as 30% is of relatively little account compared with the doubling or trebling of the value of the investment which may be anticipated over the very long term. Many funds will still have an excess of income over expenditure in forty years' time. In 1924 the *Investors Chronicle* Index of Ordinary Shares stood at 100, while in late 1965 it had reached 580. For this type of fund, therefore, the greatest importance lies in the long-term prospects of the investment, and a gradual build-up of the holding, over a period, will iron out the day-to-day fluctuations in price.

THE SELECTION OF INVESTMENTS

Much of the work of the department consists of plodding through the published information available, selecting relevant passages in reports, analysing statistics and gradually building up a survey of an industry or a case for an investment. The one vital factor which cannot be accurately established from a study of facts and figures or even company reports, however, is the future quality of management. Their success or failure in the past can be judged by an examination of the record of the concern, suitably discounted by comparison with like companies, but this gives no indication of their performance in the future. As a result, the second source of information lies in direct contact with industry, and visits to companies, combined with meetings with management at all levels, have become a much more common occurrence. The stockbroker is able to form his own judgement of the competence of the executives from personal acquaintance. The third source of information available to the Research Department lies in the work of outside experts — economists, market-research consultants and others — who are commissioned to undertake certain specific tasks.

PUBLISHED INFORMATION

Apart from the statistical services mentioned earlier, a mass of published information is available to the investment analyst, and one of the problems is to ensure that the highly qualified staff are not bogged down in reading material which they may never use again. The essence of an efficient Research Department, therefore, is to be able to refer readily and easily to information when it is required.

Most of the larger firms maintain their own reference libraries, where up-to-date files are kept on industries, companies and general subjects. A useful bibliography[1] for research departments has been produced by the Society of Investment Analysts, giving a system of indexing and a list of suitable publications.

Even the largest firms would find it uneconomical to subscribe to all the trade papers and other sources of information listed, and many analysts find that the Commercial Section of the Guildhall Library, Basinghall Street, London, E.C.2, and the Library of the London Chamber of Commerce, 92 Cannon Street, London, E.C.4. provide all the reference works they require. A larger collection of trade papers, particularly technical journals and those published in the U.S.A., are included in the Patent Office Library in Holborn (25 Southampton Buildings, London, W.C.2).

For those who want a more comprehensive source of production and trade statistics, including those of overseas areas, the Statistics and Market Intelligence Library of the Board of Trade at Hillgate House, 35 Old Bailey, London, E.C.4, may well provide the answers.

Two further sources of published information should be mentioned — the Registrar of Companies and Limited Partnerships at Companies House, 55 City Road, London, E.C.2, and the Registrar of Companies for Scotland, 102 George Street, Edinburgh 2. A study of a company's file may prove most rewarding. For those concerns with a varied product group, different subsidiaries manufacturing different articles or operating in different industries, the detailed figures from each company file may give a very fair breakdown of the group's profits in the various industries with which it is concerned.

COMPANY ACCOUNTS

It is not within the compass of this book to deal in any detail with the study of company accounts, nor to discuss the relevance

[1] *A Bibliography for Investment and Economic Analysis*, published January 1965.

of the various figures. Every shareholder, however, receives a copy of the company's accounts annually and some mention of one or two of the items seems appropriate here, even if their significance is fairly elementary in terms of the work of a Research Department.

(a) Balance Sheet Figures

The balance sheet gives the financial position of the company or group on one day in the year. The following items are worth noting:

(i) *Capital*. The capital of a public company provides some measure of its size (e.g. the provisions of the Trustee Investments Act, 1961, limits investment to those companies with issued share capital of £1 million or more). In addition, the relative amounts of various classes of capital (debentures, loans, preference and ordinary) indicate the gearing of the equity. Where the service of the prior charges takes a high proportion of available profit, the equity is said to be 'highly geared', and a small fluctuation in such available profit will have a marked effect on the earning for the equity.

(ii) *Reserves*. Reserves comprise both capital reserves and revenue reserves, and indicate the surplus worth of a company over and above its issued capital. It is common practice for companies to capitalise reserves, giving 'scrip' issues to shareholders, so that reserves large in relation to issued capital indicate the prospect and extent of future capitalisation issues.

(iii) *Fixed Assets*. Fixed assets include properties, plant and machinery. With inflation and rising values of property, there is often a measure of hidden reserve in the value of fixed assets. Where freehold property is a significant item, it is important to note the last date of revaluation. Where new values are written into the balance-sheet after a revaluation, a balancing increase will be made to the reserves.

(iv) *Current Assets*. Current assets include such items as cash, investments, debtors and stocks. The figure may reveal whether the company has a surplus of cash resources or whether it is carrying too large an amount of stock. Examined in conjunction with current liabilities (q.v.), an indication may be given as to whether there is sufficient working capital, and therefore whether a fund-raising issue is likely.

(v) *Current Liabilities.* Included under this heading are such items as creditors, tax payments due, dividend payments and bank overdrafts. Where large overdrafts are shown they may well indicate the need to raise fresh capital, particularly if they have increased sharply since the previous year.

(vi) *Net Asset Value.* The net asset value per share is calculated by ascertaining the total of net assets available for the ordinary and dividing it by the number of ordinary shares in issue. In general terms the net assets available for the ordinary are represented by the balance-sheet totals of ordinary capital, plus reserves, less fixed-interest capital, but it is usual to deduct also any figure for goodwill. Net asset values should only be used for comparison with the market prices of shares, to suggest what premium is being paid above the assets available. Great care should also be taken in comparing asset values of companies in dissimilar industries. Shipping companies, for example, may have asset values well in excess of the market values of their shares; companies carrying out services or marketing may have very low asset values relative to the market prices of their shares.

Companies in profitable industries which have produced poor results and which have high asset values may well be worth investigation, since if these assets can be better employed by another concern the company could well be the subject of a take-over bid. Estimating the true break-up value from balance-sheet figures is, however, particularly difficult, since the value of stocks in a winding-up may be either well above or well below the balance-sheet figure.

(b) Profit and Loss Account

(i) *Profit Record.* The record of net profits before tax over a period of years may prove misleading as a guide to progress, since new acquisitions during the period will have affected these figures. The profit record therefore will probably be shown in terms of earnings on the ordinary capital, adjusted for capitalisation issues and the 'bonus element' in rights issues. The adjusted record will now give a clear picture of the earnings available for ordinary shareholders over the period and will indicate the measure of growth that has taken place.

(ii) *Dividend Record.* Dividend records are adjusted in the same way. It may be that a company has never increased its dividend through the years, but that frequent capitalisation issues or rights issues have been made. In cases such as this, the effective increase in dividend can look quite startling. On the other hand, when compared with the earnings record, it may simply show that there has been virtually no growth in the company's earnings, but that the directors have been successively more generous to shareholders by distributing a greater proportion of profits.

(c) Profitability

Two measures of profitability are in common use — the ratios 'earned on total sales' and 'earned on capital employed'.

(i) *Earned on Total Sales*. The trend in the ratio of net profit from trading, before interest charges and before tax, to total sales gives an indication of whether the company is improving, maintaining or reducing its sales margins. Unfortunately the publication of sales volume is not yet compulsory and many companies do not divulge these important figures.

(ii) *Earned on Capital Employed*. The trend in the ratio of net profit before tax to the total capital employed in the business gives an indication of whether the company is improving, maintaining or reducing the return on its assets. This figure can be very valuable since it often indicates a turn-round in the fortunes of the company. The earnings on the ordinary capital of the company may continue to show an improvement while those on the capital employed may show a fall. One of the difficulties faced by the analyst is to arrive at a true figure for the capital employed. This is usually taken as the balance-sheet assets total, less current liabilities, including bank overdrafts and intangibles such as goodwill, patent rights and 'excess of cost' of subsidiaries over book value. Some analysts take the figure at the commencement of the year, some at the year-end and some as the average of the two, so that there is no standard practice in this connection. Only the trend of the amount earned on capital employed over the years is of real value, and any comparisons between these ratios for companies even in the same industry may be misleading. One company may have recently revalued its properties, for example, giving a higher figure for capital employed, or some exceptional capital expenditure may have been undertaken which cannot produce full profitability in its first few months of operation.

(d) Cash Flow

Cash flow is used to describe the amount of money the company has available for spending each year, generated from its own trading operations.

No precise definition of the term has been generally accepted, but the 'gross cash flow' is usually taken to be the net profit after tax plus the amount set aside for depreciation. The 'net cash flow' is the net profit after tax, less the dividends payable, plus depreciation. In these calculations profits from the sale of investments and tax provisions no longer required are excluded (as being non-recurring) when arriving at the net profit figure.

The figure for 'cash flow' is of interest in two respects. If the company's annual programme of capital expenditure is obviously much greater than the net cash flow, additional permanent finance may be required. Those companies which are engaged in heavy expenditure on plant and machinery, with high depreciation levels, may show an apparently misleadingly low earnings record on their ordinary capital. These are the very companies, however, which, when the new plant is fully productive, may be expected to show above-average improvement in their profits.

COMPANY VISITS

Until recently chairmen and directors of companies viewed requests for visits by stockbrokers with extreme suspicion. They took the view that no individual should be given *any* information about the company that was not available to the body of shareholders in general meeting or through the company's publications. While this is an understandable attitude of mind, it has now been proved to be somewhat dated. Stockbrokers and other investment analysts who visit companies respect and even encourage the principles of chairmen and directors. They do not request confidential details, such as the current level of profits or a forecast of the dividend. They are concerned to obtain a more balanced view of the company's activities than can be achieved by reading the chairman's reports, and to get an impression of the management by meeting the individuals face to face.

It should be emphasised here that considerable experience is required to obtain any value out of company visits, and, if used as a single tool in the investment investigation, they can prove to be extremely misleading. Unless the analyst has visited works before and knows the points to observe, he may obtain an entirely unrealistic view. Managements are inevitably shy of exhibiting the least efficient of their processes and tend to show only the divisions which are working smoothly and well. Stores of finished stock, for example, may be considerably larger than needed technically or are usually held in the industry. This may be all too easily concealed from the untrained eye. Over a period the analyst develops a nose for the well-run workshop and can detect the smell of the inefficient firm. In the same way that some highly-placed executives can be excellent talkers and indifferent, or even disastrous, managers, so the evidence of all company visits must be viewed in a highly critical light.

Managements are easily put off by too many and too pointed questions and will often talk more readily about their competitors in the same field than about their own concerns. A company visit may often produce more valuable information about another company in the same industry than about the organisation to which the visit has been paid, but any judgement of a competitor is usually a fair guide to the ability of the judge.

One of the problems facing the analyst is to remember the salient points which have been discussed and to record them. In the middle of an informal talk with the managing director, when he is just getting warmed up to the company's new developments, the production of a large pad of paper and a pencil spells death to the conversation. Every interview and visit has to be conducted with a different approach. It is usual to submit the resulting memorandum to the management for amendment or for the erasure of any information held to be confidential.

The preparatory work which must be done before a visit to a company is very considerable. The reports and accounts for at least the past five years must be studied and the chairman's remarks examined so that intelligent enquiries can be made about the company's products or services. Some firms have a standard *pro forma*, the main headings of which are committed to memory by the visiting analyst so that the ground is adequately covered and no important facts omitted. The completion of a report in this form also assists the publication of a memorandum on the company if this is to be sent to clients at a later date.

Each firm of stockbrokers will have its own method of preparing such a *pro forma*, but one specimen example might include the following details:

General	Name of company.
	Visited by
	Date of visit.
	Introduction to company.
	Issuing house to company.
Details of Visit	Works, factories, offices, etc., visited.
	Names, functions and ages of directors and executives met.
Management	Impression of existing management.
	Method of selection:
	(*a*) Internal.
	(*b*) External.
	Does management selection ensure
	(*a*) sufficient outside knowledge and experience?
	(*b*) sufficient technical experience?
	What management training provisions are there?
	What is outlook for management in future?
	(*a*) Approx. ages of existing management.
	(*b*) Are suitable replacements available?
	Management tree or chain of command of the company.
	General comments.
The Industry	Names of leading competitors.
	Company's views on competitors.
	Company's share of the market.
	Is it increasing/decreasing?
	Is the market increasing/decreasing?
	Industry's exports.
Sales	Products sold.
	Are they up to date?
	Sales outlets:
	(*a*) Wholesalers
	(*b*) Retailers
	(*c*) Direct.

Does sale pattern change?

What market research has been done?

Any special advantages or difficulties?

Experience in other countries, particularly America

Export sales.

Advertising.

General comments.

Production   Production grouping — continuous, batch, on-off, etc.

Shift work.

Layout of production flow.

Is there a Work Study Dept.?

Age and type of machines used.

Handling of products down the line.

Size of average batch and time on the shop floor.

Stock record and stock control.

General comments.

Labour   Labour relations.

Total number of employees (divided in groups if possible).

Payment, piecework, etc.

S.E.T. — net benefit or loss.

Incentive schemes.

Pensions schemes.

Training.

Special labour problems.

Raw Materials   Main raw materials.

Where are supplies drawn from?

Do stock losses/profits materially affect P. & L. account?

Method of stock valuation (last in — first out, etc.).

Finance   Methods of financial control.

Is company largely self-financing?

Major capital expenditure programmes planned.

Properties   Last date of revaluation.

Approx. area of factories.

Estimate as to whether properties are fully utilised.

Current Trading   Is the industry generally running at higher level in current year?

Are profit margins being maintained?

Is company's trade affected by any exceptional circumstances?

It is, of course, not always possible to obtain answers to all these questions, and in particular circumstances there may be other and more important points which should be made. On current trading, in particular, considerable tact must be used to avoid asking direct questions which may lead to the disclosure of confidential information.

Company visits are one of the most pleasant and interesting of the investment analyst's tasks. Generally more is learned about an industry and its prospects in half an hour's conversation with a leading member of management than in several days sitting in the back room of a stockbroker's office. In particular the emergence from the somewhat rarefied atmosphere of the City to the more realistic and down to-earth environment of the industrial North or the Midlands provides a breath of fresh air which stimulates the analyst's perception.

Conversely, members of management can be fascinated by stockbrokers, having found all too few who emerge from the confines of the City to get first-hand knowledge of their company.

ORGANISED MEETINGS AND VISITS

Meetings addressed by leading industrialists and visits to companies are arranged by the Society of Investment Analysts. This body was formed in 1961, with a founder membership of seven, and a total of ninety within a few days. At the end of 1965 it comprised a membership of almost 800, drawn not only from firms of stockbrokers but from all institutions and other investment organisations.

It is a rule of the Society that remarks made by speakers at their meetings must not be quoted in circulars or other investment material, with the result that replies to questions and the facts disclosed in these addresses tend to be more uninhibited than in more formal gatherings.

EXTERNAL WORK

Many firms employ the services of leading economists to prepare for them periodic reviews on the economic outlook and to act in a consultative capacity when specific questions require to be answered. This does not imply that the economists within the firm are incapable of a reasonable assessment of the situation, but the advantage of an outside mind, not hemmed in by current City thought, and constantly mixing with other economists in discussions of theory and practice, can be considerable.

From time to time market research consultants are employed by stockbrokers to investigate trends in the sales of consumer goods and to report on the development of new methods of merchandising. A major investigation of this type is fairly costly and is therefore not undertaken as a matter of routine.

Industrial experts are less easy to find for outside consultation. If their opinion is of real value they are most likely already fully employed in their own company and less well informed about others in the same field.

Outside financial journalists are employed by a number of firms to convert the work of the Research Department into a readable article, when a company or industry review is planned. Some journalists also work under contract to produce regular investment reviews for circulation, normally to private clients.

TIMING

It has been mentioned earlier that the investing public's yard-stick for equity share prices is still the yield (or to put it more accurately the percentage dividend/price ratio), allied to the price/earnings ratio. The yield will vary with both the price and the dividend. The share price may fluctuate for a number of reasons: in sympathy with either the market in general or the section of the market in which it lies; or the investment rating of the share itself may have changed, due to changed profits, an announcement of special importance, or a hundred and one different eventualities; or, thirdly, some technical factor may have forced the price of the share temporarily out of line. The object of the analyst in studying timing is firstly to estimate whether the market in general is likely to move upwards or downwards, and secondly to select shares which are either dear or cheap in relation to other comparable shares. At any given time investment trusts will switch from one share which looks relatively dear to another which looks relatively cheap, since by this means they will improve upon the average performance of the market. Funds with long-term liabilities and new money accruing regularly will select those shares which are cheap in relation to the whole market, since regular purchases of such stocks over a period will also give above-average performance. Some method of indicating which shares are standing out of line with their normal course must therefore be of advantage.

DIVIDEND YIELD RATIOS

The facility of computers to undertake a large number of calculations rapidly and accurately opened the way to their use in solving this problem. A team of analysts commenced operations using the B.O.A.C.-B.E.A. computer to compare the yields on selected ordinary shares with the index of yield for the whole list. The result was a comparison of both earnings yields and dividend yields, not only with the overall yield on every share in the list but with the yield on the particular industrial group in which the share lay. By comparing the figures thrown out it is possible to decide whether the share is showing an abnormal yield compared with the overall yield and whether this is due to the fact that the group is either in or out of favour or whether only the share itself is responsible. The system jogs the analyst's elbow to investigate shares which appear to be out of line.

CHARTS

A number of research departments utilise charts of share prices or price indices in attempting to forecast the movement both of the market in general and of particular securities. At its simplest a chart illustrates the movements of the past in a clear and obvious manner, but the majority of chartists expect to derive considerably more information than just a historical record. Their experience suggests that price charts move in certain identifiable patterns, and that these patterns will be repeated in the future.

OTHER METHODS

There are almost as many aids to investment timing — point and figure methods, volume and price correlations, and a range of new ratios calculated on computers — as there are invest-ment analysts. It is not within the compass of this book to name more than the most widely used. But when it is possible to increase the capital invested by 50% in a single year on a leading share (as shown by the differential between high and low mentioned earlier), it can be realised that successful timing is of even greater importance than successful selection.

RESEARCH INTO NEW METHODS AND TECHNIQUES

The work of the Research Department outlined so far deals only with the day-to-day problems of investment. Its long-term role, however, must be to find new and improved methods of selecting investments and techniques for improving timing.

The use of the computer in this connection is now only in its early stages. In America a number of firms have developed methods of examining the mass of statistics available to select and compare the performance of individual companies. One firm supplies its clients with relevant figures on over a thousand companies. In London, in 1965, a leading firm of stockbrokers commenced a weekly service on 1,200 companies, providing not only indices for a number of manufacturing groups, but balance-sheet items expressed as a proportion of the share price.

Naturally the work which is currently under examination in the research departments of stockbrokers is a highly guarded secret, but it is evident that new and more sophisticated computer techniques will be developed in the future. It is only by having one additional precision tool and acquiring the skill to use it that a firm of stockbrokers can obtain an advantage over its competitors.

5

FINANCE

THE previous chapters have been devoted to the work of individual operating departments. The financial control of a partnership may be devolved upon one individual or become the responsibility of an executive committee, depending upon the way in which the firm is managed.

Money is one of the basic raw materials of the stockbroker, and it is natural that the financial aspects of the business should be handled with particular care. These may be broken down under three main headings: the financial standing of the client; the financial stability of the firm, including the provision and best uses of the partnership funds; and budgetary control, including the costing of bargains, the annual budgets of current and capital expenditure, and trading forecasts.

THE FINANCIAL STANDING OF THE CLIENT

Except in special circumstances (arbitrage dealing, for example), the stockbroker acts as an agent for his client, rather than as a principal, but he is nevertheless responsible for the settlement with other members of The Stock Exchange of any transactions which his firm has undertaken.

A partner in a firm of stockbrokers is liable, to the extent of all his worldly goods, for the transactions of his firm. As a result clients are carefully scrutinised before they are accepted. It is normal to request a banker's reference, indicating the credit-worthiness of the individual, and also to apply to the Stock Exchange Mutual Reference Society. The Society, although not a department of The Stock Exchange, provides a centre where member firms may be introduced to one another to discuss doubtful cases in confidence.

One of the problems facing stockbrokers on the introduction of a new client is the extent of his resources. The first transaction may be for a relatively small number of shares, a sale order possibly being accompanied by a relevant certificate, so that obviously little risk is attached to the transaction. If the newly-accepted client then gives instructions to buy a large number of shares in a highly speculative concern, does the stockbroker accept the instructions or refuse to deal?

Most firms have their own internal regulations regarding this sort of dilemma, just as they take the necessary precautions against mystery voices which give telephone instructions to buy or sell securities in times of hectic trading, or individuals who identify themselves, on the telephone for example, as one of the directors in a company for whom it is known that the firm of stockbrokers acts. But some clients tend to look askance at stockbrokers, whom they accept implicitly as being of good financial standing, while on the other hand the firm makes detailed investigations as to the client's credit-worthiness.

THE FINANCIAL STANDING OF THE STOCKBROKER

The client has a number of safeguards against the failure of a firm of stockbrokers. Member firms of stockbrokers of any of the Federated Exchanges must at all times maintain a 'margin of solvency' (the amount by which net assets exceed net liabilities) of not less than £5,000 per partner. Copies of the annual balance-sheet must be submitted to independent accountants for examination. And a compensation fund is available to pay the losses to clients in the event of a failure by a member firm. Although this fund has been built up out of members' subscriptions over a number of years, it is not available to pay the losses which accrue to other firms in the event of failure. The Rules of the Federation of Stock Exchanges in Great Britain and Ireland provide for a general compensation fund, subscribed by all exchanges for the failure of a member of any one, and equal to an amount of £200 per member. The fund may call up to a total of £1,000 per member if required. While the London fund stood at £675,000 at the end of March 1966, the potential of the total Federation fund is of the order of £6 million.

Finally, members of the London Stock Exchange are not permitted to engage in other activities which may incur a liability on their finances. Rule 30 states (*inter alia*) that a member who wishes to be a principal or an employee in any business other than that of The Stock Exchange, or whose wife wishes to be a principal in any business, must obtain prior consent of the Council.

The Law Society imposes restrictions on firms of solicitors, insisting that clients' funds must be held in a separate bank account from partnership funds. The situation of stockbrokers is very different, since they act to a far smaller degree as custodians of securities and relatively rarely are given powers of attorney for their clients. Stockbrokers nevertheless have to accept delivery of securities on Settlement Day and pay for them punctually, whether they have been put in funds by their clients or not. It is true to say, therefore, that clients who are slow in paying for their purchases may be financed over the short term either by the funds of the partnership, or by those of more punctilious clients, or by a combination of both. Many institutional investors, in order only to part with securities against the receipt of a cheque in the case of a sale, or to pay against the physical delivery of the stock in the case of a purchase, arrange to have the securities delivered to or by their banks against payment.

DAY-TO-DAY FINANCE

Several problems face the stockbroker in the administration of day-to-day finance. The first is that the banks tend to place their business with those firms who maintain reasonably large current accounts. As a result the funds at the disposal of the firm may be spread between thirty or forty accounts with different banks. In order to avoid paying high rates of interest on overdrafts in some banks, while obtaining no interest on credits with others, the cashier has to maintain a careful balance between banking clients.

The second is concerned with the delays in preparing stocks for delivery. The Stock Transfer Act, 1963, has reduced many of the delays of delivery and greatly reduced the volume of dividend claims, etc., but about 50% of stock is now delivered on Settlement Day itself, whereas in the past the inefficiency of the system extended delivery throughout the following week or longer. The physical difficulty of preparing some thousands of transfer forms, having them impressed with the correct stamp duty, obtaining

certification where required and attaching the necessary documents, together with the requirement during the same short
period of checking and listing some thousands of deliveries,
requires considerable effort in management and organisation.
Priority must obviously be given to those deliveries where the
money passing is large, and particularly institutional transactions where payment is made on receipt of securities sold and
must be recouped from the buying brokers. Firms with substantial sums at their disposal may find it worth while to
arrange the acceptance of institutional or other large sale
deliveries earlier than Settlement Day, in order to prepare the
documents in advance and spread out the work of the
settlement, even if this means some delay between paying the
seller and recouping the money from the buyer. This extra
advantage of having large partnership funds occurs at a time
when the financing of partnerships is becoming increasingly
difficult.

FINANCE FOR PARTNERSHIPS

Before the Second World War finance for stockbrokers was not
normally difficult to obtain. Candidates for partnership often
qualified because of their connections and as a result were likely
to be endowed with sufficient wealth to pay for their participation. The emphasis since the war, on service rather than connections, allied to the high rates of taxation and swingeing
estate duties, has brought in a new membership of technocrats,
often with little capital behind them. Partnerships have therefore been faced with two problems: increasing the total funds
to cope with expanding business, while the remuneration of
the partners suffers the full rates of income and surtax; and
finding methods of buying out the elder retiring partners in
order to make room for the younger men.

The plight of the firms of jobbers in this respect is much worse,
but a detailed discussion is not within the scope of this book.
They act as principals, not as agents, and their capital is truly
on risk. While the banks will provide temporary finance against
the security of the stocks in the hands of the jobbers, the freedom
of dealing in large amounts is obviously curtailed when the
jobbers appreciate that a sudden move in the market could
virtually wipe out the greater part of their capital. The oppor-

tunity of making large capital sums has gone, while the chance
of losing them is ever present.

LIMITED PARTNERS

In order to alleviate the problem of obtaining additional funds,
the Council introduced in June 1966 regulations permitting
external members and limited partnerships. Risk capital may
now be obtained from persons and corporations not actively
engaged in Stock Exchange business, entitling them to a participation in profits (and losses) of the firm but limiting their
liability to the capital introduced.

These provisions are of particular assistance in allowing
retired members to retain a share in profits without unlimited
liability and giving similar opportunities to widows, family
trusts and other connections of members. Members of Lloyd's,
provided they have the approval of that institution, may also
participate.

Among the corporations eligible for membership, those
actively engaged in investment (e.g. banks, insurance companies, pension funds and investment trusts) are specifically
excluded, except in the case of consortium companies formed to
assist in the finance of jobbing firms where no individual institution may hold more than 35 % of the capital of the consortium
company.

Limited partners may also not hold more than 50% of the
capital owned by the general partners, thus effectively limiting
them to one-third of the capital of the firm. Under the Limited
Partnership Act, a limited partner may not take part in the
management of the firm.

The introduction of these new regulations offered several
advantages over previous practice. Time may now be given to
members of a partnership to pay out a retiring partner or beneficiaries of a deceased estate, causing less strain on surviving
partners. Corporations not active in Stock Exchange investment may be interested to invest in forward-looking firms to
finance expansion, and this may, in turn, give existing partners
an opportunity of realising some of the goodwill which they
have built up over the years.

Member firms who have formed corporate memberships are
not prohibited from having limited partners.

CORPORATE MEMBERSHIPS

No provision for reserves can be made out of partnership profits, which must be distributed each year between the partners, and which suffer tax in the hands of each individual at his personal rate. The full earned-income allowance may, however, be claimed.

In order to provide reserves at a less penal rate of taxation, a number of firms elected in the past to form themselves into unlimited private companies (corporate members). A number of advantages and disadvantages attached to this action. Provided that a reasonable proportion of the profit is distributed by way of dividend, the Inland Revenue has been prepared to give surtax clearance to such companies. As a result reserves have been built up after suffering tax at only the company's rate (previously profits tax of 15% and income tax of 8s. 3d., making a total rate of 11s. 3d.) as against the individual partner's rate of income and surtax which could amount to as high a rate as 18s. 3d. in the £.

A build-up of capital within a corporate membership has been relatively easy and painless, and has resulted in funds being available for the provision of new and expensive data-processing apparatus, as well as providing the liquid resources for expanding the business. The principal disadvantage lies in the difficulty of freeing these reserves to outgoing partners. Young men joining a corporate membership are naturally reluctant to lock up free capital in paying out retiring members when they have themselves gained none of the advantage in the process of accumulating it. The incoming partners would prefer to put up capital for the partnership which is free of any problem of withdrawal, since the capital of the partnership may be adjusted freely from time to time as the situation warrants.

The corporate membership can, however, be put into liquidation at any time and, provided that the Inland Revenue is satisfied that the reason for liquidation is valid and is not primarily a method of tax evasion, the assets of the company can be distributed to members. Once this action has been taken it is unlikely that the Inland Revenue would give surtax clearance to another corporate membership for some considerable time unless very special circumstances warranted it.

SERVICE COMPANIES

A halfway house between a partnership and a corporate membership has been offered by the formation of a service company. This is also an unlimited private company owned, jointly or severally, by the partners. The physical operation of the business can be carried out by the service company on a fee basis, and the service company can justly be expected to make a reasonable profit, reducing the profits of the partnership accordingly. Provided once more that a sufficient proportion of the service company profits is paid to the partnership by way of dividend, the Inland Revenue has been in the habit of granting surtax clearance. The amount of profit which can be put to reserve in the service company is naturally less than in the case of a corporate membership, since the service company's fee will be unlikely to absorb all the partnership profits. Some capital reserves can, however, be built up, while the taxation advantages of a partnership are retained.

PARTNERSHIP TAXATION

In the following context the term 'year' refers to the fiscal year ended 5 April.

Partnerships pay income tax on their business profits on a preceding-year basis. That is to say, the assessment for a given year is based on the profits of an accounting year ended in the preceding fiscal year. When a business is set up, or when it is permanently discontinued, special rules apply. Further, in the 'commencement' period an option is available to the taxpayer (but not to the Revenue) if it is to his advantage to elect for it and in the 'cessation' period the Revenue (but not the taxpayer) will, in relevant circumstances, increase the assessments for the penultimate and pre-penultimate years of assessment. A detailed exposé of the rules regulating the assessments of the 'commencement' and 'cessation' periods is quite outside the scope of this book, but their general effect is that in the 'commencement' period some profits will be assessed twice whilst in the 'cessation' period some profits will fall out of assessment altogether. *Any* change in the partners will be an event which will give rise to the application of these special rules. In fact, the rules will apply as though the business carried on by the old group of partners were a different business from that carried on

by the new. The application of these special rules may substantially increase the taxation liability of the firm and, con-
sequentially, of its partners (in relation to that which it would
have been had the change not taken place) and, in mitigation,
an election is available which has the effect of securing that the
assessments are made as though no change had taken place.
This election must be made, in writing, and within one calendar
year of the change by *all* the partners engaged in the business
both before and after the change. Whether or not to make this
election is a matter of some complexity and it is essential, in all
cases, that the firm's professional advisers be consulted. In
addition, it should be borne in mind that the application of the
special rules can have sufficiently material effects to be a de-
termining factor when deciding on the date when a partner
should retire or a new one be admitted.

The great advantage of the 'commencement and cessation'
provisions is that it may be possible, if the figures fit, to cause
a 'bad' year to be the basis of more than one assessment, to the
exclusion, effectively, of a 'good' year.

FINANCE ACT, 1965

The Finance Act, 1965, has made it much more difficult for
stockbrokers to accumulate capital. Both the corporate membership and the service companies are controlled by the partners, who are considered to be one 'person' in deciding whether
the company is a 'close company' or not. The Finance Act
specifies that at least 60% of earnings must be distributed by
way of dividend. A combination of 40% corporation tax and
income tax deducted at 8s. 3d. in the £ on a distribution of this
proportion of earnings is in itself a disincentive to continue with
unlimited companies. Added to this, however, the funds put to
reserve will bear capital gains tax at 30% if the company is
put into liquidation.

GOODWILL

Stockbroking is such a personal profession and so much depends
upon the confidence of the client in the reliability of the stockbroker's advice that, in general, most firms specifically exclude
any goodwill element from the cost of becoming a partner. It
seems hard, however, when both doctors and accountants still

cling to the practice of selling goodwill, that a stockbroker who
has built up a successful business should be unable to capitalise
on it at his retirement, unless a limited partner can be interested
in acquiring a share. The same problem is now facing firms of accountants, as new entrants are either unable or unwilling to subscribe for goodwill. Some years ago, in an address presented to
the Institute of Chartered Accountants in England and Wales,
Mr. Neil McLaren, F.C.A., made some suggestions which could
well bear consideration by firms of stockbrokers. He pointed
out that, for the new generation of accountants coming into
partnership, finance for their declining years could well be
provided through the provisions of Part III of the Finance Act,
1956. This Act permits self-employed persons not covered by
other pension provisions to allocate up to 10% of their gross
earnings, with a maximum of £750 in any one year, towards a
recognised pension scheme. The result is that the top 10% of
earnings, free of tax, may be put towards the finance of one's
declining years.

Mr. McLaren goes on to say:

> ... and if no payment for goodwill were required, but in its
> place there existed an obligation on an incoming partner to
> make the maximum annual payment under this Act, it would
> seem that a very worth-while annuity would be available at
> retirement date.
>
> If a young man aged thirty applied the sum of £200 per
> annum in a 'self-employed annuity' policy and every five years
> increased this allocation by £50, so that in the last five years
> up to age sixty-five he would be paying £500 per annum, then
> by carefully choosing when to switch from with-profits to
> without-profits, and assuming that present premium rates and
> bonus rates are maintained, he could get a 'pension' at age
> sixty-five of about £3,000 per annum; or should he require
> an annuity for joint lives and survivor, and assuming he and
> his wife were of similar age, an annual sum of £2,000 would be
> available.[1]

In cases where goodwill is specifically excluded from partnerships, it is important that the partnership deed should include

[1] 'Financing an Accountant's Practice', address presented on 20 September 1963 by Neil McLaren, F.C.A.

a statement to this effect, since otherwise the Estate Duty Office may demand evidence of the fact in assessing the duty payable by a deceased partner.

INSURANCE COMPANY FINANCE

One further suggestion made by Mr. McLaren in his paper is of interest. In discussing the provisions of capital for a firm, he says:

> It seems that such a fund might well be provided if the present partners of a firm felt it proper to take the necessary steps in the interest and for the benefit of the future of the firm, and it might be provided through the agency of the insurance companies.
>
> The present partners of a firm might well be able to borrow from an insurance company a very substantial part of the hard core of capital required by the firm, securing the repayment of the loan by endowment policies on the lives of the younger partners, all partners agreeing that the endowment policies are held in trust for the partners for the time being and not owned by any of them individually.
>
> The loan would very substantially take the place of the partners' capital accounts and it would be necessary for the firm to allocate as a first slice of the profits such an amount as would enable each insured partner to pay the premium on his endowment policy at no cost to himself other than his propor-tion of the first slice of profit.
>
> The interest on the loan would most likely be at a higher rate than partners normally allow on their own capital, but not substantially more, so that the cost to the firm which is borne by the partners in their profit-sharing ratio is the excess interest and the first slice of profit. Both these items fall to be deducted from the top slices of income if surtax is involved.
>
> When the policies mature the obligation to the insurance company is extinguished and the original loan becomes a fund of capital for the firm. In effect it becomes 'fixed capital of the firm', to be repaid only when the firm no longer needs it, and if all the partners at that time so agree.
>
> A side-effect of a transaction of this description is that in the event of an untimely death of an insured partner who would normally be a young man, the premium on his life and the interest on that slice of the loan will no longer be payable, thus

freeing some of the previously earmarked profits, some of which might, by agreement of the partners, be used to assist a widow or children.

FINANCIAL CONTROL

COSTING

The unit of transaction in stockbroking is the 'bargain', irrespective of whether the amount of money passing is £10 or £10,000. In the various processes of production that have already been mentioned, the amount of work involved, ledger entries, paper circulated, etc., between bargains varies relatively little. The bargain therefore is the most convenient unit to cost, and it should be made clear here that each bargain refers to an individual transaction with a jobber. To buy 10,000 shares may require either one bargain with one jobber, or perhaps three bargains with three different jobbers. Here the purchase by three separate deals would be considered to be three separate bargains.

Occasionally the 'cost of a bargain' appears in the Press and figures of between £3 and £4 have been quoted. It is not clear exactly how these costs have been calculated, but it is safe to assume that they refer to purchases and sales of ordinary shares (gilt-edged and fixed-interest securities represent a small proportion of the number of transactions of the majority of firms). It seems likely that the cost figure has been calculated simply by dividing the total number of bargains executed in a given period by the overall expenses of the firm, probably before allowing any remuneration to the profit-sharing partners. On this evidence the conclusion might easily be reached that, if the commission does not amount to something over £3 to £4, a bargain is being executed at a loss.

The immediate counter to this argument which has often been put forward is that, if the economic business is sufficient to warrant a given size of Production Department, any additional business, however small, adds grist to the mill. Most brokers also find that, if all small business is rejected, then apart from failing to provide a service in the national interest, they throw away the chance of a small account growing into a large one in time, or introducing a large one if the service is sufficiently good. It is extremely difficult, therefore, to be too selective in accepting business on cost grounds alone.

The fallacy in drawing any conclusion from such rudimentary costing lies in the fact that a high proportion of effort and expense is incurred outside the Production Department, and this is more closely related to the class of client than to the number of bargains. A private client with only £200 to invest may involve far greater expense in the sales-and-service and research departments than dealing as a post office for a country broker in ten times that amount. Various systems of costing have been applied in my own office, but the basic difficulty lies in the flexibility of each individual's operations. No member of the sales-and-service organisations, for example, is doing the same work two hours running, nor is the proportion of his time on one class of client uniform over a period.

One method which has proved satisfactory is to break the costing down under the four basic headings — sales-and-service, production, research, administration — and allocate a proportion of the total cost of each department to each class of client. A number of further assumptions have had to be made:

(*a*) In all departments other than the general office, allocations of an individual's time were made to each of the client classes, confirmed by spot checks over a period.

(*b*) As far as the dealing time of the House staff was concerned (as against the time they spent in reporting price movements, dividend announcements, South American revolutions, etc.) and the time of the general office staff, the time taken to process a 'bargain' in ordinary shares, however large the order, was uniform.

(*c*) Profit-sharing partners, irrespective of their seniority or performance, were adjudged to be paid identical salaries.

(*d*) No bonus payment to the staff, a traditional part of Stock Exchange remuneration, was included in the expenses.

(*e*) Adjustments were made for the exclusion of gilt-edged and other fixed-interest bargains which had been carried out at the instigation or on the advice of these departments. The relatively small orders in fixed-interest securities which originated in the Private Clients

Department were included, since they did not affect the figure materially.

The review on which the figures quoted below in Table 6 were based was taken over the six-month period from May to October 1964. The general office at this time was operating on a machine accounting system, and shortly after the end of the period a number of sections were progressively moved on to a computer system, which is not yet complete. The period under review coincided with the latter months of the Conservative administration, when investment business was necessarily reduced pending the results of the October election. In my own opinion it was operating at only two-thirds of optimum production.

These figures have been quoted as an example of the costing carried out by one firm. It should be noted that research expenditure has been almost entirely devoted to institutional and pension-fund business. The reason for this is that, over this period, all research projects were initiated for institutional investment. The results of the research are passed on to the investment departments serving tied trusts and private clients through the circulation of written reports or by verbal discussion at the daily morning investment meetings. It should also be noted that the major part of company visits as a research item are conducted in my own firm by partners, most of whom are concerned with sales-and-service. Our current policy is to devote a much higher proportion of costs to research.

One inescapable conclusion to be drawn from these figures is that the free service given to certain private clients, in the shape of voluminous correspondence, regular valuations, meetings and the like, is inevitably paid for by those others who either give the stockbroker *carte blanche* to manage their portfolios or make up their own minds and use the stockbroker only as an agent for carrying out their transactions.

TABLE 6

TABLE OF COSTS

Client	Department	Cost per bargain			Total cost			Total cost at optimum production		
		£	s.	d.	£	s.	d.	£	s.	d.
Institutions (insurance companies, investment and unit trusts, merchant banks)	Sales-and-Service	6	16	9						
	Research	4	9	5						
	Production	2	6	5						
	Administration		11	4	14	3	11	9	9	3
Pension and Superannuation Funds	Sales-and-Service	6	–	10						
	Research	1	4	–						
	Production	2	1	10						
	Administration		11	4	9	18	–	6	8	8
Tied Trusts, Branch Banks and Agents	Sales-and-Service	1	11	2						
	Research		2	9						
	Production	1	15	10						
	Administration		11	3	4	1	–	2	14	–
Country Brokers	Sales-and-Service		1	2						
	Research		—							
	Production	1	19	1						
	Administration		11	3	2	11	6	1	14	4
Private Clients	Sales-and-Service	1	15	1						
	Research		4	6						
	Production	1	15	4						
	Administration		11	4	4	6	3	2	17	6

TRADING PROJECTIONS

In every industrial concern the new financial year is heralded by a general review of trading and a budget of sales for the next twelve months. In stockbroking this exercise is rarely, if ever, attempted. The excuse is made that so many variables affect the mood of the investor — international affairs, Government decrees, even the weather plays its part — that no useful prediction can be made. Many of these factors, however, make the task of the industrialist equally arduous — particularly in those industries which are traditionally Aunt Sallies for Government tax adjustments or are very vulnerable to the English climate. The motor-car manufacturers and the soft-drink companies still produce their production and sales targets, however often they require to be adjusted. Theoretically the stockbroker is in a much stronger position to fulfil his trading targets, whatever the economic climate, since the majority of his clients will act if he so advises them. It is this knowledge, that he is in a position of trust, coupled with the natural feeling that it is very often easier and safer to do nothing than to stick one's neck out, that keeps the stockbroker from trading just for the sake of trading, or turning his clients' holdings over just for the sake of the commission involved. This very conflict of interest between himself and his client tends to make him lean over backwards not to take any undue risk, with the result that he is very often accused of being too conservative or too uninterested by the client he is endeavouring to protect.

In my own view some sort of trading forecast is essential in almost any business, even if it simply retraces the graph of last year's history, with suitable corrections for known variations and some factor applied for growth. A budget of trading, broken down between the different classifications of clients, gives a series of monthly target figures for the various departments. If these targets are not being achieved, then some remedial action may be taken with a flexible organisation. The institutions may be 'waiting on the sidelines' so that some of the staff in that department could be more profitably employed in increasing the coverage of the Research Department by studying some particular project. Without a series of trading targets it becomes too easy simply to complain that business is slack without taking any action to improve the position, with resultant deterioration in the morale of the staff.

BUDGETS OF CURRENT AND CAPITAL EXPENDITURE

The preparation of the trading forecast for the following year also gives rise to an examination of the salaries of personnel and of the needs for increased staff throughout each department. In examining the costing of bargains and the profitability of each class of client a decision must be made whether the firm intends to give an even more comprehensive coverage to institutions, both of sales-and-service and of research, in the hopes of increasing this very competitive but profitable business, or to streamline the private-client business on the chain-store principle of providing a very efficient service in a limited range of products to a large clientele. At the preparation of the annual budgets of current and capital expenditure, therefore, some indication can be given of the expected overall increase in expenses during the year ahead, and departments will be making out their cases for any increases in staff and equipment which they require.

In recent years the move by some of the leading stockbroking firms from machine accounting to computers has made this type of annual budget of much greater importance. As far as I am aware, none of the firms who have made this change has seen any saving in overheads, and many have been faced with higher costs. On the other hand none of them would be likely to suffer again the appalling production crises of the 1959 boom, their business could expand to a considerable extent without marked increase in production costs, and the figures on which their costing and trading forecasts are based are much more easily and accurately obtainable.

6

FIXED-INTEREST

So far the only classification of investment which has been considered in any detail is the ordinary share, the risk-bearing capital of the company. The other broad class of securities is the fixed-interest group, covering gilt-edged securities, company loan capital and preference shares.

The volume of business transacted on the London Stock Exchange in fixed-interest sections of the market is very large. For the calendar years 1965 and 1966, the comparative figures are given below in Table 7.

While every firm of stockbrokers carried out some business in fixed-interest securities, probably 80% of the turnover in gilt-edged is handled by a dozen firms with specialist departments in this field, and the greater part of the debenture and preference-share business (other than dealings immediately following a new issue) lies in even fewer hands, notably one specialist firm and departments of half a dozen others.

It will be seen from the turnover figures just quoted that the business in fixed-interest securities, other than gilt-edged, is relatively small. Some firms divide the two into completely separate departments, but in the management tree I have quoted they are considered as independent sections working under one control.

Before looking at the operation of the department in more detail, some explanation of the quotations and terminology of the market in fixed-interest securities should be made. The majority of gilt-edged stocks are redeemable, so that the borrower must repay them (or offer an alternative issue of equal value) at the end of the period. Most stocks give the borrower a choice of repayment date, so that Funding 5¼% 1978–80 must be repaid at £100 for each nominal £100 of stock at earliest on 15 June 1978 and at latest on 15 June 1980. These two dates are termed the 'earliest redemption date' and the 'final redemption date'. During the life of the stock, for every £100 nominal

TABLE 7

TURNOVER ON THE LONDON STOCK EXCHANGE

(Calculated as the aggregate of all purchases and sales)

| | Calendar Year | | | |
| | 1965 | | 1966 | |
	Number of Bargains	Value (£ million)	Number of Bargains	Value (£ million)
1. British Government and British Government guaranteed:				
Short-dated (having five years or less to run)	96,109	10,594	117,656	10,581
Others	264,520	5,402	254,547	6,025
2. U.K. local authority	96,282	331	97,887	694
3. Overseas Government, provincial and municipal	53,791	201	50,574	138
4. Fixed-interest stock, preference and preferred ordinary shares	430,485	480	503,989	585
5. Ordinary shares	3,417,395	3,479	3,118,894	3,565

Source: The Stock Exchange, London.

the investor will receive £5 5s. per annum before tax. The rate of interest paid on the nominal value is termed the 'coupon', in this case a '5¼% coupon'. On all gilt-edged securities, with the exception of Consolidated 2½%, Annuities 2½% and Annuities 2¾% interest payments are made twice yearly on fixed dates.

The prices of both gilt-edged and company loan stocks are quoted per cent. On 20 December 1966, Funding 5½% 1978–80 stood at 86. The value of £100 nominal of this stock, therefore, amounted to £86. The annual return on an investment of £100 in this security (income yield) can also be calculated by dividing the coupon by the price and multiplying by 100. In this case the income yield amounts to £6 2s. 4d.

But if the stock is held to redemption the return is obviously greater, since over the period of 11½ years to the earliest date or 13½ years to the final date, a capital appreciation of £14 % must occur. In order to compare the merits of such fixed-interest stocks, a 'redemption yield' is calculated, apportioning the capital appreciation in annual instalments over the period. In the case of stocks standing *below* par it is normal to take the period to the *final* redemption date, and for those standing *above* par to the *earliest* date, thus giving the most conservative picture in either case. If held to maturity, the 'gross redemption yield' gives the effective annual return to an investor who is not subject to tax and, in the example quoted, amounts to £6 15s. 5d.

For the investor who is subject to tax, the capital appreciation may be more important than the income, and the 'net redemption yield' is calculated with both income tax and capital-gains tax at the appropriate rates.

The prices of gilt-edged and loan capital, with the exception of those British Government stocks with less than five years to final redemption, are quoted to include the accrued interest which has built up since the previous 'ex dividend' date. In order that the comparison shall be accurate, the 'clean' price of the security is taken for calculating these yields, the accrued interest having been deducted.

GILT-EDGED

The gilt-edged market covers securities issued by the British Government, the Dominions and colonies, the local authorities

and most of the public boards. The section entitled 'British
Funds' on the back page of the *Financial Times* divides the list
of British Government securities into four sections — short-
dated (due to be redeemed within five years), medium-dated
(with redemption between five and fifteen years), long-dated
(over fifteen years) and undated (where either there is no final
date of redemption or the date is unspecified and at the option
of the Government).

SHORT-DATED

Securities which have less than five years to redemption are
termed 'money stocks', since they provide an alternative to other
forms of short-term lending. The rate of commission on purchase
and sale is extremely low, the rate being left to the discretion of
the broker and, in large amounts, being as low as $\frac{1}{64}$% ($3\frac{3}{4}$d.
per £100) on the nominal value of the stock or even half that
figure in very large amounts.

The principal investors in the short-dated market are the
banks and discount houses, who require investments which are
easily liquidated and which can be bought or sold in large
quantities. Stockbrokers who specialise in this field spend much
of their time walking round the City between The Stock
Exchange, the clearing banks, the merchant banks and the
discount market. Their expertise lies in judging the future trend
of short-term interest rates, selecting the stocks which appear to
be the most attractive on the list and enjoying the confidence
of the jobbers in the gilt-edged market, which enables them to
deal in very large quantities of stock.

OTHER GILT-EDGED SECURITIES

The largest holders of medium-dated, long-dated and undated
gilt-edged securities are institutional. The short end of the
medium-dated market is within the reach of the banks, who
generally dislike moving beyond a redemption date of about
seven years for their funds, other than superannuation funds.
Insurance companies with liabilities accruing at given dates may
adopt a policy of matching some at least of their assets against
these liabilities, obtaining a spread of dated securities in the
medium range.

The long-dated stocks are particularly favoured by the life

offices and the pension funds, whose liabilities are long-term and whose investment policy is designed to obtain the highest rate for the longest period.

Undated securities are generally regarded with disfavour by the majority of institutions, although they may be purchased in times of high long-term interest rates as a policy move in the management of a gilt-edged portfolio.

MANAGEMENT OF A PORTFOLIO

The service which a Gilt-Edged Department offers to its clients lies primarily in two directions:

(a) advice on future trends in interest rates;

(b) advice on the attractions of one stock as compared with another.

Judgement on both these matters is required, not only in selecting investments for new money, but also in switching an existing holding into a more attractive security.

SWITCHING

The basic principle of 'switching' is to take advantage of price movements to exchange from one gilt-edged stock to another and later switch back again to the original stock, taking a profit on the completed transaction. In effect, at the end of the operation, the fund has the same gilt-edged holdings as at the start, with a profit as well.

While at first sight this savours of speculation, switching is a normal part of the day-to-day investment of all well-known insurance companies and a number of the larger pension funds.

(a) Policy Switches

A policy switch results from taking a view on the trend of interest rates and the resulting prices of gilt-edged stocks. If it is considered that long-term interest rates will rise, longer-dated stocks are sold and shorter-dated stocks purchased. In due course, when it is anticipated that the long-term trend in interest rates is downward, the exchange is reversed by selling the shorter-dated stocks and repurchasing the longer-dated ones. If the interpretation of the movement in interest rates is right, a substantial profit may result, although there is normally a fairly lengthy period before such switches are completed.

In many cases the reversal of the policy switch does not put back into the portfolio the original stock that was sold, since some other stock of approximately the same life may look more attractive at the time of the reversal.

Evidence for a policy switch is largely a matter for the economist. Part of his stock-in-trade is to look forward at the likely pressures on the economy, from which some assessment of trends in long- and short-term interest rates may be made.

Policy switches from medium-dated to long-dated gilt-edged securities may be carried out with no intention of a reversal, being based purely on the fact that longer-dated stocks tend to yield more than medium-dated under normal market conditions.

(b) Jobbing or Anomaly Switches

A jobbing switch consists of taking advantage of an anomaly in the relative prices of two gilt-edged stocks. For a number of reasons the supply and demand of different stocks varies, so that from time to time one stock will move abnormally compared with another. This can apply even to stocks of similar date. The stock which is relatively high is therefore sold and the other, which is relatively low, bought. If the switch can be reversed within twenty-eight days, commission is only payable on the initial transaction, with the result that most short-term switches are started in the hopes of reversal within a month.

Comparisons between different stocks are kept either in chart form, or, more recently, in terms of figures produced daily on a computer. To give some indication of the value of gilt-edged switching, a number of pension funds have stated that profits derived from switches closed during a year amount to an average of $\frac{1}{2}$% on the gilt-edged portfolio.

TAP STOCKS

When the Government makes a new issue of one of its loans, the full amount of the issue is not generally subscribed by the public, and a large proportion of the stock may be taken up by Government departments or departments under the control of the Government, notably the Ministry of Social Security, and to a lesser degree the Colonial Office and the Ministry of Agriculture and Fisheries. The management of the Government debt is carried out through the Bank of England and the Government Broker, so that interest rates can be influenced, or the market supported, in various sectors of the market by increasing or decreasing the departments' holdings of certain stocks. The stock that is currently being released by the departments is called a 'tap stock' and is generally offered at a slightly more advantageous price than others of a similar redemption date. From time to time the Government Broker may be instructed to raise the selling price at which the stock is released to the market — the 'tap price' — until the Bank of England considers that sufficient stock has been released to achieve its object and the 'tap is off'.

The release of stock on tap usually presents opportunities to switch from other securities into the tap stock and may provide an attractive home for new money destined for the gilt-edged market.

GILT-EDGED LISTS

As an aid to selecting gilt-edged securities, most firms with specialist departments circularise their institutional clients with lists of securities, giving the relevant details of price, redemption dates, dates of interest payments, together with interest yield and redemption yields both gross and after tax. One or two firms who are renowned in the gilt-edged market even produce lists at regular intervals throughout the day updating their earlier lists with the changes which have occurred during the day's trading.

For the firms who do not publish their own lists, the leading jobbers in the gilt-edged market provide a similar service, noting in addition offers of the somewhat rarer issues among the Dominion and colonial stocks, the public boards and the local authorities.

The only stocks which are subject to *ad valorem* stamp duty are those contained in the list of securities guaranteed by the Government and those of certain Public Boards.

NON-INSTITUTIONAL GILT-EDGED HOLDERS

While the majority of the really substantial gilt-edged *business* emanates from the banks and other institutions, the trusts and private individuals still hold by far the larger proportion of the stocks issued. Some indication of this is given in Table 8 below:

TABLE 8

INSTITUTIONAL SHARE OF GILT-EDGED MARKET: HOLDINGS AT 31 MARCH 1964[1]

	Under 5-year stocks £ millions nominal	%	Over 5-year stocks £ millions nominal	%
Insurance companies	61	1	2,029	14
Pension funds:				
Private	(20)	(—)	(700)	(5)
Local authorities	2	—	225	2
Nationalised industries, etc.	6	—	229	2
Building societies	134	2	167	1
Investment trusts	7	—	31	—
Hire-purchase finance companies	3	—	—	—
Trustee savings banks (special investment departments)	50	1	150	1
Unit trusts	1	—	2	—
Special finance agencies	—	—	4	—
Total institutions	(284)	(5)	(3,537)	(24)
Other non-official holdings	(3,734)	(69)	(6,871)	(47)
Official holdings	1,384	26	4,183	29
TOTAL	5,402	100	14,591	100

[1] Some of these figures were later revised.
Source: The Bank of England. Estimated figures shown in brackets.

A number of the issues not only pay interest free of tax to overseas residents, but are also free of U.K. death duties if held by them. In times of high interest rates in Britain, therefore, they provide a useful income-producer. Victory 4% Bonds also have the attraction that they may be surrendered at par in payment of estate duty (provided that they have been held for a minimum period of six months), and the stock is redeemed by annual drawings at par.

Before 1961 funds which were subject to the Trustee Act 1925 were required to hold virtually all their stock-exchange investments in gilt-edged securities, until the new Act of 1961 gave permission to hold up to half the total in certain ordinary shares and to substitute certain company loan capital for gilt-edged in the other half. Funds administered under the Friendly Societies Act were similarly restricted in their investment powers, and the majority of trustees responsible for charities and private trusts felt it prudent to hold a reasonable proportion in Government securities. Many individuals too have deemed it safe to hold a proportion of their portfolios in gilt-edged securities, if only to provide a security which can be realised easily and inexpensively at times when the ordinary share market may be in the doldrums. The cost of this policy of 'safety' to the holder, in terms of the depreciating purchasing power of gilt-edged stocks, has only recently received the full attention it deserves.

All firms of stockbrokers have clients who are interested in the gilt-edged market to some extent, and must keep themselves informed of the trends in this market.

THE DEBENTURE MARKET

The debenture market is a loose term which covers the market in principal issues of company loan capital:

(a) Mortgage debentures, which are loans secured upon a specific part of the assets of the company, normally its land and buildings, and sometimes in addition by a floating charge on other assets.

(b) Debenture stocks, which are loans normally secured by a floating charge on all the assets of the company remaining after meeting any prior claim.

(c) Unsecured loan stocks or notes, which are loans without any specific security, other than the recognised financial strength of the company concerned.

(d) Convertible stocks, which cover all the above types of loan, with the additional right conferred upon the holder that he may elect to exchange the stock for ordinary shares at certain specified dates and in certain conditions.

Issues of loan capital have the advantage over gilt-edged securities with similar redemption dates that they normally offer a somewhat higher yield to redemption. They have the disadvantages that a purchase is subject to the payment of *ad valorem* stamp duty, the expenses of dealing are much higher and the marketability is much more restricted. The greatest volume of dealing in a debenture or other issue of loan capital is likely to occur in the days immediately after its issue, for during this period the stock is usually transferable on allotment letter. It is thus free of the *ad valorem* stamp duty, and also in many cases it is partly paid (i.e. only a down-payment of say £25 per £100 stock requires to be paid, the balance of the issue price being payable at a later date or dates), with the result that commission charges are lower.

The section of the Fixed-Interest Department dealing with debentures will examine each offer of stock from the market, or each new issue, for a number of factors, in particular:

(i) *Size of the Issue.* If the issue is very small the marketability becomes practically non-existent. Very small issues must thus be placed in the hands of institutions, who are likely to hold them until redemption, and who may require a somewhat higher return for the lack of ability to sell.

(ii) *Security.* The security of the loan is normally quoted as 'asset cover'. If the assets available, at balance-sheet valuation, including the principal of the loan, amount to three times the principal of the loan, the asset cover will be described as 'three times'. Members of the department will be concerned to investigate just what assets are available as security. An investment-trust debenture, secured upon the assets of the underlying portfolio, obviously has assets which may be readily disposable. A chain-store debenture may be secured by freehold shops in first-class areas, and thus have assets far more easily viable than those of a textile company, whose loan is secured by a mill and machinery which may be of little use to any other concern in the event of a textile slump. Ever since the famous St. Martin Preserving or Tickler case in 1958, where a sale of the undertaking was agreed by the board, without infringing the trust deed of the debenture, investors in debentures have been careful to check in detail the particulars of the issue.

(iii) *Security of Income.* The security of income is indicated by the amount of earnings available to cover the interest payment on the loan. This figure may refer either to the year immediately past, or, if this may have been exceptional, to the average of the past three or five years. Interest cover may be given either as a factor, i.e. 'five times', or as a priority percentage, i.e. '15–20%'. The former method may be misleading, for it does not always indicate that there may be a prior charge, standing before the loan stock in question. The latter method clearly indicates that the prior charge takes the first 15% of earnings, leaving the second stock to take the next 5%.

(iv) *Terms*. In particular the department will examine the terms of the offer: the price; the rate of interest; the dates and terms of repayment of the principal; where the loan stock ranks in relation to other loans made to the company; the powers relating to future borrowings; the provisions in the event of a default; and the provisions for a sinking fund, if any.

From this information the essential yields can be calculated — interest yield, gross redemption yield and net redemption yield after applying taxes at the rates applicable to any particular class of client. These yields will probably be compared with those of the nearest British Government security to establish whether sufficient extra yield is obtainable to make the stock attractive.

The operation of a sinking fund is important for two reasons. Firstly, if the security offers a high return for a relatively long period, sinking-fund drawings may be unattractive to long-term funds, since part of their holding could be redeemed in the future when interest rates may be lower and it would be impossible to secure such a good return for the balance of the term; secondly, powers to increase the sinking fund from time to time virtually give the company the option to redeem the stock at an earlier date if it suits it.

On the other hand, for those funds which pursue a flexible policy regarding their debenture portfolios, the restricted market in some issues standing below par provides them with an opportunity of selling at an artificially high level to the sinking fund towards the date when otherwise drawings must be made.

CORPORATION AND CAPITAL-GAINS TAXES

The taxation reforms introduced in the Finance Act, 1965, have made the raising of new funds by means of loan capital more attractive to companies than issues of ordinary or preference shares. Interest paid on debentures and other loan stocks may be deducted from profits before the application of corporation tax. In the simplest example, therefore, taking corporation tax at 40%, the net profits before tax required to pay a rate of 7% on a preference share or a dividend of 7% on a £1 ordinary share would be sufficient to pay interest of 11·7% on a debenture.

The application of capital-gains tax to insurance companies has restricted the market in new debenture issues. Some funds, who had accepted placings of debentures and seen them reach a premium over the short term, were content in the past to take their profits and use the funds on subsequent stock issues. Liability to capital-gains tax now inhibits this type of operation.

It seems likely that, when investors have become acclimatised to the new taxes, some improvement in the freedom of the market will be seen.

PREFERENCE SHARES

There are two basic forms of capital under English company law. Loan capital represents borrowings, repayable before any distribution of surplus assets to shareholders. Share capital represents the member's participation in the enterprise, whether or not on terms which afford a preference as to return of capital or to dividend.

Preference capital is classified in the share capital of a company, and thus bears more of the risks of the enterprise than the loan capital. It consists principally of two types:

(a) *Preference shares*, the holders of which have certain preferential rights, defined in the Articles of Association, as to the rate of and entitlement to dividend, the distribution of surplus assets, and to voting. The dividend is payable at a fixed rate and may be cumulative (i.e. a dividend unpaid one year will be payable out of the profits of the company in succeeding years), or non-cumulative; the shares may be redeemable, although issues of redeemable preference are now uncommon;

and in some cases they may be convertible into shares of another class.

(*b*) *Participating preference shares*, which confer, in addition to the normal rights of preference shares, a further participation in profits, often related to the dividend payable on the ordinary capital.

For many years preference shares have been the unwanted child of the stock market. They have neither the security of gilt-edged or debentures, nor the possibility of increased income in good times given by equities. Since the majority have no final date of redemption, their yields can be compared with those obtainable from undated debentures or undated gilt-edged issues, such as War Loan. Preference shares have always been looked on as the highest-yielding class of fixed-interest security.

Unfortunately they have not provided the best return for those most interested in income — the individual enjoying only a low rate of tax or the pension fund which is able to reclaim all U.K. income tax from investment income. The reason for this has been the effect of double tax relief on dividends paid by companies trading overseas.

From April 1966 onwards, however, the tax reforms introduced in 1965 removed this disadvantage. The 'dividend-withholding tax' deducted by the company before payment of the dividend (initially 8s. 3d. in the £) is fully reclaimable.

'FRANKED' INCOME

Preference shares have one advantage over debentures for those funds (particularly investment-trust companies) paying corporation tax. Dividends from preference shares of U.K.-registered companies will have been paid after deduction of corporation tax on the profits of those companies. Provided that a sufficient proportion of these dividends are passed on to shareholders, they will not be brought into the computations for corporation tax on the investment company's profits. Income which has already borne corporation tax is known as 'franked' income.

VOTING RIGHTS

Preference shares which enjoy a substantial proportion of the voting rights of a company have also commanded a higher price than the return on the investment warranted. In several cases a purchase of the voting preference shares has helped to secure control of a company with much less outlay of capital than would have been necessary to acquire the same number of votes through purchases of the ordinary. Companies faced with possible danger from this direction have reorganised their capital, offering the preference holders a stake in the ordinary or other inducement to agree to the change in exchange for their votes.

RIGHTS IN A LIQUIDATION

Many preference shares are entitled only to repayment at par in a liquidation, although they may have been standing at much higher prices immediately prior to the liquidation date. Following the famous Union Cold Storage case in 1933, where the company sought to repay the three preference issues with only a modest premium over par value by way of compensation, and the decisions in the Wilsons and Clyde Coal Company and Chatterley-Whitfield cases in 1949, where the courts upheld the companies in their decision to extinguish the preference shares at par, many investors have fought shy of high-coupon preference issues. Recent issues of preference capital normally include the provision that repayment may be at par or the average price over a period before the liquidation takes place, whichever is the higher. There may also be the provision that the consent of preference shareholders must be obtained, at a separate meeting, to any liquidation.

SERVICE BY THE DEPARTMENT

Apart from internal advice to other departments on action regarding loan capital or preference shares, this section is likely to act directly with institutional clients.

(i) OFFERS AND BIDS FOR QUOTED SECURITIES

The department will examine the 'marks' each day to ascertain if dealing in any issues has taken place at prices which made them obviously attractive either to buy or sell. It will then keep informed those institutions who normally operate in this field. In particular it will operate for the sinking funds of those debentures issued by companies for whom the firm acts, or bid holders for stock where a sinking fund is operating in the market.

(ii) NEW ISSUES

As mentioned earlier, the greatest activity in debenture and preference issues takes place during the early days after quotation when the stock or shares may be transferred free of *ad valorem* stamp duty. When a placing of new fixed-interest capital is made in the market, not less than 20% (or a smaller proportion in placings of very large amounts) must be offered to the jobbers for passing on to brokers other than the firm involved in the issue. The section's role therefore is to examine the details of new issues as they occur, to obtain as much stock as they can in attractive placings and to ration participations equitably between clients. Where their own firm is acting as sponsor to an issue of fixed-interest capital, the section will be required to advise on the terms of the issue and the institutions who are likely to take a participation either of underwriting or a placing of stock. The mechanics of such an issue are described in the next chapter.

7

NEW ISSUES

ONE of the most fascinating sides of a stockbroking business is the New Issues Department, since its duties cover not only the midwifery of bringing new companies to the market, but the cut and thrust of the battle to take over other companies or to defend them against take-over bids. The partners in charge must spend much of their time visiting companies up and down the country — and often overseas — assessing the management, estimating the price which shares in a relatively unknown concern can command at some date in the future, and advising the management on how best they can solve the particular financial problem that faces them. In some cases it may require several years of careful nurturing before a company is ready to obtain a quotation on the London market, and in almost every case it requires an after-sales service to keep clients who have invested in the company abreast of the latest developments.

The new money raised on The Stock Exchange, London, during the year to 31 March 1967 is shown in Appendix 3.

All issues by the British Government are handled by the Government Broker. Other gilt-edged issues, whether for Dominion or colonial Governments or for the local authorities, are spread between a wider range of firms who specialise in acting for these particular clients. One firm also has a reputation as an issuing broker to water undertakings, most of which are offered by tender.

Issues of capital by companies are more widely spread throughout stockbroking firms. They can be divided into two classes — companies seeking a quotation for the first time and companies whose capital is already quoted. So little has been written about the advantages and disadvantages of a quotation from the point of view of the owners of the company that, before looking into the detailed work of the New Issues Department, it is worth looking at the general problems facing company directors in taking the decision to 'go public'.

COMPANIES SEEKING A QUOTATION FOR THE FIRST TIME

There are a number of reasons why companies seek quotations for their shares, but in the majority of cases they fall into three categories:

(i) To obtain additional capital, whether by the issue of shares or the borrowing of money, as part of the financial development of the enterprise.

(ii) To enable members of the family, for fiscal, financial or other reasons, to make part of their holdings available to the public.

(iii) To improve the marketability of the company's capital and hence the standing of the concern and its products.

(i) PRESENT OR FUTURE FINANCIAL REQUIREMENTS

When a company is unable to generate sufficient capital for its future expansion, either internally from retained profits or by subscription from its present members, or externally from its overdraft facilities, a number of courses are open to it. A mortgage may be raised privately on the fixed assets with one of the insurance companies or other funds; a link may be established with one of the City 'nurseries' which are prepared to take minority interests in private companies; or the decision may be taken to create additional capital which may be offered to the public by obtaining a quotation on either The Stock Exchange, London, one of the other Federated Exchanges, or both. In any event it is likely that the company's bankers or auditors will be consulted, and it is possible that they may pass on the enquiry to a firm of stockbrokers who are known to specialise in this field. The New Issues Department of the firm will then be consulted as to which of the alternatives appears to be the most attractive and, with their connections among the City institutions, will be able to give the necessary introductions if one of the first two alternatives is adopted. In many cases, however, the recommendations may include the issue of share or loan capital, by combining a quotation on a recognised stock exchange with the raising of new permanent finance from the public.

Once a quotation has been obtained, the company will find that it can raise new capital more easily and cheaply. Institutional investors are unwilling to invest a large proportion of their funds in unquoted securities. The investigation which they must carry out before deciding whether shares or debentures of a private company should be included in their portfolios and the difficulty of keeping an eye on the investment over the years, together with the inability to sell easily should they decide to dispose of their holding, does not encourage investment in private companies. As a result, institutions expect a considerably higher return on their money from unquoted securities, and this can be expensive to the borrower or the seller of shares.

(ii) FAMILY INVESTMENT AND FISCAL CONSIDERATIONS

Where a business has been carried on by one family for a number of years, almost all the assets of members of the family may be tied up in the one company. They have, therefore, no spread of interest in their investments. Their advisers may suggest that, however good the prospects for the family concern, they should endeavour to obtain a wider spread among their assets.

As well as the broader aspect of investment, the family may be faced with fiscal problems. Where one member is elderly and his heirs may be faced in due course with a substantial payment of estate duty, the need for a quotation becomes doubly important. Money may be raised at a time when public interest in this type of share is active, thus providing a cash reserve from which part at least of the duty can be paid. At the same time a quotation on a recognised stock exchange (with the condition that dealings take place at least once a year) provides a price which the Estate Duty Office will accept in the probate valuation without undue delay.

Where an estate contains shares in a private or unquoted public company of which the control is in a limited number of hands, the value for estate-duty purposes may be based on asset valuation. Broadly speaking this arises under the Finance Act, 1940, as amended, where the deceased, within five years of death, had control of the company or received more than 50% of dividends paid by the company or owned more than half the share and debenture capital. A quotation may not be of benefit to an estate in reducing the probate value, but it does furnish an upper limit which is acceptable to the Estate Duty Office, and perhaps more important it provides a means by which the actual duty may be realised in due course.

Prior to the Finance Act, 1965, a number of applications were made for quotation in order to establish a price for long-term capital-gains tax. Since that date one or two companies have come to the market because of the penalties attached to being a 'close' company.

Occasionally quotations are obtained for the shares of companies which have previously been under the control of not more than five persons, in order to avoid the risk of surtax direction if, in the opinion of the Special Commissioners, a reasonable part of the company's profit has not been distributed. When the public holds shares carrying not less than 35% of the voting power of the company, which have been the subject of dealings on a stock exchange in the United Kingdom, the company is outside the scope of surtax directions.

On average, quoted companies tend to distribute approximately half their available earnings as dividend on ordinary share capital. This may result in the controlling shareholders paying unnecessarily large sums in surtax instead of ploughing back more into the company. There are, however, technical methods of avoiding this difficulty, which are considered later.

It should be emphasised that there is a fundamental difference between the issue of shares discussed here and that in section (i) above. In the earlier section the company received additional capital, subscribed either directly or indirectly by the public. In the latter case the vendors of the shares are the existing owners, so that the company does not benefit financially. In a large number of cases, however, issues are arranged to give advantage to both parties.

(iii) MARKETABILITY AND PUBLICITY

Marketability has obvious advantages for family concerns, since it provides the owners with the opportunity of liquidating part of their holdings whenever they require to raise money. It also assists growing companies in the acquisition of other businesses by putting a price tag on their shares, which can then be offered in exchange for those of the company they intend to acquire.

In addition to the advantage of easier marketability, the publicity value of a quotation is not so immediately obvious. This is probably appreciated more in America than in Britain, owing to the wider spread of share ownership in the United States. A principal reason for the quotation in London of shares of overseas companies is to keep the name of the concern before a growing investing public, as well as to attract funds from new sources. For British companies also, regular mention in the financial Press, noticed by the majority of executives in the U.K., can provide an efficient and inexpensive form of advertising. Where a public company or its products enjoy a well-known name, its shareholders may become loyal and active customers.

In some industries where the business is very largely carried out by small local concerns, the fact that a company is large enough and respectable enough to be quoted can have a marked effect on the relations with its customers and on the engagement of executive staff. The dissemination of information in accordance with Stock Exchange requirements gives confidence both to customers and to employees.

The coin of publicity has a reverse side to it, and this is the principal disadvantage. From being a private company with a small family of shareholders, most of whom are probably known personally to the board, a quoted company emerges into the public eye. Its accounts, which may only have been available to investigators at Companies House, are now publicised through statistical services and the Press. If the company is progressive and business expands, the directors will have to remember that they must be more reticent about facts and figures to their friends and acquaintances in order to ensure that all members are treated equally. They will almost certainly receive requests from financial journalists and stockbrokers to visit their factories and meet their top-level management. And they will be spurred on by the fact that the public will come to expect a steady trend of rising profits from a well-managed concern. So long as the public has the image of a progressive company, Press and investment publicity can only be of value. When things go badly, this additional publicity may become a nuisance, but both investment analysts and financial journalists are sufficiently realistic to appreciate that

few companies can maintain an unblemished record without the
occasional lapse in the rate of growth.

SIZE OF THE COMPANY

The boards of many companies turn down the suggestion of a
quotation out of hand because they consider that the size of
their company is small compared with other quoted companies
with which they are familiar. The limit laid down by the
Federated Stock Exchanges is that the market value of the
company's capital shall not be less than £250,000, with any
one security having a minimum market value of £100,000.

One consideration which must be borne in mind is the cost
of obtaining a quotation. There are a number of fixed charges
which cannot be reduced, so that, for a small company, these
can become very costly in proportion to the cash proceeds of
an issue.

As a rule of thumb it might be unduly expensive to arrange
for the quotation on The Stock Exchange, London, of a debenture for a company with net assets of less than about £1 million,
and for the shares of a company having net profits before
taxation of less than around £50,000.

Size alone does not rule out the possibility of eventual
quotation, since the City 'nurseries' mentioned earlier often
arrange for the merger of smaller concerns working in the same
field with a view to quotation in due course.

INITIATING THE ISSUE

The directors of most private companies of standing have at
one time or another thought about obtaining a quotation. Often
this has been shelved until the pressure of day-to-day work is
less severe, or until the expansion of profits has brought the
concern into line with others of the smaller quoted companies
with which the board is familiar. Very often the matter is raised
later as a matter of some urgency.

If management had authorised an investigation into the pos-
sibilities of obtaining a quotation at an earlier date, there is
little doubt that in most cases a more satisfactory result could
have been obtained, since the timing of the issue could have

been chosen to coincide with a rising trend in the company's profits and with market conditions which were favourable to share issues. Too often the timing of an issue is left to the last moment and becomes a matter of urgency.

New issues are introduced to stockbrokers usually from one of the company's various professional advisers — accountants, solicitors or bank managers — by some personal connection in the company or close to it, or by one of the issuing houses who have been approached to sponsor the issue.

The operation may be sponsored by the stockbrokers acting either on their own (assisted by the New Issues Department of one of the clearing banks) or in conjunction with an issuing house. From the stockbroker's point of view it is both more remunerative and more satisfying to act as sponsor, but for a number of reasons the company in question may prefer to be associated with an issuing house. Where a company is not yet ready for quotation, the issuing house may be able to provide temporary finance within its own organisation, either through its private company nursery, or through the medium of funds managed by it. Where a considerable capital reconstruction is required or the issue is very complicated, a leading issuing house probably has more experience than any single firm of stockbrokers, and stockbroking firms who do not have specialist New Issues Departments may not be equipped with the staff who are qualified to carry out the detailed investigation that is necessary before an issue is accepted. The name of a well-known issuing house on the prospectus of a new issue also automatically indicates to the investor (particularly the institutional investor) that a further team of experts have investigated the company.

The disadvantage lies almost entirely in the increased costs which are charged by issuing houses, against those charged by stockbrokers, as sponsors.

NEW-ISSUE PROCEDURES

In order to examine the work of the department, the following procedures will probably be adopted during an issue sponsored by the stockbrokers alone.

PRELIMINARY INVESTIGATION

After the initial approach has been made, representatives of the company will probably want to attend an introductory meeting with the partner in charge of the New Issues Department, so that each can assess the quality of the people with whom they are likely to be dealing. The company's problem can then be discussed informally. Either at this meeting or subsequently in a memorandum prepared by the company, the partner in charge of the New Issues Department will want to know certain salient facts about the business — a general outline of the company's products and services, the management structure, premises, labour force and competitors, together with copies of the accounts for the last five years. He will also want to know the company's exact requirements and, if a public issue is likely to be the most satisfactory solution, the distribution of major shareholdings.

From the accounts and the memorandum the stockbrokers can tell immediately if a quotation is quite out of the question. If, on the other hand, this seems feasible, the next step is probably a visit to the company itself to study it at closer quarters and to meet members of the management at the lower levels. At the same time a thorough investigation is undertaken by an independent firm of accountants, nominated by the stockbrokers.

Following a satisfactory report, the New Issues Department then has to prepare a proposal for the company, which is usually divided into four parts:

(a) The capital reorganisation required to fit the company for quotation.

(b) The form of capital to be issued.

(c) The method of quotation.

(d) The terms of the issue.

(a) *Capital Reorganisation*

Most companies seeking quotation are private companies, so that the transition to a public company and the quotation of its shares are achieved at the same time. Some form of capital reorganisation is almost always required, but each case necessitates individual treatment. It may be necessary to form a holding company or to acquire subsidiaries by the parent company to build up a sufficiently substantial concern for quotation. Outstanding loans may have to be repaid. The properties and other assets may need to be revalued. This action in turn may increase the reserves of the parent company from which a capitalisation issue may be made.

A public issue gives an opportunity of simplifying the capital structure and tidying up the classes of capital which are no longer appropriate, e.g. founders' shares, deferred shares and shares with restricted or multiple voting rights.

The essence of any capital reorganisation is to produce the simplest and most straightforward structure which will achieve the required object. All these points will be considered by the New Issues Department and put forward in a written proposal to the company.

(b) The Form of Capital to be Issued

As explained earlier, the two basic forms of capital under British law are *share capital*, representing the member's participation in the enterprise, and *loan capital*, representing borrowings, repayable before any distribution of surplus assets to the shareholders. In the great majority of companies whose share or loan capital has not yet achieved quotation, the issue will take the form of ordinary share capital, since only this form of issue satisfies the various conditions of improved marketability, estate-duty requirements and the spread of family portfolios, mentioned at the beginning of this chapter. Issues of loan capital are normally only undertaken by companies with existing quotations for their ordinary capital, and as such are discussed later in this chapter.

Application for quotation will thus be most likely in the ordinary shares of the company.

(c) Method of Issue

The department must next decide upon the best method of making the company's capital available to the public. Quotation on The Stock Exchange, London, is obtainable by any one of three methods, depending largely upon the size of the issue involved, the public interest in it and the spread of existing shareholdings.

(i) *Issue by Public Subscription/Offer for Sale.* The Companies

Act, 1948, stipulates in considerable detail the main headings of information which must be given to potential investors on the issue of share or loan capital, and the requirements of The Stock Exchange are even more stringent. Even when the Companies Act does not require a full prospectus, a Stock Exchange advertisement may have to be published, containing virtually the same information, so that the document setting out the particulars of the issue and fulfilling either the requirements of the Act or The Stock Exchange is commonly called a 'prospectus'. For the technical-minded a summary of the information to be published, in the order in which it is likely to appear, is given in Appendix 5.

All offers to the general public, as opposed to existing shareholders, must comply with these requirements unless specific exemption is granted by the Council of The Stock Exchange, to whom application for quotation is made. In the case of substantial issues by well-known concerns (the offer to the public of denationalised steel companies is an example), new shares are sometimes offered direct to the public by means of a full prospectus. This is normally called an issue by *public subscription*. In the case of smaller or less well-known companies, or where existing shares are being sold, the firm of stockbrokers sponsoring the issue may offer to purchase the entire issue on a given date, subject to the quotation being granted, and that capital is subsequently resold to the public by the stockbrokers. This is called an *offer for sale*. The detailed procedure by which these two methods are carried out is almost identical, the only difference being that in the case of a public subscription the sponsoring broker is probably paid a fee for his services, while in the case of an offer for sale his remuneration may be taken either partly or wholly out of a differential between the price which the company and/or vendors receive and the price at which the capital is offered to the public.

From the company's viewpoint the advantage of an issue by full prospectus or offer for sale lies in the wide publicity which it will attract, since every member of the public has an equal chance of obtaining an allotment of stock or shares. The disadvantage lies in the fact that, where the amount subscribed by the public is small, the cost is high in relation to the money involved. A variation on this method of issue, which safeguards

the vendors against a very large premium on the price developing immediately after the issue, is the *offer for sale by tender*. This
method has been employed for many years in issues by water
companies and has been adapted in the course of the last few
years for issues by industrial companies.

In the case of water companies, shares are offered for sale at
a minimum issue price, but in the form of application the subscriber states not only the number of shares required but also
the price, above the minimum, which he is prepared to pay.
Allotments are then made from the highest price downwards
until the issue is fully subscribed. As the ordinary shares of
water companies are normally entitled to a maximum dividend,
and since one water company does not differ vastly from
another, there is ample evidence on which to tender. The price
difference between highest and lowest tenders should not therefore be of great significance.

In the case of ordinary shares of companies in other fields
where comparison with existing quoted shares is difficult, the
tender method may be worth consideration. Allotment is made
on a somewhat different basis from that in water company
issues. Applications are listed at each price-level, from the
highest to the lowest. Working from the highest price downwards, at some price-level the total number of shares for which
tenders have been made will fully subscribe the issue.

Theoretically all tenders are accepted at this price. In practice
one of the objects of the issue is to obtain a reasonable spread of
shareholdings among the public and, if the method were taken
to its ultimate conclusion, one application might subscribe for
the whole issue at the highest price. It is also unlikely that the
total number of shares tendered down to the allotment price
would exactly match the number of shares to be issued. The
sponsoring stockbroker must be given discretion in deter-
mining the basis for acceptance, reducing large or multiple
tenders, and, if necessary, accepting a slightly lower level to
increase the spread of holders, scaling down all applications
accordingly.

The advantage of the tender method is that, if a very high
level of public demand is expected in a share which is difficult
to evaluate, the vendor receives the benefit of the popularity
of the issue, and not the successful speculator who 'stags' it.

The disadvantage is that the discretion which must be given in fixing the price and scaling down allotments lays the sponsor open to possible criticism from dissatisfied applicants. In addition few of the recent offers for sale by tender have proved to be very successful from the point of view of the investor, many of the issues failing to recover their opening price for some considerable time.

(ii) *Placing*. In the case of small issues or issues of shares in which there is unlikely to be much public interest, the Council of The Stock Exchange will permit a *placing*.

In a public placing it is normal for the stockbrokers sponsoring the issue to subscribe or purchase the capital to be issued and to sell it direct to their own clients. Under the Stock Exchange regulations a minimum of 35% of the issued ordinary shares must be the subject of the placing, and of that amount at least 25% must be offered to the public through the medium of the jobbers in the market and their connections with other firms of brokers. This increased distribution of shares also assists in providing an orderly market when dealings commence. When there is likely to be public interest in a small issue, the Council may require that a higher proportion shall be placed through the market.

A placing has the advantage of lower cost since there is no need to underwrite the issue, and advertising, printing and bank charges will be lower. It has the disadvantage that the general public are not given the same opportunity to subscribe for shares as the clients of the sponsoring brokers, and the Council therefore does not normally permit placings of ordinary shares (or fixed-interest stocks convertible into ordinary shares) except in very small issues.

(iii) *Introduction*. Although it has been assumed that the application for a quotation is linked with an issue or sale of capital to the public, there are cases where a reasonable distribution of shares already exists. The quotation is required simply to establish a market or to bring the company's name before the public for other reasons. Under these conditions the Council of The Stock Exchange may permit an *introduction*. Since no capital is being offered, no prospectus is required under the Companies Act, but the requirements of The Stock Exchange provide for a similar advertisement to be prepared for circulation by the two accredited statistical services, Moodies Services Ltd. and the Exchange Telegraph Co. Ltd.

No rule of thumb as to the number of shareholders or the spread of holdings which will provide eligibility for an introduction can be applied, since each case must be judged on its merits. The majority of London quotations for overseas companies, whose shares are normally widely spread in the country of origin, are by means of introductions. Since there will be a market in an overseas centre, no problem arises in the establishment of a fair price for the shares. In the case of a U.K. company, an introduction will only be allowed if it is considered that the normal supply and demand among new and existing holders will provide a satisfactory market in the shares.

(d) The Terms of the Issue

Part of the expertise of the New Issues Department lies in its judgement of the price at which a placing or an offer for sale may be made. In the early stages only an indication of the terms will be given, and the meeting to finalise the prospectus is left as close as possible to the date when quotation is granted so that there is the least risk that a general movement of the stock market will upset the success of the issue. Some indication of the terms will, however, be given in the initial proposal, subject to the approval of the Council of The Stock Exchange to the basis of the issue and subject to market conditions being satisfactory at the time when the issue is planned to take place.

The value which can be placed upon a company's share capital depends upon a number of interrelated factors, including the capital structure, the denomination of the shares, the present and prospective dividends, the present and prospective earnings, etc. Reference to the *terms of issue* covers all these factors.

Gauging the terms of issue is largely a combination of experience and a statistical comparison with other quoted securities in the same field. The latter exercise can only give an approximate indication, since no two companies are ever identical, but a yardstick can usually be obtained as to terms which will attract a response from the public. Prospective investors will examine a new issue in just the same way that they will investigate shares in an existing company, so that most of the investment criteria discussed in earlier chapters will be applied in establishing a value for new shares. In addition the public must be given some temptation to attract them towards a new investment, so that the price must be slightly below that of an equivalent quoted stock. Otherwise there is no reason for the investor to take the risk on the new share rather than invest in the established concern with the long public record.

The old adage of success breeding success applies to some extent in new issues. Where investors have seen a successful original issue, they tend to support succeeding issues by the same company, provided that the terms are satisfactory. While the stockbroker sponsoring the issue will endeavour to obtain the best possible price for the shares being issued, he will probably advise the company that it usually pays, when first marketing shares, to err slightly on the side of generosity.

While The Stock Exchange requires that at least 35% of ordinary capital shall end up in the hands of the public, quotation will be obtained for the whole of the ordinary share capital, even if only a part is to be marketed.

COST OF THE ISSUE

The proposal will also give some estimate of the cost of the issue. Individual expenses vary with the complexity and the amount of work carried out by the professional firms involved, so that it is not possible to give more than a general indication here. A study of some twenty ordinary share quotations on The Stock Exchange, London, granted during the calendar year 1966, has produced the figures set out in Table 9 below. All the companies included were previously without quotation for their capital.

TABLE 9

Group	Number of companies	Average amount paid by public	Average total costs	(iv) as % of (iii)
(i)	(ii)	(iii)	(iv)	(v)
(a) Up to £200,000	5	£144,275	£15,030	10·4
(b) £200,000–£500,000	5	£300,412	£26,030	8·7
(c) £500,000–£750,000	5	£569,561	£44,026	7·7
(d) Over £750,000	5	£1,976,147	£76,180	3·9

Column (i) shows the group, measured by the market value of the shares sold to the public (i.e. the number of shares multiplied by the price per share paid by the public).

Column (ii) shows the number of companies in each group.

Column (iii) shows the average amount of money raised from the public, being the total within the group divided by the number of issues.

Column (iv) shows the average total costs.

Column (v) shows the total expenses as a percentage of the amount paid by the public.

Where the sponsor has derived his remuneration as a difference between the proceeds paid to the company and/or vendors and the cash proceeds subscribed by the public, this difference has been included, together with the figure published in the prospectus, in the column headed 'average total costs'.

The principal value of the table is to indicate the magnitude of the figures involved and to show that costs as a percentage of the amount raised decrease rapidly as the size of the issue grows. This is due to the fact that certain basic expenses must be incurred, irrespective of the amount of money which the public is asked to subscribe, while others are directly, or almost directly, proportional to this figure.

THE TIME-TABLE

Although much of the basic work will have been completed by the New Issues Department in setting out its detailed proposal in writing, it is after the proposal has been accepted that the work begins to intensify and the snowball of paper mounts towards its peak. The main role of the department is now as the co-ordinator of a team of solicitors, accountants, printers and Press agents. Every separate stage must be completed to a time-table, so that nothing is left undone for the final grant of quotation and the commencement of dealing. The simplified time-table shown below (Table 10) has been constructed to apply either to a placing or an offer for sale, although the completion date may be postponed to the Friday in the latter case. It is also assumed that meetings of shareholders can be held at short notice.

Quotation is normally granted by the Quotations Committee of The Stock Exchange either on a Wednesday or a Friday

(D-Day in the time-table), and the days of the week have been shown in brackets in the example. In this case a Wednesday has been selected.

TABLE 10

SIMPLIFIED TIME-TABLE

Date	Event	Action by
About D – 40	Meeting to draw up time-table and finalise procedures.	Stockbrokers, company and solicitors.
About D – 40	Drafting of proofs of: (a) prospectus; (b) allotment letter or letter of acceptance; (c) form of acceptance; (d) underwriting agreement.	Stockbrokers, solicitors, accountants and company.
About D – 30	Proof prospectus and attached documents to Stock Exchange for comment.	Stockbrokers.
D – 12 (Friday)	Meeting to finalise prospectus.	Stockbrokers, solicitors, accountants and company.
D – 7 (Wednesday)	Extraordinary General Meeting and separate class meetings to approve capital reorganisation, adoption of new Memorandum and Articles, etc.	Company and solicitors.
	Board meeting to allot new shares, approve prospectus, exchange share purchase and sale agreement, etc.	Company, stock-brokers, solicitors and accountants.
	Documents filed with Registrar of Companies.	Solicitors.
	Bulk printing order given.	Stockbrokers and printers.
	Start underwriting.	Stockbrokers.
D – 6 (Thursday)	Press conference	Stockbrokers.

Date	Event	Action by
D – 2 (Monday)	Prospectus advertised in London morning papers.	Stockbrokers through advertising agents.
	Final documents lodged with Stock Exchange.	Stockbrokers.
D-Day (Wednesday)	Permission to deal and quotation granted, subject to the posting of allotment letters, or letters of acceptance.	Stockbrokers.
D + 1 (Thursday)	Application lists open and close.	Bankers.
D + 2 (Friday)	Allotment meeting.	Stockbrokers, company and bankers to the issue.
	Press announcement on basis of allotment.	Stockbrokers.
D + 3 (Saturday)	Allotment letters or letters of acceptance posted.	Bankers to the issue.
D + 5 (Monday)	Dealings begin.	Stockbrokers.
D + 42 (Wednesday)	Last day for split allotment letters.	Bankers to the issue.
D + 44 (Friday)	Last day for renunciation.	Bankers to the issue.
D + 72 (Friday)	Share certificates ready.	Company.
	File return of allotments.	Company through solicitors.
	Statutory declaration filed with Stock Exchange.	Company and solicitors.

UNDERWRITING

An offer for sale, whether the price is fixed before the prospectus is issued or is fixed by tender, requires to be underwritten. In other words a premium is paid to assure that the shares issued are subscribed in full. If the public fail to apply for sufficient shares, the balance is allotted to the underwriters in proportion to their underwriting commitment.

Every firm of stockbrokers specialising in new issues has its own list of underwriters, mostly the institutions and tied trusts, but possibly some private clients also. In recent years inclusion in a list of underwriters of a firm with a reputable issue business has been extremely profitable, since on relatively few occasions have the underwriters been required to take up stock or shares. The task of the New Issues Department on about D − 7 is therefore to allot underwriting among the firm's clients, so that a balance is kept between the large institutions who must be offered a reasonable slice of underwriting commitment and all the other clients who must somehow be sandwiched into an allocation, however small. No issue ever seems quite large enough to accommodate all the underwriters in the size which the issuing brokers could wish, and in the case of small issues it is usually a matter of taking underwriters in some form of rotation, so that those who were not included in the previous issue are given an opportunity in the next.

PLACING

Similarly, in a placing, the department will collaborate with the partners engaged in servicing the institutions, tied trusts and private clients in selecting firm hands to whom the shares can be offered. No brokers will accept the sponsorship of an issue unless they believe that it is a sound investment, so that they should have no difficulty in recommending the acceptance of a placing to any client for whom the investment might be suitable.

SUBMISSION OF DOCUMENTS TO THE STOCK EXCHANGE

One of the requirements of The Stock Exchange is that draft copies of almost all documents prepared in connection with the issue, particularly the prospectus itself, must be submitted to the Quotations Department for approval. Where the stockbrokers are acting in conjunction with an issuing house, their principal role in the initial stages is to act as a channel between the issuing house and this department.

The Quotations Department is concerned that any prospectus shall put before the public as full and fair a picture of the company and its prospects as possible. In almost every issue the department will have some comment to make or some amend-

ment to suggest to the prospectus that will be of advantage to
the public.

THE GRANT OF QUOTATION

The finalised documents must be submitted to The Stock Exchange two clear days before the date when permission is given
to deal in the new shares and when quotation is officially
granted. By this time all the problems regarding the issue will
have been resolved, and it is only rarely that the Quotations
Committee will want to make a last-minute enquiry. Nevertheless a partner of the firm must attend to answer any questions
that may arise.

COMMENCEMENT OF DEALINGS

It will be seen from the time-table that between the grant of
quotation and the commencement of dealings about five days
have elapsed, including a weekend. In the case of an introduction where there is no quotation elsewhere, two clear days must
be allowed to elapse, so that some estimate of the demand for
shares may be obtained through the jobbers, in order to establish a fair price at the commencement of dealings. In a placing,
dealings may begin the day after the grant of quotation.

One of the duties of the stockbrokers to an issue is to obtain
the confidence of the market in the issue. They will hold meetings with the relevant firms of jobbers prior to the first day of
dealing, to fill in any additional information which may be
required. Sometimes the New Issues Department will prepare
a précis of the information published, together if necessary
with some comparative statistics drawn from companies in the
same field.

Every new issue requires a certain amount of nursing in its
early stages, until the market in the shares settles down.

COMPANIES ALREADY QUOTED

Companies which already enjoy a quotation may make two
different types of issue to their ordinary shareholders:

(*a*) Capitalisation issue.
(*b*) Rights issue.

(a) CAPITALISATION ISSUES

Where a company has built up substantial reserves and where the capital employed by the company is large compared with the issued ordinary capital, a strong case exists for bringing the two more closely into line. For example, a company with an issued ordinary capital of £500,000 may have reserves of perhaps £1,500,000. The dividend on the ordinary shares may be 40% and the £1 ordinary shares may stand at £8 to give a dividend yield of 5%. The company has fully adequate reserves to capitalise £500,000 by giving a capitalisation issue of one new £1 share for every old £1 share. This is, in fact, nothing more than a book entry. The issued share capital will rise from £500,000 to £1 million, and the reserves will fall equivalently from £1,500,000 to £1 million. Unless otherwise stated the dividend would be likely to drop from 40% to 20% and the share price would halve from £8 to £4.

What then are the advantages of the issue? There are several:

Marketability. By doubling the number of shares in issue, the marketability improves. Similarly, by reducing the share price from the very 'heavy' £8 to a more reasonable £4, a new class of investor is interested in them. At the same time (in this particular example) the £1 shares might be reduced to a nominal value of 5s., increasing the number of shares by a further three times, reducing the price to £1, and increasing both the marketability and the number of prospective investors accordingly.

Rate of Dividend. The rate of dividend is reduced from 40% to 20%. Politically this is a sound move, for there are still unsophisticated members of the public who believe that, by buying a share which pays a dividend of 40% of nominal value, the capitalist will recoup his investment by way of income in only two and a half years. A lower rate of dividend defeats this objection.

Eligibility under the Trustee Investments Act, 1961. The provisions of this Act limit investment in ordinary shares to those companies whose issued share capital is £1 million or more. The increase of the issued capital to this figure, therefore, makes the shares eligible to another class of investor.

For many years Press reference to capitalisation issues was

made under the misleading title of 'bonus' shares, as though the shareholder were receiving something for nothing. It should be stressed that such shares can only be issued by the capitalisation of reserves which have been built up over the years, either as earnings which have suffered tax and been ploughed back into the company, or from the improved value of the assets. The term 'plough-share' which has been adopted by certain popular newspapers is much more descriptive of the true nature of the issue.

The above explanation does not indicate why the market price of a share generally improves after the announcement of a capitalisation issue. The answer is simply that, unless it is specifically stated that the dividend will only be maintained at the lower level, public opinion optimistically expects that some slight increase will be made.

The paperwork of a capitalisation issue is carried out between the company, their solicitors, the stockbrokers and The Stock Exchange. Draft documents must again be sent to the Quotations Department for approval and the necessary resolutions passed by shareholders in general meeting. The work involved, however, is largely formal.

(b) RIGHTS ISSUES

Where a company requires additional funds, it may obtain these either from the public at large or from its own shareholders. In the case of loan capital or preference share capital, where the rights of existing ordinary shareholders are not affected, shares may be offered to the public at large. In the case of ordinary shares or loan capital which may be converted into ordinary shares, except under special circumstances (such as the purchase of an asset, a trade link-up, etc.), such funds must be obtained (under Stock Exchange rules) by an issue of capital to ordinary shareholders in proportion to their existing holdings unless shareholders in general meeting agree otherwise.

The term 'rights' therefore refers to the entitlement of the shareholder to a participation in the new issue.

Rights issues of ordinary shares are somewhat more complicated than capitalisation issues, for a decision must first be reached as to whether an ordinary share issue is the best means of obtaining finance at the particular time. Then the terms of the issue must be established.

The new shares must obviously be issued at a price somewhat lower than the price of the existing ordinary shares in order to make them an attractive investment. A decision has to be taken as to whether this price can be so reduced that, allowing for fluctuations in the market during the period of subscription (usually about three weeks), all the shares will be subscribed by shareholders or any left over can be sold in the market without loss; otherwise the issue must be underwritten. The criticism of underwriting such issues is that the discount which could have been offered to the shareholder is being paid away to a third party.

Shares not subscribed by those to whom they have been offered are (unless shareholders in general meeting have agreed otherwise) normally required by the Council to be dealt with by one of the following methods:

(i) sold for the benefit of the shareholders entitled to them;
(ii) offered to existing shareholders by the provision of application forms for excess shares;
(iii) sold for the benefit of the company.

On occasions a combined capitalisation issue and rights issue is made, and the rights issue may be underwritten. Under such conditions the advantages of reducing the two issues to a larger rights issue, at or near par, may be considered. In Australia and Japan particularly, regular rights issues are made at par. If the rate of dividend is maintained and the price of the shares continues to stand substantially above the nominal value, the shareholders, while contributing new capital to the company, are obtaining an improvement in both capital and income.

ISSUES OF LOAN CAPITAL

Types of loan capital were discussed in Chapter 6 from the point of view of the investor. Somewhat different criteria apply from the point of view of the company issuing the security.

Mortgage debentures (loans secured upon a specific part of the assets of the company, normally its land and buildings) are most suitable for companies where the freehold or long leasehold element is large. Property companies, retail outlets, breweries, etc., can usually provide the specific assets for such securities, although in recent years many companies have preferred not to create a charge over specific assets, but to issue debenture stocks.

Debenture stocks (normally secured by a floating charge on all the assets of the company remaining after meeting any prior claims) have been a favourite form of investment for insurance companies and pension funds. The application of corporation tax in the 1965 Finance Act has, however, somewhat reduced the attraction to the former class of investor. As a form of loan capital the debenture with final redemption dates is probably the most suitable form of fixed-interest issue for the majority of companies.

Unsecured loan stocks (having no specific security other than the recognised financial strength of the company concerned) are appropriate only for larger companies. The majority of institutional investors do not view unsecured loans of smaller or lesser-known companies with approval, since, if loan capital is required, the security should be available. The various restrictive covenants which are substituted for the security are often such that a small company cannot prudently accept them without too great a surrender of flexibility.

Convertible stocks (covering all loan capital with the additional right that the holder may elect to exchange the stock for ordinary shares at certain specified dates and in certain proportions) may provide a useful means of raising finance on the best terms from the point of view of the company. The interest rate is not normally as high as would have been necessary for a loan stock without the attraction of a future stake in the equity of the company, and the conversion terms are usually at a premium above the price of the ordinary shares at the time of issue, thus providing finance which would not have been available on the basis of a rights issue of ordinary shares. Convertible issues are particularly suitable either when market conditions do not permit a rights issue of ordinary shares, or when there may be some delay between the raising of the finance and the eventual effect upon the profits of the company.

Issues of loan capital have two advantages to the borrower. Firstly, interest payments are met out of earnings before the charging of corporation tax, so that, in the majority of cases, they provide a cheaper form of fixed-interest capital than preference shares. Secondly, where a company is earning a reasonably high rate on the capital it employs, the difference between the earnings on the loan capital and the interest payments accrue to the benefit of the ordinary shareholders.

The disadvantage of loan capital lies in the creation of a charge or some other restriction on the assets. Many companies are reluctant to entertain this, since it may affect the scope of their existing overdraft facilities with their banks.

The issue of loan capital does not, however, limit the company to a further issue of additional stock of the same class in the future. Nowadays most debenture issues are made on a 'formula' basis. The formula permits further issues, providing that the relation of the total amount of debenture in issue to total assets and earnings is maintained.

METHOD OF ISSUE

Loan capital may be issued by any of three methods:

(a) As an offer for sale.
(b) As a placing.
(c) As an offer restricted to shareholders.

(a) Offer for Sale

The offer for sale has the advantage that close terms can usually be obtained, but this is counterbalanced by the expenses of the issue, which are high. A full prospectus is required, with the high cost of advertising, underwriting, bank charges, etc. Preferential treatment may be offered to applications from existing shareholders.

(b) Placing

Unlike equity issues, no limit is put on the size of fixed-interest issues which are the subject of a placing, since there is a limited class of investor (primarily insurance companies and pension funds) interested in this type of security. Where the amount placed does not exceed £1 million, not less than 20% must be offered to the market for distribution through other firms of brokers. For amounts in excess of £1 million, provisions are in force to obtain a balance between ensuring sufficient distribution and not prejudicing the success of the issue.

Placings of fixed-interest securities, in particular loan capital, are frequently more advantageous to the borrower, despite the fact that a narrower section of the public may be able to participate. Not only are the costs of the issue lower than for an offer for sale, but the terms (price and life of the security) need not be fixed until about a few days before the placing, as opposed to three or even four weeks before a public offer. In the most recent 'crash programmes' for loan issues the terms are fixed on the day before the placing. Consequently the borrower (or the company) secures terms most closely in accord with current market conditions.

(c) *Offer to Shareholders*

The cost of an issue to shareholders is again reduced, but it requires to be underwritten, since it is unlikely that existing shareholders will fully subscribe most debenture issues, unless they contain some conversion terms. Underwriters will thus expect to be left to take up stock, so that the terms must be relatively attractive.

In the majority of cases, therefore, a placing will probably be found to be the most satisfactory method. At least 30% of any class of fixed-income capital for which quotation is sought must end up in the hands of the public.

ADDITIONAL ADMINISTRATIVE MATTERS

Issues of loan capital require additional administration in a number of directions. Trustees must be appointed to ensure that the company adheres to its various undertakings. Usually one of the insurance companies, often the office which undertakes the company's own insurance, will accept the appointment. The trust or mortgage deed must be prepared, and the prospectus will contain a number of new paragraphs, the principal of which are given at the end of Appendix 5.

QUOTATION OF FOREIGN COMPANIES

In recent years a number of overseas companies have realised the value of a quotation in London, just as a number of leading British companies have taken steps to arrange quotation for their shares in the United States and in leading European centres.

Normally the initiation of an overseas issue will come to the New Issues Department through the Foreign Department of the firm, and one of the duties of the partner in charge will be to explain the advantages of a London quotation and the requirements of The Stock Exchange to the overseas client.

ADVANTAGES OF A LONDON QUOTATION

The general advantages of a quotation have already been discussed, but for the foreign company two factors are of the greatest importance.

(a) *An Additional Source of Finance*

London provides the largest source of investment finance in Europe and, next to New York, in the world. The investment trusts provide the largest closed-end trust organisation in the world, and their traditional outlook has caused them to place a relatively large proportion of their investments in overseas securities. The insurance companies also have tended to hold a higher proportion of their investments in ordinary shares than have insurance companies in other countries, and, although they may not have liabilities in certain overseas countries, many offices have considered it wise investment policy to give their portfolios a global spread.

The foreign company which, by reason of its London quotation, publishes its reports in English and produces its accounts in a form with which U.K. investors are acquainted thus has a distinct advantage as a recipient of British institutional funds over its counterpart who does not have a quotation.

Institutions are forced to rely on the advice of bankers or brokers close to foreign companies as to the progress of the concerns and their outlook for future growth. Where a London merchant bank and a firm of stockbrokers have been engaged in introducing shares to the London market, institutions are able to make enquiries from people with whom they are probably in daily contact, and, other factors being equal, will prefer to invest in the concern with which they can keep in the closest touch and whose share price they can follow daily in the financial Press.

(b) *Publicity Value*

Compared with the cost of mounting even a fairly small advertising campaign in the British Press, the cost of a quotation on

The Stock Exchange gives remarkable value. The names of the leading foreign stocks are still relatively unknown in Britain and the number of quotations relatively few, so that any innovation receives very considerable editorial coverage in the Press. A quotation in the leading national financial papers also provides a regular reminder of the company's existence to a wide range of executive and professional men who read these journals.

REQUIREMENTS FOR A QUOTATION

The requirements for the quotation of the shares of a foreign company do not differ much from those of shares in companies incorporated in the United Kingdom, since it is the policy of The Stock Exchange that, if a company wishes to enjoy the facilities provided by London, it must provide investors with the same information and undertake the same pledges as a domestic concern. The requirements are sufficiently flexible, however, for there to be no absolute limitation on the quotation of a foreign security which cannot for good reason comply with every requirement of the regulations. The Council are also prepared to consider some slight amendment to the requirements of the General Undertaking which would obviously be either unduly burdensome or inapplicable to overseas companies.

The principal difficulties arise in connection with the publication of consolidated accounts, with the qualifications of the auditors and with the paragraph entitled 'Profits, Prospects and Dividends' in the prospectus.

In order to make clear the requirements of The Stock Exchange to companies incorporated outside Great Britain, the Quotations Department has published a memorandum on the subject.[1]

PROFITS, PROSPECTS AND DIVIDENDS

One of the requirements of The Stock Exchange is that a paragraph on the current profits, the future outlook for the company and the directors' intention with regard to dividends shall be included in the prospectus at the time of an issue. This may conflict with the regulations in the country in which the

[1] 'Foreign Companies Memorandum' (June 1964).

company is incorporated. It may be found desirable, therefore, to seek a London quotation immediately after the end of an accounting period, when up-to-date figures will be available for the prospectus and when the 'Profits, Prospects and Dividends' paragraph can be drawn from the statement recently made to the company's shareholders.

EXPENSES

Since quotation of a foreign company's shares is often undertaken partly for advertising and prestige, it is normally advisable to utilise the services of an issuing house, and preferably one with a reputation for international coverage. The translation of documents and the preparation of accounts in the form required for quotation, together with the travelling expenses of members of the issuing house and possibly of the reporting accountants, may increase the expenses over those which would be applicable to a similar introduction of a company incorporated in the U.K. Application for the reduction of the Stock Exchange quotation fee may be made, however, for securities where less than 20% of the issue is held by U.K. investors.

There is no requirement to state the costs of an introduction in the published particulars, but the costs of three introductions of leading foreign companies which did publish their figures in recent years were £7,750, £12,500 and £20,000.

TAKE-OVER BIDS

The most exciting part of a stockbroker's life comes when he is concerned with either an attempt to take over a company or the defence of one of the companies which he represents in the face of a bid. Unlike the sole responsibility of a new issue, however, stockbrokers are not normally given sole charge of advising a company in a take-over situation, unless both managements have agreed to recommend the terms to their shareholders. Where a bid is likely to meet opposition, one of the issuing houses with considerable experience in this field is likely to be employed. The duties of the stockbroker are largely confined to market operations where shares have to be acquired, to advising on whether the terms of the bid or the counter-bid moves will be acceptable to the public or not, and to arranging meetings with institutional investors and with other firms of brokers at which the management of the company they represent can put its case and answer questions.

A code of conduct in take-over bids[1] was issued by the Issuing Houses Association in October 1959 and revised in a publication entitled 'Revised Notes on Company Amalgamations and Mergers' in October 1963. It is currently the subject of further investigation.

The first essential in the planning stage is security. If a possible bid may be expected to meet with opposition, the bidder may consider it wise to acquire a holding of the other company's shares before negotiations commence. The role of the stockbroker is then to make purchases without disturbing the price. If the bid should fail it is likely that the price of the shares will be materially higher, since the company to be taken over must give reasonable grounds for refusing to support it. The bidder is thus protected to some extent from the loss of time and effort in the negotiations by a profit on his initial holding.

Security in such cases is extremely difficult to keep. The jobbers, seeing a firm quietly acquiring a substantial line of shares, are inclined to put two and two together and make four. A code name for the operation may have to be used, and both contract notes and shares will be delivered to a third party, such as one of the clearing banks. In addition the bidder faces the problem that, if a purchase of shares in the market or any suggestion of a take-over causes the price to rise, his bid price, when disclosed, will look less attractive compared with the market price.

Both sides will want to try and keep the initiative in the battle. The classical attack is the offer of either cash, loan stock or shares very considerably above the current market price, with some indication of the progress of the bidder company and the benefits of the merger of interests. This may be matched by the defending company increasing its dividend, distributing cash assets to shareholders where these are available, and often showing some dramatic change in management to prove that the lethargy of the past has been shaken off. Private shareholders tend to be loyal to their boards of directors and their sympathy is often with the under-dog. Institutional holders, being more professional, are concerned with obtaining the greatest possible

[1] 'Notes on Amalgamations of British Business'.

financial advantage for their own shareholders or policy-holders, but they too will normally stand behind existing management unless the case for accepting a bid is irrefutable.

During the course of the battle both sides may be operating in the market. The defence may form a syndicate to keep up the price of their shares, and thus make the bid unattractive. The attack, where their own shares are offered in exchange, may be supporting these. As the date for acceptance of the bid approaches and meetings are being held by both sides to elicit support for their particular cause, the excitement becomes intense. The life of the partner concerned is very different from the quiet City existence imagined by the public.

CONCLUSION

I may have been guilty of devoting too much space to the work of the New Issues Department, which is essentially a specialised part of any stockbroker's office. Little appears to have been written about it in the past and the mechanics of an issue are still shrouded in mystery for most people. It also happens to be the department which I myself find the most fascinating and the most exciting.

8

FOREIGN SECURITIES

MUCH of the success of the investment policies of British institutions has been due to their foresight in spreading their interests throughout the world. At 31 December 1964 investment and unit trusts alone had securities in overseas companies worth over £1,000 million out of total assets of £3,300 million. Comparative figures from insurance companies are not so easy to establish, but the 256 companies making returns through the British Insurance Association to the Board of Trade held almost £400 million of overseas company securities, by book value. In view of the high proportion in the United States and the many years during which regular investment abroad has been carried out, the market value was likely to have been considerably greater.

Among the firms of stockbrokers in London a number have acquired the reputation of being specialists in some particular area — usually Canada, America, Europe, South Africa, Australia or, in more recent years, Japan. One or two firms have opened branch offices in European centres, since the Council first gave permission in July 1962. On the other hand no less than thirty-seven firms of overseas stockbrokers have offices in London, twenty from the United States, eleven from Canada, four from Japan, one from Australia and one from the Bahamas. A firm which does not possess a specialised department dealing with foreign securities is thus able to obtain information at first hand from one of these branch offices.

In recent years the foreign departments of London firms have prepared the way for a two-way traffic, recommending overseas investments to U.K. investors and recommending British securities to foreign investors. Residents in a number of countries (including Australia and Japan) are not permitted to buy securities outside their own countries, and the introduction of the temporary 15% interest equalisation tax in the U.S.A. effectively reduced the large-scale buying of British securities by Americans in the early 1960s. Foreign portfolio investment in the U.K., much of which was on American account, has therefore fallen to a very low figure during the past few years.

Overseas investments currently offer three advantages over domestic securities to U.K. residents. Firstly, it is possible to select those economies or industries which are growing at a faster rate than in Britain. By exercising a flexible policy, investments may be switched from countries that are riding on an economic boom to those which are currently depressed. For example, in post-war years, it has been possible to switch investment between France, West Germany and Italy, to considerable advantage. Secondly, it is possible to invest in certain industries which have no investment counterpart at home. The gas and electric utilities of the United States give possibly the best example of sustained growth, but in various areas coal, railroads, mining and other commodity shares offer interesting investment opportunities. Finally, at times when the U.K. appears to be weak and the possibility of a devaluation of sterling cannot be disregarded, certain other currencies, notably in recent times the American dollar, offer a safer haven than sterling.

Overseas investments are not, however, without their disadvantages also. With the exception of America, where accounting requirements are of a very high order and where disclosure of such important figures as turnover is obligatory, the accounts of few foreign companies give sufficient information to be of real value to an investment analyst. In many countries the accounts of parent and subsidiaries are not consolidated, so that transfers between the two parties can make the figures virtually meaningless. In some the auditor is in fact an officer of the company and not an independent inspector of the accounts.

In many centres the marketability of the shares of even the major companies is very restricted. As a result a purchase of a unit of investment that might be appropriate for an institution can take several days or even weeks to execute, and the possibility of selling the shares easily at a later date is remote.

There is also the difficulty of keeping in close touch with an investment when made. In the case of domestic securities any announcement of importance will be seen through the medium of the Press. Alternatively the stockbroker to the company will normally be well informed about current progress. Overseas stockbrokers have not developed the same after-service to their clients, and on this situation many British stockbrokers have capitalised. A number of institutions prefer to deal through the medium of a British firm, although this may be more expensive because of the additional commission charged, since they feel that they will be kept in closer touch with their investment as a result.

STERLING AREA INVESTMENTS

All those countries in the Sterling Area are termed the Scheduled Territories. They include the United Kingdom, all British Dominions, colonies, protectorates and trust territories (with the exception of Canada), the Republic of South Africa, Rhodesia and Eire. For investment in these areas no special Exchange Control permission is required. The permission to withdraw funds, however, lies under the jurisdiction of the country concerned. In both Australia and New Zealand permission must be obtained through the Exchange Control authorities, via the Reserve Banks, although this is normally a formality. In South Africa the immediate withdrawal of funds following the sale of securities by a non-resident is blocked. As a result the London market in South African securities, which is free of such restrictions, values the securities on a very different basis from that ruling in the Johannesburg market.

In order to deal in overseas securities within the Scheduled Territories, the Foreign Department will first check whether it is cheaper to transact the business through the London market or through one of the stock exchanges in the area concerned. In certain shares, where there are large London holdings, it may well be to the advantage of the client to deal in London. The rules of The Stock Exchange do not permit the London stockbroker to deal with the London branch of an overseas firm of stockbrokers, so the transaction must be carried out by telephone or cable to the overseas centre. Arrangements are then made with one of the banks to settle the transaction in the relevant currency, for which the bank makes a small transmission charge.

Brief details of the markets in Australia, New Zealand and

South Africa, and the expenses of dealing direct with brokers in those countries, are given in Appendices 9, 10 and 21.

INVESTMENTS OUTSIDE THE SCHEDULED TERRITORIES

Investment in non-Sterling Area countries requires a supply of currency for the purpose. In practice the Bank of England does not make currency available at the time of each investment, but a buyer of foreign securities purchases dollars from the pool. These dollars are quoted at the official rate of $2·80 to the £, but, because the pool is limited in size, where there is an excess of demand over supply a premium is established. The premium has varied between about 30% at the time of the devaluation of sterling in 1949 and again in 1967, to nothing when the dollar itself was under pressure in 1960. Investment dollars purchased may be exchanged into any other investment currency.

All securities in Common Market countries can be purchased through the medium of the investment dollar, but in Scandinavian countries, such as Sweden, local regulations affect the premium paid for the currency.

A slight complication arises in understanding the quotation of Canadian securities. For administrative reasons the foreign exchange market quotes both the U.S. and the Canadian dollar as a premium on a rate of $2·80, although the official rate for the Canadian dollar is $3·00 to the £.

When dealing in securities outside the Scheduled Territories, the Foreign Department will again check whether it is to the advantage of the client to deal in the London market or in the overseas stock exchange. A purchase of a security requires a series of calculations: the calculation of the net price in the country concerned (the offered price of the security plus expenses); the conversion of this price to dollars at the official rate; the conversion of dollars to sterling at the premium quoted by a dealer in the foreign exchange market; a comparison with the offered price of the security in London.

If it is to the advantage of the client to deal overseas, the department will instruct the agents in the country concerned to make the purchase. The currency must then be covered through the foreign exchange market, with instructions given for payment and delivery of the security.

The sale of a security quoted outside the Scheduled Territories has been made more complicated since the Finance Act of 1965. This Act included the provision that, whenever a sale of such a security was made, one-quarter of the investment dollar proceeds must be returned to the Bank of England at the par rate ($2·80). If the investor does not wish to repatriate dollar funds, this quarter must be repurchased through the dollar pool at the ruling premium. As a result any switching operation attracts an additional cost of one-quarter of the premium overall.

The effect of the 1965 Finance Act has been both to stultify switching of investments and to provide additional paperwork for the foreign departments of stockbrokers' offices. To comply with the Bank of England regulations approximately twice as many entries are now required for deals in foreign securities as was necessary under previous regulations.

SALES-AND-SERVICE

One of the problems of operating an effective Foreign Department lies in the immensity of the area to be covered. No firm can expect to be expert on every country which offers investment prospects, or on more than a limited spectrum of the security market in any one country. The first essential is to establish relations with reliable and well-informed correspondents or agents in the areas concerned, particularly those who are trained to present their material in a manner acceptable to British institutions. American, Canadian, Australian and Japanese stockbrokers, in particular, present a wealth of statistical and other research material. To a lesser extent, but of an extremely high quality, reports are published by some of the leading banking houses in France, Belgium, West Germany and Switzerland.

The second essential is to select the areas on which the department is planning to concentrate and to maintain a service on industries and companies within these areas. It is painfully easy to develop an interest in a country when the market is rising and prospects appear rosy, only to lose interest and contact when things go wrong. The only advantage enjoyed by the London stockbroker over his foreign counterpart is the close association with his institutional client. If the service is good enough, the client will prefer to pay the additional expenses involved in dealing through the London broker.

The U.S. is traditionally the home of the greater part of U.K. overseas investment. The information disclosed by companies is more detailed than in other countries, accounts of parent and subsidiaries are consolidated, and conditions of audit provide adequate protection to the shareholder. Boards of U.S. companies are more conscious of the importance of their shareholders as owners of the business than in most other countries and are free with their information at meetings or on visits. In addition the U.S. dollar has been one of the strongest of world currencies, certain areas have shown continued growth over many years, and there is a ready market in many of the shares of the leading concerns.

Outstanding post-war growth, however, has been shown by a number of other countries, particularly West Germany, Italy and Japan. Some indication of growth rates, together with indices of security prices in the five years from 1958 to 1963, is shown in Tables 11 and 12 below.

ARBITRAGE

Reference was made in an earlier chapter to 'shunting' transactions between London and the provincial exchanges, where the same security is traded in both centres. Exactly the same operations take place on an international scale between London and New York, Paris, Tokyo, etc. This type of business, buying in one centre and selling in another with the object of making a profit on the transaction, is termed 'arbitrage' and the firms or individuals operating it 'arbitrageurs'.

Whereas it is possible, in shunting transactions, to be fairly certain of the price differential on which the dual transactions take place, additional complications arise in arbitrage due both to the time differential and to fluctuations in the rate of exchange or the dollar premium. The true arbitrageur will have to take a position in a security between the time he deals in London and the time he is able to carry out the second half of the operation on the opening of the overseas market. New York, for example, opens at 3 p.m. G.M.T. Tokyo opens at midnight

TABLE 11

A COMPARISON OF (a) GROSS FIXED CAPITAL FORMATION WITH (b) GROSS NATIONAL PRODUCT OF SELECTED COUNTRIES

		1958	1960	1961	1962	1963	Compound growth rate (% per annum)
			(calendar years unless otherwise stated)				
Australia (£A million year to 30 June)	(a) Private and local govt. investment	1,319	1,633	1,923	1,513	1,933	1958–63 (5 periods) 8·0
	(b) G.N.P.	5,695	6,736	7,099	7,205	7,732	1958–63 (5 periods) 6·25
	(a) as % of (b)	23·2	24·2	27·1	21·0	25·0	
Belgium (billion francs)	(a)	83	105	112	116	n.a.	1958–62 (4 periods) 8·125
	(b)	523	572	605	646	695	1958–62 (4 periods) 5·5
	(a) as % of (b)	15·9	18·4	18·5	18·0	n.a.	
Canada ($ billion)	(a)	7·69	8·30	7·66	8·90	n.a.	1958–62 (4 periods) 3·75
	(b)	32·89	36·29	37·39	40·34	43·01	1958–62 (4 periods) 5·25
	(a) as % of (b)	23·4	22·9	20·5	22·1	n.a.	

France (billion francs)	(a)	51·2	60·5	63·0	72·2	n.a.	1958–62 (4 periods)	9·0
	(b)	244·7	296·2	319·7	353·6	391·8	1958–62 (4 periods)	9·75
	(a) as % of (b)	20·9	20·4	19·7	20·4	n.a.		
W. Germany (billion DM)	(a)	54·1	79·2	86·6	93·8	97·9	1958–63 (5 periods)	12·5
	(b)	231·5	296·8	326·2	354·5	376·5	1958–63 (5 periods)	10·0
	(a) as % of (b)	23·4	26·7	26·5	26·5	26·0		
Italy (billion lire)	(a)	3,473	4,618	5,264	5,937	n.a.	1958–62 (4 periods)	14·3
	(b)	17,114	19,937	22,022	24,693	28,186	1958–63 (5 periods)	9·5
	(a) as % of (b)	20·3	23·2	23·9	24·0	n.a.		
Japan (billion yen)	(a)	2,469	5,127	7,476	7,295	8,177	1958–63 (5 periods)	27·0
	(b)	9,973	14,065	17,203	19,004	21,482	1958–63 (5 periods)	16·5
	(a) as % of (b)	24·8	36·5	43·5	38·4	38·0		
Netherlands (billion guilders)	(a)	8·15	11·49	12·18	12·29	13·21	1958–63 (5 periods)	10·1
	(b)	35·93	42·73	45·29	48·09	52·16	1958–63 (5 periods)	7·6
	(a) as % of (b)	22·7	26·9	26·9	25·6	25·3		

TABLE 11 (contd.)

		1958	1960	1961	1962	1963	Compound growth (rate % per annum)
			(calender years unless otherwise stated)				
New Zealand (£NZ million; year beginning 1 April)	(a)	268	324	326	336	404	1958–63 (5 periods) 8·5
	(b)	1,135	1,311	1,357	1,453	1,595	1958–63 (5 periods) 7·0
	(a) as % of (b)	23·6	24·7	24·0	23·1	25·3	
South Africa (million rands)	(a)	1,105	1,135	1,113	1,140	1,410	1958–63 (5 periods) 5·0
	(b)	4,723	5,355	5,584	6,067	6,667	1958–63 (5 periods) 7·2
	(a) as % of (b)	23·4	21·2	19·9	18·8	21·2	
Spain (billion pesetas)	(a)	111·4	99·7	138·6	194·2		1958–62 (4 periods) 14·9
	(b)	574·7	615·2	697·0	795·5		1958–62 (4 periods) 6·75
	(a) as % of (b)	19·4	16·2	19·9	24·4		

United Kingdom (£ billion)	(a)	3·34	4·46	4·67	4·54	4·74	1958–63 (5 periods) 7·2
	(b)	21·67	24·09	25·65	26·85	28·30	1958–63 (5 periods) 5·5
	(a) as % of (b)	15·4	18·5	18·2	16·9	16·8	
U.S.A. ($ billion)	(a)	56·6	71·8	68·8	79·1	82·0	1958–63 (5 periods) 7·7
	(b)	444·5	502·6	518·7	556·2	583·9	1958–63 (5 periods) 5·6
	(a) as % of (b)	12·7	14·3	13·3	14·2	14·1	

Source: International Financial Statistics, International Monetary Fund, March 1965.

Note: The U.N. system of national accounting differs in some respects from traditional national systems, but differences in end results are not significant. Exports, central Government expenditure, private and local government investment (approximating to gross fixed capital formation in the U.K. system) are totalled; imports and expenditure not on product (transfer and interest payments and subsidies) are then subtracted to reach the figure for Gross National Product.

TABLE 12

A COMPARISON OF SHARE PRICES
(*Base 1958 = 100*)

	1958	*1960*	*1961*	*1962*	*1963*	*1964*
Australia (adjusted average of daily Sydney industrial shares)	100	148	140	149	149	167
Belgium (industrials)	100	114	123	122	120	125
Canada (manufacturing industrials)	100	112	143	138	148	180
France (industrials)	100	160	187	198	171	150 (est.)
W. Germany (industrials)	100	272	282	221	215	243
Italy (industrials)	100	230	262	223	193	148
Japan (Tokyo Stock Exchange index)	100	195	271	248	252	221
Netherlands (industrials)	100	201	255	230	232	233
New Zealand (industrials)	100	152	150	145	166	199 (est.)
South Africa (industrials)	100	95	94	129	190	261
Spain (industrials)	100	90	97	105	104	93
United Kingdom (London, industrials)	100	166	171	158	181	192
U.S.A. (industrials)	100	120	142	133	149	175

Source: International Financial Statistics, International Monetary Fund, March 1965.

London time, Johannesburg at 8 a.m. The risks of being unable to complete the operation are thus greater than in domestic 'shunting' and the margin of profit accordingly wider.

Arbitrage is not undertaken by all firms who maintain foreign departments, but is confined to those specialists who are predared to run the risks involved. It is more akin to a form of jobbing than the normal stockbroking business, and firms engaged in arbitrage are permitted to open joint accounts with their overseas partners, buying and selling securities as principals, and thus reducing the margins that would have been necessary if they had treated the overseas correspondent as an agent and had charged commission at the minimum rates.

PRODUCTION

It is not possible to discuss in detail the peculiarities of each of the foreign markets in which U.K. investors may be interested. Appendices 7 to 23 give a brief summary of the principal markets listed in the *Financial Times* at the present time. There are, however, some general points which can conveniently be discussed here.

(a) DEALING

It has already been explained that the purchase or sale of overseas securities may take place either on the London market or in the overseas centre concerned.

Foreign shares are usually quoted in London either in sterling or, in the case of American and Canadian issues, in 'London dollars'. Prices under the headings 'American' and 'Canadian' on the back page of the *Financial Times* will be found in this form. The London dollar is a hangover from the days when the official rate for the U.S. dollar was $4·86⅔ to the £ and, to aid rapid mental calculation, the London dollar was fixed at $5 to the £. The price of the share was then varied by the jobber to take into account any fluctuation in the rate of exchange. Quotations in London dollars may still be converted to sterling at the rate of $5 to the £, and the prices take into account the premium on the investment dollar. The quotation of prices by this method, however, is a constant source of irritation to brokers and clients alike, who find the two dollar prices for stocks (New York and London, or Canadian and London) extremely confusing. It is difficult to see why these securities cannot be quoted in sterling only and the London dollar finally abolished.

(b) DELIVERY AND REGISTRATION

Foreign securities may be delivered in a variety of ways. Some are registered in a central nominee company (French and West German). Some are delivered by renounceable certificates (American common stocks). Some are bearer. A decision must be made as to whether the security is to be brought home for safe custody in the U.K. or left in the country where it has been purchased. In the former case there may be insurance and shipping charges; in the latter bank safe-custody charges. Where securities are registered, in most cases it will prove most economical to have shares put in the name of a nominee company in the country concerned. Where a substantial investment has been made in shares delivered by bearer document or renounceable certificate, it is probably most economical to bring the scrip home for safe custody in the U.K. Under British Exchange Control Regulations, such securities must be held in safe custody by an authorised depositary (such as a bank).

Renounceable certificates of foreign shares traded in the London market are normally in 'good marking names' and as such are termed 'good delivery'. A list of marking names is set out in *The Stock Exchange Official Year Book* and a member need not accept delivery of shares registered in any other name. In fact the seller of shares not registered in a good marking name is liable to receive a lower price. The reason for this regulation lies largely in the complications that occur in North America when the registered owner of shares dies and it is necessary to prove the estate. The delays and legal fees can be considerable.

Overseas Deliveries

On a number of occasions transactions in foreign securities will be carried out by brokers with the jobbers in London, although the security is held abroad. In the case of a sale the Foreign Transfer Department will ascertain where the security is held and to whose order. The jobber or overseas agent will provide the information as to where the security is to be delivered and to whose order, and this information, together with authority to release the security, is arranged. In the case of a purchase for delivery abroad the Foreign Transfer Department will check where the stock is required and to whose order it should be held. This information is given to the jobber, or overseas agent, who arranges to deliver the security accordingly. Payment is made in either case on confirmation from overseas that the stock has been delivered.

Deposit Receipts

A number of foreign shares are quoted in London as E.D.R. (European Deposit Receipts) or B.D.R. (Bearer Deposit Receipts). Usually the deposit receipt represents either a fraction or a multiple of the shares quoted in the foreign centre. For example General Motors are quoted in London both as shares of U.S. $1\frac{2}{3}$ par value and also as B.D.R. of $\frac{1}{20}$ share. The reason for quoting a different unit lies in the price. At the end of 1966 the price of General Motors shares was over £28. The U.K. private investor dislikes 'heavy' shares, of which he can afford to buy only a few, preferring lower-priced units. The market in the B.D.R. is therefore wider.

Honda Motor, on the other hand, is quoted in E.D.R. of 5 shares each, since the price of each share in Tokyo at the time of obtaining the London quotation was only about 6s. Shares of too small a price are suspect, so that the happy medium of somewhere over 10s. and under £3 appears to satisfy the requirements of the public.

(c) FOREIGN DIVIDENDS

(i) Stocks in Own Marking Names

Most of the brokers with specialist departments dealing in foreign securities are included in the list of 'good marking names'. The name of the firm is thus included in the register of shareholders in the books of the foreign company. For each such company the Foreign Dividend Department will open an account, showing for each dividend distribution (usually quarterly) the dates the books closed, the dividend payable, the rate of the dividend, the date the dividend is received in London, the ex-dividend date and the 'Stock Exchange valuation'.

All but the final entry are self-explanatory. The Stock Exchange valuation is the value of the dividend in sterling, calculated at a rate of exchange published weekly by the Stock Exchange Marking Names Committee. The rate is based on the average $ rate for the week, taking into account also an allowance for the costs of collecting and distributing the dividend which is due to the firm. (It should be noted that the premium on the investment dollar does not enter into calculations on dividends, which are paid at the spot rate.)

Where marking names leave mandates with companies to pay dividends to their foreign banks, these are transferred to the London branches and credited to the firm's account in sterling. The authorised depositaries who hold the securities, usually the banks of the clients who own the securities, claim on the marking names for dividend payments, which are made in sterling.

(ii) *Stocks in Other Names*

The Foreign Dividend Department will examine all foreign stock passing through the office, either bought or sold. Where a dividend is due to be claimed, either from the selling client or on behalf of the buyer, the Foreign Dividend Department stamps the back of the renounceable certificates 'Dividend due on (date) claimed by . . .' and despatches the claim accordingly.

INFORMATION

(*a*) COMPARISON OF DIFFERENT AREAS

In addition to the statistics for comparison of past and prospective growth, many foreign departments maintain charts of the stock-market movements in the countries in which they specialise. These give the historical price record (and often the record of price/earnings ratios) of the indices in each of the major areas. An assessment can be made as to whether prices in one centre over-discount future prosperity, indicating a switch in emphasis to an area of prospective recovery.

(b) SELECTION OF INDIVIDUAL SECURITIES

The selection of shares is little different from that in the United Kingdom, with the exception that accounts of companies in many overseas areas are less detailed and less revealing than those of their British counterparts. A personal visit to an overseas company is almost always worth the trouble and expense, and some arrangement for a continuous flow of information about the company is essential. Most of the stockbrokers who specialise in a particular area send a partner on a visit at least once a year, and sometimes more often. In European countries a knowledge of languages is important, but in such countries as Japan the British broker inevitably has to accept an interpreter's translation both at verbal interviews and of written reports.

NEW ISSUES

The quotation of foreign companies' shares in London has already been discussed in Chapter 7.

CONCLUSION

There seems little doubt that, as methods of communication improve and as countries become more sophisticated in the publication of essential information and the preparation of accounts, increasing interest will be shown in overseas securities. Firms which have established a reputation in this field should reap a future harvest.

9

STOCKBROKING AS
A PROFESSION

I HAVE endeavoured, in the preceding pages, to give some
indication of the operations which take place in a stockbroker's
office today. A young man who is considering stockbroking as
a profession will want to know the answers to other and broader
questions. What is the future of stockbroking? What are the
advantages and disadvantages of the profession? What qualifications does he require? How do firms recruit their new
entrants? What will it cost him to become a member of The
Stock Exchange?

THE FUTURE OF THE STOCK EXCHANGE

In answer to the first question, the future of The Stock Exchange, I can only express my personal opinion, and Part II of
this book is devoted entirely to the outlook for stockbroking. In
summary, while capitalism exists, some market for the exchange
of securities must also exist. The Stock Exchange, although I
believe its structure will change more rapidly in the next quarter
of a century than it has in the past hundred years, should still
provide a reasonable livelihood for forward-looking stockbrokers.

ADVANTAGES AND DISADVANTAGES

The advantages and disadvantages are more easily enumerated.
I shall deal with the disadvantages first. Stockbroking is an
uncreative profession. The engineer or the architect can look
at some physical result of his labour. Even the doctor can be
certain in his own mind that he has saved a life or cured an ill-
ness. The stockbroker may make a great deal of money for his
clients, but he rarely receives much praise for it and can never

boast about it. It is a worrying profession, particularly for those who deal with the affairs of private clients. Duodenal ulcers are a common occupational hazard among stockbrokers, caused during busy times by rushing meals, worrying over clients' affairs and by the demands of the non-stop telephone. And the stockbroker, like the doctor, carries his work with him out of office hours. Certain clients will wait until the comparative calm of the evening to discuss their own investment problems on the telephone. A stockbroker is always fair game for free advice at a cocktail party.

Stockbroking is also a precarious profession. The swings of fortune can be very wide and sharp. The Stock Exchange is the barometer of the country's economic strength, a target for Left-wing politicians, and it is not uncommon for firms who have enjoyed boom conditions in one year to experience heavy losses the next. Unfortunately the training of a stockbroker does not fit the individual for any other profession. The accounting procedures are peculiar to the industry, and even the examination syllabus agreed by the Federated Exchanges does not fit the successful candidate for alternative employment.

Finally, in common with the professions as opposed to trade, stockbroking gives less opportunity for the build-up of capital through the business itself. The man who expands a small company into a large concern is rewarded by the increase in the value of his shares. A stockbroker leaving his firm may well take out of it only the capital which he put in, since few succeeding partners nowadays are prepared to make a substantial payment for goodwill, and little interest has yet been shown by limited-member corporations. There is also a widespread impression that, as a stockbroker works close to the centre of investment, he is in a privileged position, able to take advantage of much secret information which is not available to the public. Any stockbroker worth his salt should be able to invest his own funds with reasonable success, but this is a far cry from making a large personal fortune. On the few occasions when he is in possession of guaranteed information, such as a take-over bid, he is almost certainly (and rightly) prevented from using the information to his own advantage by being professionally involved in the case.

The advantages, in my opinion, far outweigh the disadvantages of the profession. Possibly the variety of the work is one of its chief attractions. No two days are ever the same. No one, on arriving at the office, has the faintest notion of the business of the day, the surprises, disappointments and the successes to come. In every department the daily contact is with people and all stockbrokers have a wide circle of acquaintances, many in every quarter of the globe. In the smaller firms, where the control is more centralised, the stockbroker is like a general practitioner, having to deal single-handed with every facet from the book-keeping in the office to the whole range of the sales-and-service departments. He may be advising a widow with two children to support on a small pension at one moment of the day and discussing the best means of defence against a take-over bid an hour later. When actual trading is slack, it is impossible to leave the office altogether for a few days each week. It is a job in which keeping abreast of events is vitally important and endeavouring to predict the outcome of events wholly fascinating.

The financial rewards of stockbroking are considerable. While it may be difficult to create a large capital, a partnership in a successful firm may produce a very sizeable annual income. In comparison with positions of equal responsibility in industry, these rewards are often considerably greater. But the risk of greatly diminished profits in bad times compensates for the high earnings during boom periods.

The Stock Exchange, in common with Parliament, has often been called a first-class club. This phrase has something of the pre-war ring of the Establishment about it, the closed shop of the moneyed ranks. In fact it means something totally different. Working within the confines of the City, a communal influence embraces all firms and all employees of them. Every sort of sport and interest is encouraged by someone, who voluntarily organises an association to cater for it. Cricket, football, rugby, hockey, athletics, swimming, golf, boxing, rifle clubs are all available as well as the chess, darts, billiards and bowls clubs. The London to Brighton walk is an annual feature in the nation's athletics calendar. For those with artistic interests, there are societies devoted to art and drama, with an orchestra and a male-voice choir. And so widespread are the interests of the members that, however unusual a hobby a new member may have, someone else is likely to be either interested, or even expert, in the same field.

The very fact of having one central place of business, the House itself, instils a certain comradeship between members of The Stock Exchange, although this spirit has become sadly reduced as the technician, working from the confines of his office, has overtaken the old-time stockbroker who operated almost exclusively on the floor of the House. Nevertheless it still remains. Most members will count other members, not necessarily of their own firms, among their closest friends. A member signifies to another member someone whom he can trust, for his business is based on trust.

Lastly, for the member who falls on difficult times, The Stock Exchange Benevolent Fund was formed over 150 years ago. It caters for those members or their dependants who are in need of financial help, and operates in addition a residential home in Surrey.

RECRUITMENT

Different firms have different methods of recruiting new members of their staff, but in practice three doors are open to a young man seeking employment in stockbroking: to the general office, working his way up the clerical tree; to one of the specialist departments, depending upon his qualifications and experience; and the traditional entry, to one of the sales-and-service departments, depending upon his business connections.

(a) TO THE GENERAL OFFICE

Stockbrokers require, in their clerical staff, just the same qualities that are demanded from clerks in any walk of life. No particular mathematical ability is required, provided that the man is accurate and neat with figures. Any complicated sums are worked out on machines. A young man with ambition, a reasonable level of intelligence, and a conscientious approach to his work can rise through the production departments to the partnership. In my own office one of the partners started life as the office boy.

Vacancies are filled either through the medium of the Press; the register of those desiring employment kept at the Stock Exchange Employments Bureau, for the higher grades; the

Stock Exchange Clerks Provident Fund, for existing employees
and the more junior grades; or, usually as a last resort, through
the City Labour Exchange.

The fluctuating fortunes of stockbroking, coupled with the
rather unwieldy procedures that have held back the progress of
automation, have resulted in severe shortages of staff during
boom periods. Both men and women found it easy to move
from job to job at increasing salaries as one firm bids against
another to maintain its staff in active conditions.

Owing to these severe fluctuations in profits, salaries in stockbroking offices were traditionally low, with a high level of
profit-sharing bonus added. As a result, in the past, over 100%
of salary might have been received by the older and more
responsible members in particularly good years. This situation
has materially changed in recent times, and salary levels are
now more closely comparable with those in other financial
institutions, the bonus element being relatively small.

In addition employees may be entitled to a share of the commission charged on business which they introduce. The maximum proportion which can be allowed to a clerk is one-third
and to a member of The Stock Exchange is normally one-half.
With the increase in overheads during the last decade, however,
some firms have abolished the sharing of commission with
employees, while others have reduced the maximum to members
to 40% or a lower figure, or made a charge for the firm's
services which effectively brought down the proportion allotted
to the employee.

(b) TO ONE OF THE SPECIALIST DEPARTMENTS

With the increasing emphasis on technology, the man with
suitable qualifications is now actively sought by the larger
firms. The chartered accountant is probably the most suitably
qualified individual, since his training enables him to seek employment in the production side of the office, in the Research
Department where a knowledge of company accounts is essential, in the sales-and-service departments, or in the new-issue
side of the business. Of somewhat more specialised knowledge
is an actuarial qualification, the examination for which alone
contains the papers on investment. The investment managers of
many insurance companies have actuarial qualifications, so

that the ability to talk and think on the same lines can be of advantage both in presenting the case for investment and in selecting the security. The precise mathematical techniques of gilt-edged switching have also proved to be fields where actuaries can use their talents to advantage.

In the research departments economists and statisticians are also required, for the long-term prediction of economic trends and the interpretation of particular statistics. In recent years a number of financial journalists have left their earlier calling to join research departments. They have not only the flair to write their material in simple straightforward language and a knowledge of presentation, but many of them have developed close connections in industry which can be invaluable as sources of background information.

Managers or assistants in the investment departments of institutions such as insurance companies and investment trusts have also been tempted to cross over from customer to salesman. They have the advantage of possessing the knowledge of how the institutional investor likes the case for a purchase or sale presented to him. The more senior managers have been offered immediate partnerships in the past, although the conditions of membership introduced in 1965 make this more difficult for the future.

A number of firms make a regular policy of interviewing graduates from the universities, in the hope of finding those who may prove to be outstanding material. Some are assisted financially to broaden their viewpoint by being sent abroad for a few months before they join the firm. Other firms offer undergraduates holiday work during the summer vacations, thus saving the problems of carrying too excessive a staff, and offering future employment to those young men who seem particularly suitable. The importance of some recognised qualification is becoming more and more important in obtaining employment in the City.

Finally, the growth of data processing both as an aid to investment and as a tool in the accounting departments has opened the field to electronic engineers and programmers. These skills, which are in short supply in industry itself, will soon be required in ever greater numbers by stockbrokers and the central administration of The Stock Exchange.

(c) TO THE SALES-AND-SERVICE DEPARTMENTS

In common with most walks of life where no particular qualifications are obligatory, opportunities in The Stock Exchange
are still open to young men whose personal connections can
guarantee substantial business to the firm. The guarantee,
however, is much less easy to secure than it has been in the past.
Neither private clients nor institutional investors are prepared
to spoon-feed a young man because of his family connections.
Business is placed primarily in recognition of the investment
service provided. It would, however, be blinking the obvious if
it were denied that good connections can still assist in providing
a reasonable livelihood in stockbroking.

TRAINING

The size of most firms on The Stock Exchange makes it difficult
to arrange any formal training during their early years, nor is
there any joint training college under Stock Exchange control.
The City of London College has a special course of evening
classes devoted to the subject, however, and this can prove of
invaluable assistance to the young stockbroker.

Most firms lay out a two-year course of apprenticeship for
the promising young man who may eventually come into their
partnership stream, so that he spends sufficient time in each of
the departments to become proficient. At the end of this period
it should be evident, from the progress reports of the heads of
the departments, where his ultimate future lies and how valuable a member he is likely to be.

In the future I believe that, if stockbroking is to progress in
step with the more advanced sections of industry, the larger
firms will have to engage men who are specifically trained in
management skills to ensure that the best output is obtained
from the individual and that communication from the partnership
to the lowest member of the departments is rapid and complete.

The conclusions which can be drawn from these few paragraphs can be summarised in a few words. The opportunities
for a nice chap, without connections and with no particular
qualifications, are becoming fewer and fewer. The opportunities for the qualified man are, I believe, considerable.

ELIGIBILITY FOR MEMBERSHIP

Three methods of entry into the membership of the London Stock Exchange existed in the past: through long service as a clerk, which was limited to a few vacancies each year; through serving a normal apprenticeship; or, by paying higher entrance fees and subscriptions, it was possible to achieve immediate membership.

The rules covering membership have been altered from time to time, but a complete revision was made effective from 25 June 1965. It had long been felt that, with the increasing emphasis on research and on the servicing of institutional and other clients from the office, the contact between the broker and jobber was becoming increasingly tenuous. Many broker members, who had spent no time in the House itself, were largely ignorant of the techniques of dealing. As a result misunderstandings with jobbing firms became more frequent. At the same time a Federal Examination was desirable.

The requirements for membership under the Federation Prospectus include the following provisions:

(*a*) A candidate for membership must be at least twenty-one.

(*b*) Unless the Council permit in the case of a candidate with commercial experience or a suitable professional qualification, he shall have completed not less than three years' training of which not less than three months shall have been spent as an unauthorised clerk.

(*c*) He shall have attained a minimum standard in a written Federal Examination.

(*d*) He shall be separately proposed and seconded by two members who shall each be members of a Federated Exchange and who can satisfy the exchange committee that he is a fit person to become a member. They must not be partners of, or members associated with, the candidate's future firm.

EXAMINATIONS

The first Stock Exchange examination is planned for June 1970, and thereafter examinations will be held in June of each year. The syllabus indicated in a memorandum to all members of Federated Exchanges in November 1966 consisted of six subjects.

Section A: Law
Monetary Economics
Taxation.
Section B: Stock Exchange Practice
Interpretation of Company Reports and Accounts
The Technique of Investment.

All six subjects can be taken in one examination or Section A and Section B can be taken separately. A candidate cannot take Section B until he has passed Section A.

The memorandum indicated that facilities could be arranged in most centres for tuition in the subjects included in the syllabus, with the possible exception of Stock Exchange Practice and the Technique of Investment. Courses would be arranged in these subjects in conjunction with the committees of the exchanges.

COST OF MEMBERSHIP

A new member of The Stock Exchange, London, has three separate costs to bear:

(i) A nomination, costing about £100 in December 1966 (high since 1945, £1,980; low virtually nil).
(ii) The entrance fee of 1,000 guineas.
(iii) The annual subscription of 250 guineas.

The cost of the nomination and the entrance fee is usually borne by the member himself, while the annual subscription may be paid each year by his firm. A total of approximately 3,500 nominations are currently in existence. Dealings in these take place in much the same way as in stocks and shares, although they can only be held by a non-member for a limited time. Additional nominations may be created by the Council, if necessary.

PARTNERSHIP

The ultimate aim of most young men after achieving membership is to be taken into partnership. Owing to the amalgamation of stockbroking firms into larger units, competition for a place in the partnership of the larger firms is becoming increasingly fierce. A first step to partnership may therefore be the inclusion of the name of the member on the writing-paper and other of the firm's documents, as an associate member 'below the line'.

Different firms use this facility for different purposes. Those who have a number of members, operating for their own clientele on a commission basis, may insert their names to add to their prestige. Others may show recognition of the managers of their specialist departments, such as Research or Foreign. It can therefore either be a step towards partnership or a recognition in lieu of it.

It has already been mentioned (Chapter 1) that the names in the partnership of stockbroking firms may not all be profit-sharing partners. Some may be salaried, some paid on a commission-sharing basis, and some may directly share a proportion of the profits. Very often young men being accepted into partnership may start on a purely salary basis, with some form of bonus or commission-sharing payment, graduating to profit-sharing at a later date.

It should be stressed at this point that a partner, whether he derives his remuneration from salary or a share of the profits, is liable for the whole of his personal assets in the event of a failure of his firm. This factor is too often disregarded by young men, accepting partnerships with firms who undertake speculative business.

The cost of becoming a partner will obviously vary from firm to firm. The Stock Exchange regulations state that, in the firm's balance-sheet submitted annually to independent accountants, the surplus of assets over liabilities must amount to not less than £5,000 per partner. Many firms have appreciated the difficulty of attracting the best young men into their partnerships if a large amount of capital must be put up at the time of entry. As a result it is now commonplace for incoming partners to be given a period of some years to contribute their full requirements of capital and tax reserves, while those partners whose shares are being reduced to make room for the new-comers accept repayment in instalments over the period.

One final word of advice. Having started life myself in a small firm, with a total complement including partners of only eight, and having then been particularly lucky in being offered a partnership in a larger firm, I would advise any other prospective stockbroker to enter the business in the reverse order. A young man who has been trained with one of the larger firms has a valuable background to investment. He has experience of research methods, possibly personal connections with institutions, and the overall outlook that only a widespread business can give. If, after he has worked with the larger firm for some years, he then decides that his future there is uncertain, he has something to offer to the smaller firm. There is also the possibility that the larger firm will not want to lose him and will offer him some additional incentive to stay.

PART TWO

STOCKBROKING TOMORROW

10

THE INVESTOR OF
THE FUTURE

THE future of stockbroking is linked primarily to the future destination of the nation's savings. Is a new generation growing up whose philosophy is antagonistic to thrift, so that they live for the minute, mortgaged to the neck by hire-purchase and other debts, relying upon the State to care for their old age? Or are their savings to be chanelled through indirect media of investment —life assurance, the building societies, the savings banks, etc? Or are they becoming more sophisticated, following the American pattern of individual investment in stocks and shares, either directly or through the medium of the unit-trust movement?

The available evidence suggests that there is no simple answer to these alternatives. But personal savings continue to increase in real terms, new issues of unit trusts exceed encashments, and the institutional share of ordinary share investment does not appear to be growing at a higher rate than direct investment by individuals.

It is my own belief that investors in the United Kingdom will gradually follow the American trend of direct share ownership. Every political party accepts as a cornerstone of its electoral attack on the Government of the day the increase in the cost of living and the depreciating value of the currency. Bank deposits, national savings, pensions based on fixed retirement benefits are all losing face as safe havens of investment, owing to the steady erosion caused by inflation. The growth of the unit-trust movement and the formation of investment clubs each year is evidence that the traditional media of saving are on the decline. At the same time the national popular Press has become much more investment-conscious. The *Daily Mirror* had no City column until 1960. The double column of the *Daily Mail* has expanded to a City page. The *Sunday Times*, *Daily Telegraph* and *The Times* have complete Business Supplements. And the circulation of the *Financial Times* has more than doubled over the last ten years.

To this must be added the growth of technicians among stockbrokers, many of whom believe in the 'hard sell' technique. Firms no longer wait for their clients to write and telephone asking for advice, but circulate them with suggestions or actively manage their investment portfolios.

It will be a long time, I trust, before stockbrokers employ the travelling bond salesmen of the United States, knocking at the doors of prospective clients and selling them securities over the doorstep. Nor do I look forward to seeing stockbrokers' kiosks on the railway stations, as in Japan. But I do believe that a far more virile approach will be seen in the profession in years to come and that fewer clients will have cause to complain that they never hear from their stockbrokers from one year's end to the next.

If we are to see the small client become an economic factor in stockbroking, then the costs of sales-and-service, and more particularly the cost of production, must be reduced. Reduction in production costs depends to some extent upon a united move by all stockbrokers. Costs of sales-and-service are much more directly under the control of the individual firm.

NUMBER OF SECURITIES

The moral that can be learned from the growth of the great retail organisations is that costs per unit of sale can be dramatically reduced if the range of articles sold is sufficiently reduced and if the volume of sales is sufficiently expanded. The London Stock Exchange suffers from the total of over 4,000 quotations of ordinary shares, so that the choice of goods laid out before the client is so vast that it is virtually impossible for the stockbroker to advise him adequately over more than a limited range.

The future outlook of stockbrokers towards the smaller private clients may therefore be to limit their specialist advice to perhaps one or two hundred securities. The amount of research and statistical work would thus be considerably reduced and working files, including visits and discussions with management, would be possible on the majority of companies covered. Many of the best managed investment trusts limit their portfolios to a number not greatly in excess of this, and one or two investment trusts whose performance is measured against their competitors might well be included in the securities under review.

The small private client has the advantage that there is usually a market in the quantity of shares he is likely to buy or sell in almost every quoted share. However attractive to the stockbroker, therefore, to reduce his list to the hundred largest companies, on the principle that no one can criticise such blue chips in a portfolio, this course of action would seem to limit the performance of his clients' holdings to a fairly mediocre average. Most firms have among the securities they particularly favour several which have not yet achieved the status of leading concerns and which can be more easily reviewed than the giants since they have a smaller spread of interest both industrially or geographically.

MANAGED UNIT TRUSTS

It can be argued that the simplest method of ensuring an adequate spread of investment, and also of reducing substantially the sales-and-service side of private-client business, would be for stockbrokers either to advise their clients to invest in investment trust company shares or in quoted unit trusts, or to manage their own unit-trust portfolios. Many stockbrokers advise their private clients to put at least a proportion of their funds in one of the first two, and one or two firms manage their own unit trusts. The problem in this respect is that no two clients have exactly the same requirements. Some want income, some capital appreciation, some are old and conservative, some young and dashing. Very few, even with relatively small amounts of capital, are prepared to put it all into a unit or investment trust, however well spread its interests. They like to be able to follow the fortunes of their particular shares in the newspapers. On the whole they dislike not knowing from day to day the components that make up their indirect investment.

A stockbroker's unit trust has, of course, the advantage that its performance gives a yardstick of the stockbroker's expertise. This may be one of the reasons why so few have been formed so far.

ADVERTISING

Volume of trade is the second major factor in making economic the small investment order. Under the present regulations stockbrokers are not only not permitted to advertise for business, but an even more stringent etiquette of unwritten rules prevents the name of a firm of stockbrokers being disclosed on any material which may be circulated outside the firm's direct connection of clients. Only recently has reference to a firm of stockbrokers by name in the Press been permitted.

An investigation into the cost of advertising indicates that something over £50,000 per annum would have to be spent by any firm in order to obtain sufficient coverage and effective impact in the early stages of a campaign. Such a cost would be prohibitive to small and medium-sized firms, but might well be worth while for the very large units produced by the over-twenty partnership mergers following the Companies Act, 1967. While large advertising expenditure would be unlikely to have much effect on the more lucrative institutional investors and would result in a direct cost against the marginal private-client business, it could bring with it a number of side-effects, such as new issues. The type of investor introduced in this way might add to the burden of bad debts or speculative and unsatisfactory clients, and the long-term effect of individual advertising, once the initial impact has abated, is also difficult to assess. Many firms have the impression that, once started, it is virtually impossible to stop in the face of competition from other firms.

It seems more important to me to leave the question of individual advertising to a time when the procedures of transacting business in The Stock Exchange have been so streamlined that small business is economic. The next chapter is devoted to the future developments in the 'production' departments which will lead to that end. In the meantime a gradual relaxation of the very stringent Rule 78 seems likely.

BRANCH OFFICES

The second method of increasing the volume of trade is to permit firms to open branch offices. Regulation III of the Pros-

pectus of the Federation of Stock Exchanges permits the opening of a branch office under certain conditions, the limiting
factor being that it shall not be within twenty-five miles of any
of the Associated Exchanges, including the four incorporated in
the Scottish Stock Exchange, nor within this distance of any
city or town where a member of one of the Federated Exchanges continues to be in practice, without the specific permission of the committee of the relevant exchange. As the
Provincial Brokers Stock Exchange contains 220 members
operating in 110 towns throughout Great Britain and Ireland,
the localities open for successful branch offices seem restricted
to say the least.

The way is open, however, for amalgamation of member
firms of the Provincial Brokers Stock Exchange with member
firms of any of the Federated Stock Exchanges. This is the
first step towards a widespread branch-office network in the
future. Central accounting, research and other production
facilities could reduce costs very considerably, so that a high
volume of small business might produce a profitable return.
The take-over of provincial firms by London stockbrokers will
not be confined to a one-way traffic, and a number of the
larger provincial firms would willingly absorb a smaller London
firm to provide a London sales office and a medium for dealing
direct on the London market. The advantages of having the
bulk of overheads in a lower cost area than the City might even
put these firms at an advantage.

The disadvantage, from the point of view of the provincial
stockbroker, of a direct merger with a London firm is that this
must reduce his spread of information and service from a
number of London correspondents. Since the majority of the
business carried out through the Associated Exchanges finds its
way to the London market, a provincial broker is able to offer
business to more than one London firm. In exchange he has the
call on all their research establishments and may obtain a participation in underwriting or other benefits. It seems likely,
however, with the concentration of business moving into fewer
hands, that many provincial firms will prefer to merge with
London concerns.

PORTFOLIO MANAGEMENT

One of the great criticisms levied against stockbroking firms, and mentioned earlier, is that they fail to look after their clients, by leaving their portfolios static for long periods of time. Reviews and valuations may be made at regular intervals, but all too often the policy is to leave the client in a blue-chip security and advise no action.

The merchant banks have for many years actively managed their customers' portfolios, often taking action without reference and charging a fee for their services. In recent years an increasing number of investment consultants have begun to practise in the U.K., following the American pattern, and these individuals have accepted portfolios which were considerably smaller than those normally managed by merchant banks.

The growth of the investment consultant and merchant banks' investment business is largely due to the reluctance of stockbrokers to act for their clients without prior consultation. They fear the stigma of 'turning over' their clients' investments for the sake of earning commission. To take no action can incur no blame. As a result, when particularly attractive lines of stock pass through their hands, the majority of these are passed on to institutional clients, rather than broken up into smaller amounts and divided among the private-client portfolios.

The introduction of technicians into stockbroking firms means that these larger concerns are equally, or better, equipped to manage clients' portfolios than any of the investment consultants and than most of the merchant banks. It seems to me, therefore, that a more active approach will be given to private clients, with action taken to take advantage of opportunities and not just to make sporadic reviews and recommendations.

CHARGES FOR SERVICES

The alternative to reducing costs on actual transactions is to introduce a scale of charges for services rendered. At the present time a client who demands a quarterly valuation and review of all his securities with regular lists of suggestions and opinions, and never carries out a transaction, receives a highly expensive service completely free of charge. The unremunerative private-client accounts are, in fact, paid for largely by the very remunerative institutional business. While the institutions appreciate that the private client still makes the market, there is obviously a limit to the amount which they should pay to support and encourage small business.

In my own opinion the introduction of charges for valuations, reviews, recommendations, etc., would be a retrograde step, unless this were accompanied by a reduction in rates of commission. I am hopeful that the improvement in methods of production described in the next chapter will render any increased charges unnecessary in the foreseeable future.

II

THE NEW HOUSE

THE rebuilding of the London Stock Exchange has been discussed for many years, but only in November 1964 did the Council decide to proceed with the new building, and only in November 1965 did the members endorse this decision in general meeting. I have selected this single feature as the heading for this chapter, for it seems to me to be symbolic of the change in the outlook of the industry. A wind of change is blowing through the world of stockbroking. Stockbrokers are now facing up to investigating their own industry with something of the intensity with which they investigate others.

Four of the major questions which face the London Stock Exchange today are:

(i) Is the jobbing system out of date?

(ii) What will be the effect on stockbroking of the provisions of the Companies Act, 1967, permitting an unlimited number of partners?

(iii) How can the provincial stock exchanges be united more closely with London?

(iv) How can the systems operated in London be made more economic and more efficient to cope with the probable increase of business in the future?

THE JOBBING SYSTEM

The jobbing system, as mentioned briefly in Chapter 1, is constantly under fire: from merchant banks and other institutions, as increasing the cost of dealing without acting as more than a negotiator of large lines of stock, except in a small number of securities where the turnover is particularly high; from investment analysts, for preventing the issue of statistics (particularly daily turnover in individual securities) which are obtainable in other centres; from stockbrokers, for occasionally restricting rather than encouraging the free transactions between clients (trading with provincial centres, for example, and between the same clients of the stockbroker's firm); and from the Press, for all and any of the above reasons. It is seldom that any authoritative and disinterested party says anything favourable about the jobbing system.

But when the alternatives to the jobbing system are investigated in detail, their attractions are not so obvious. The call-over system operates effectively only where the number of members and the list of quotations is limited. The only alternative is therefore the trading-post system, with its specialists in particular securities. But the specialist acts not only as a marriage bureau for orders in opposite directions, he is also permitted to take a position in the securities in which he deals, when there are no orders to match in the opposite direction *and when it suits him.* In order to ensure that he is not, therefore, always trading for his own account at the most remunerative times and is actively assisting in maintaining a free and orderly market, his activities must be hedged round with all sorts of rules and regulations. In many cases the jobbing system operates more efficiently and to the greater advantage of the investor.

In my own opinion there are two faults in the jobbing system as it is now operated. The first is the problem of control over the number of jobbers making books in any individual security. Too many jobbers have been acting in certain leading securities, with cut-throat competition and losses to all in some stocks, while in others there have been too few. Too strict control by the Council may close the doors to new and efficient firms and only protect the inefficient. The aim should be to have three genuine competitors in every marketable security. At the end of 1966, the Council in fact introduced new regulations regarding the opening of books by jobbers in new securities.

As this book goes to press, a Committee is at work examining the future structure of jobbing and reviewing a report prepared on the subject by an outside firm of consultants.

The second fault lies, not so much in the lack of risk capital among the jobbers, as in the difficulty of increasing that capital through the profession of jobbing. The Finance Act, 1965, has made it increasingly difficult to make and retain capital, without reducing the liability to loss.

Jobbers thrive on activity. When there is a free two-way market in shares they can take positions in the relative certainty that, over a period, they can get their books straight again and that, taking the swings and the roundabouts, there will be an overall profit. The capital gains taxes have made an immediate impact on the freedom of markets and thus on activity.

The taxation position of jobbers is also not conducive to taking risks. Prior to the Second World War, jobbing firms were given preferential treatment in taxation, tax being paid on the basis of a three-year average of profits. The very sharp fluctuations between years were thus evened out. During the last twenty years, however, the basis of taxation has been the same as for any other professional occupation and the incidence of income and surtaxes has been levied at much higher rates. As a result high taxation is levied in the good years, making it virtually impossible to maintain the freedom of markets in bad times.

There is no evidence to show that the jobbing system is short of overall finance. The banks are willing to advance a substantial proportion of the funds required to take up stock which the jobbers acquire on their books, on the security of the underlying stock. But there is a shortage of *risk* capital, the equity of the jobbing firms, and this problem is likely to become more acute as younger and less well-endowed members take the places of the older generation.

My own view is that, sooner or later, the London market must be divided into two sections, the first and second floor. The first floor should contain a limited list of major securities, in which there is a ready market. The second floor should contain all other securities. From time to time a security may be upgraded from the second to the first floor, or vice versa.

It seems likely that the contraction in the number of firms of jobbers will continue in the future, possibly at a higher pace than in the past, and the market may be reduced to only four or five firms in the gilt-edged market, a dozen or so in industrials, and three or four in each of the other markets. If, under these conditions, the jobbing system operates reasonably well for the first floor of marketable securities, the second floor may well be operated on a specialist system. There is no reason why the same firm should not have different individuals acting as specialists in one market and jobbers in others.

The consolidation of the jobbing system into more and larger units may be hastened by the difficulty in finding young men with sufficient capital to enter the business. The financial rewards are precarious, and so much risk capital is required for the running of the firm that it cannot be invested in some security which will improve in monetary value to combat inflation.

It seems very unlikely, however, that the alteration in the existing system will be anything but prolonged. The proposals for the federation of the stock exchanges throughout the country (discussed below) seem largely designed to strengthen the system in its present form. The change will inevitably be slow, but the evidence of change is growing each day.

As far as the second problem is concerned, the provision of risk capital from outside sources is now permitted, although few financial organisations have shown much enthusiasm for taking part in consortium companies to assist in financing jobbers. The external member provisions, allowing families, friends and trusts of past and present members to take a share in the firm with limited liability, may, however, prove very useful. More important, perhaps, the abolition of the twenty-partner limitation permits the formation of much larger concerns with a spread of activity in both the industrial and gilt-edged markets. When activity in one sector is restricted because of market conditions, the other may provide more profitable use of the firm's resources.

INCREASE IN PARTNERSHIP NUMBERS

In Chapter 1 the number of stockbroking firms in The Stock Exchange, London, at 24 March 1967 was given as 225. It does not require much imagination to see this figure falling to one-half, or less, within the next five years. Today is the day of the large-scale enterprise, in the City no less than in industry and commerce. Only the large firm can afford the sophisticated electronic equipment to reduce production costs per unit of sale; or the highly-qualified specialists to provide research information for a much wider spread of clientele; or, in time, the substantial advertising expenditure mentioned in the previous chapter; or possibly the national coverage of a branch-office system which many believe will be the ultimate goal of a number of the larger firms.

This leads to the thorny question of more direct participation in firms of stockbrokers by financial institutions, such as merchant banks. In my own view (and this is entirely a personal opinion) the time is not too far distant when merchant banks should be offered a direct equity stake in stockbroking firms. If the U.K. eventually joins the Common Market the traditional lead that London has developed in providing a capital market must be developed with all the resources at our disposal. The financial strength of the issuing houses, in partnership with the technical expertise of the firms of stockbrokers, would provide a formidable combination.

FEDERATION

On 1 June 1965 the London Stock Exchange, the Associated Stock Exchanges and the Provincial Brokers Stock Exchange all voted to accept the Articles of Constitution and the Prescribed Rules set out in the draft Prospectus of Federation. The main provisions include the following:

(a) The establishment and administration of compensation funds, under which all members are ultimately liable for contribution towards the default of a member or member firm, irrespective of the exchange to which he belongs.

(b) The requirements for the grant of quotations, which will be based on those of the London Stock Exchange, overseen by a New Issues Panel appointed by the Federal Committee.

(c) The requirements for membership of a Federated Exchange, which include (unless other commercial or professional qualifications exempt the candidate) not less than three years' training with a member firm and the passing of a written examination.

(d) The provision of an annual report from an independent qualified accountant on the firm's balance-sheet, which shall be submitted to the exchange committee, and which shall show a minimum excess of assets over liabilities of £5,000 per partner, with a minimum of £15,000 per member firm.

(e) Revised dealing arrangements between London and the provincial exchanges.

It is the last mentioned of these that provides the greatest interest for the future. The possible amalgamation between firms of brokers in London and the provinces, to which reference was made in the previous chapter, may well lead to more centralisation of dealings in the national leaders in the London market, and more specialisation in the local companies in the provinces. Country brokers are naturally loath to lose the facility of a local floor, with all transactions passed through one national centre, but the advent of a two-floor system, one jobbing and one specialist, might well assist them in the long run.

PRODUCTION FACILITIES

The plans for the rebuilding of The Stock Exchange received the final sanction of the Board of Trade in September 1965.

Improvement in production facilities can be considered under two heads: facilities for trading and facilities for centralised accounting.

(a) DEALING FACILITIES

The improvement in dealing facilities depends largely upon the rebuilding. While plans were originally drawn up by the Surveyor to the Council in 1948, and outline planning permission granted a year later, all schemes foundered on the difficulty of there being insufficient space to allow for rebuilding on the existing site while the market was still in operation, and it was considered impracticable to move to another site during the rebuilding. In 1961, however, additional freeholds of adjoining sites were purchased to overcome this problem. Twelve months after final Board of Trade sanction had been given, demolition of the existing building commenced, in September 1966, and the whole rebuilding operation should be completed by August 1972.

The chief hazard faced by this ambitious scheme (the contract cost is approximately £8¾ million) is that the jobbing system will have decreased so substantially over the next few years that the functions of the building when it is completed will not be those for which it was designed. It seems, however, that the design has sufficient flexibility to meet this problem, if it arises.

The improvements in dealing facilities which the new House will offer include a vastly improved communications network, so that paging will be quicker and more efficient, telephone calls will be routed through an automatic exchange and delays between giving orders and receiving confirmation should be considerably reduced. The number of dealing 'boxes' will also be very considerably increased and these will be sited much more conveniently for access to the trading floor, those on the half-floor levels above and below being linked to the trading floor by escalators. All these improvements should result in better productive capacity of the dealing staff, with a consequent economy of manpower.

The problem of financing the new building and other improved facilities has been occupying the attention of the Council and other members for many years. As far back as 1958 I was the joint author with Michael Bennett of an article for the summer edition of the *Stock Exchange Journal*. At the time the plans for rebuilding The Stock Exchange had just been postponed, possibly for a period of twenty years, and we wrote:

> The House itself is probably one of the greatest wastes of valuable space in the City of London, but plans for rebuilding are well under way — in twenty years' time. . . . The traditional techniques continue unabated; Members still queue for telephones in busy times; the clearing house still issues impassioned pleas to firms either to deliver names earlier or collect them later . . . there has been no specialist work-study, to the public knowledge at least, to improve this situation. . . . Advertising — well the gallery undoubtedly has been a step in the right direction, although it seems a pity that the only time the Stock Exchange gets a full-scale press is when a firm has been hammered or a Bank rate leak alleged.
>
> We said that Finance was the key to most of our problems, and there's been a rare old hubbub about the increased subscriptions announced recently, not to mention the new issue charges. When the small firms find it difficult to make ends meet in bad times and the big ones have permanent institutional investment to tide them over, even a small increase in subscriptions hits the small firms very hard. Why should the big firms get a relatively greater advantage when the improved facilities will be available to all? Be that as it may, suppose in

fact the big firms were made to pay the greater part of the cost. How would the members react to a levy on net profits before tax . . . say, at a guess, of as little as ½ per cent or 1 per cent on the profits over £5,000 of all firms? The figures are a cockshy, but the proceeds should be pretty considerable. If you wanted, you could make it a heavier tax for a limited number of years . . . nasty medicine but soon over.

Then we could think about rebuilding the House in earnest. We might consider an electronic department that centralised all broker-jobber accounting. If jobbers could be persuaded to report bargains into this machine as they were carried out it would clear all stocks automatically and, not only that, it would give a running record of dealing prices in every broker's office, reducing the staff required in boxes and order rooms and the House itself. And if sufficient finance were available we could begin to advertise the House as a serious place of business to attract new classes of investors. We might even manage to reduce the costs to such an extent that small orders became profitable and the ideal of the Cloth Cap Investor at last became a reality.

Much water has flowed under the bridge since these words were written, but a number of the suggestions made have come much closer to fruition. The new Stock Exchange, the electronic accounting department, and the consultant study of the jobbing system have already been mentioned. A central price-distribution scheme is also currently under consideration. In New York each bargain is immediately reported to the Tape and transmitted, usually within a few minutes, except in periods of exceptional activity, to the trading rooms of all subscribers. In London almost every firm now employs unauthorised clerks to move continuously round the market, noting price changes and reporting these to its sales-and-service departments. The wastage of both the jobbers' and the brokers' time caused by this incessant stream of enquiry is very considerable. Under the jobbing system, however, the automatic transmission of prices at which deals are carried out would immediately inform competitive firms of jobbers of what their rivals were doing and would make a jobbing book increasingly unremunerative. The system under consideration employs a number of clerks obtaining a continuous service of middle market prices from the jobbers and relaying these to the offices of subscribers, both member firms and possibly outside financial institutions, by closed-circuit television or similar means.

(b) STOCK EXCHANGE CENTRAL SERVICES

Concurrent with the rebuilding programme, The Stock Exchange administration has been moving forward at a remarkable pace. The 'electronic department that centralised all broker-jobber accounting' has indeed taken shape, with the installation in 1966 of an ICT 1903 computer. The first stage towards the goal which we light-heartedly forecast in 1958 has already taken place with one cheque settlement. The final aim is much more comprehensive. To those readers who waded bravely through the accounting procedures of Chapter 3, the use of the computer should make it possible to dispose with making-up prices altogether, and thereafter bring about the centralisation of all jobbers' accounts. Checking of bargains could also be carried out centrally by the computer working overnight, which would eliminate about 80% of the bargains, leaving only the 20% for firm-to-firm adjustment.

Taking the use of the computer a stage further, the tickets themselves could be issued by the centre and in such a form that the computer could read them again when they were returned to the Central Stock Payment Office, so that firms would no longer be required to complete the stock delivery sets.

The computer could check the record of all tickets issued against that of the tickets returned on Account Day and periodically thereafter. When books close for the payment of a dividend it could take out all items open in that particular stock and claim and credit dividends accordingly.

The ultimate service would, of course, be comprehensive centralised accounting, including that of broker/client, but for a number of reasons this seems unlikely, at least in the foreseeable future.

(c) OFFICE PROCEDURES

The procedures explained in Chapter 3 are those carried out, with individual variations, by the majority of stockbroking offices. Several firms have now moved from the mechanical accounting procedures on which the illustrations were based to punch-card systems, or directly on to computers. Several have already installed computers of their own.

The great advantage of the computer is the high speed of its calculations. This is not, in fact, normally a requirement in a stockbroking office and there is a danger that, unless the equipment is used for other important functions (such as valuations, research or fixed-interest yields), insufficient use will be made of expensive plant. On the other hand the peripheral equipment, particularly the magnetic stores, can save an enormous amount of time and effort, since each purchase and sale can automatically update a client's portfolio, and rights and capitalisation issues can be entered with the minimum of effort. The rapid calculation of yields, either for portfolio valuation or for regular lists of fixed-interest securities, can also be programmed.

In my own opinion the use of the computer may, oddly enough, divert the trend away from the amalgamations of the medium-sized firms into the giants, while extending the trend towards co-operative general offices. A number of firms now support the co-operative use of a central computer with input and print-out equipment in their own offices. A group of sixteen smaller firms have borne the expenses of a joint investigation into a computer centre for their communal use. The principal disadvantage of full amalgamation of these smaller firms lies in the inevitable differences of opinion on matters of traditional policy and procedures between members of different teams immediately following a merger. If the economies of a large-scale organisation can be obtained without loss of individuality, a co-operative office organisation must appeal to a number of medium-sized firms.

As far as can be judged at the present time, no firm anticipates immediate or substantial savings in overheads by the individual or communal use of a computer. The advantage should come in two directions. The capacity of a computer should enable a considerable expansion of business to be undertaken without proportional increase in staff. This expansion may take place either by further mergers or additions to the co-operative members, or from the increase in investment business in the future. Some protection will also be given against the inevitable rise in salaries of Stock Exchange staff, and the difficulty in finding suitable trained personnel.

There is no doubt in my own mind that a firm which is deliberately geared to the acceptance and satisfaction of small business will be able to make this type of client profitable in the future without any increase in commission rates or other charges to the public.

12

THE SPECIALIST
DEPARTMENTS

THIS chapter is intended to deal, very briefly, with some of the advances which may be made in the four specialist departments — fixed-interest, research, new issues and overseas securities.

FIXED-INTEREST SECURITIES

In the earlier discussion of the Gilt-Edged Department it was shown (Table 8, p. 142) that the institutions (insurance companies, pension funds, building societies, investment trusts, special investment departments of trustee savings banks and unit trusts) at 31 March 1964 owned only just over 5% of the short-dated gilt-edged stocks and about 24% of the outstanding issues with redemption dates over five years. The short-dated total would no doubt have been considerably larger had the holdings of banks, particularly the clearing banks, the discount houses and Lloyd's underwriters, been included, but these are specialist organisations whose day-to-day investments are to a great extent concerned with securities which are largely the equivalent of cash. The 47% of issues with redemption dates over five years which are in the hands of other members of the public indicates the sizeable total made up by relatively small holdings distributed widely among individuals and trusts.

The activity of the institutions, however, is proportionately greater than their total investment. During the fourth quarter of 1964, transactions on their behalf amounted to 26% of the total turnover in over-five-year stocks. This comprised principally switching between similar stocks, although there was some noticeable lengthening of dates at this time to take advantage of higher yields at the longer end of the market.

At the present time, with the probability of continuing inflation over the longer term, few stockbrokers or other investment advisers seem disposed to recommend the sale of ordinary shares and the reinvestment of the proceeds in gilt-edged securities, except on short-term considerations with a view to returning to the equity market at lower levels. Gilt-edged holdings are often maintained in private portfolios as a suitable source for raising money required for rights issues or for other cash payments. It seems probable, therefore, that the institutional share of the gilt-edged market will continue to grow while private holdings will gradually be reduced.

DEBENTURE AND PREFERENCE SHARES

At 31 March 1964 the institutions held just over two-thirds of the outstanding debenture and loan-stock issues by market value and almost 40% of preference shares (see Table 13 below). The turnover in this section of the market is relatively small, since stocks tend to be locked away in firm hands until redemption. Preference shares have traditionally been the haven for investors wanting relatively high income, but corporation tax, introduced in the 1965 Finance Act, makes this type of security expensive to service and, while they may be attractive to investment trusts and other investors requiring franked income, they lack the security of loan capital and fail to provide the hedge against the inflation offered by ordinary shares. It seems likely therefore that the debenture market will remain largely institutional and that preference issues may become less frequent in the future.

SERVICE ON FIXED-INTEREST SECURITIES

In recent years the computer has revolutionised the labour attached to providing a comprehensive service on fixed-interest securities. Calculations of ratios and differences between a wide range of gilt-edged securities, to facilitate switching decisions, can now be produced on a relatively simple programme. It would not be surprising if a detailed comparison of the charts over a relatively long period did not produce some significant figure (such as the acceleration immediately prior to a change in trend) which would give further indicators to assist in switching decisions.

TABLE 13

INSTITUTIONAL SHARE OF MARKET-QUOTED FIXED-INTEREST SECURITIES OF U.K. COMPANIES

| | Holdings, 31 March 1964 (market value) | | | | | | Turnover, 4th quarter 1964 | |
| | Debenture and loan stocks | | Preference shares | | Total fixed-interest | | Total fixed-interest | |
	£ millions	%	£ millions	%	£ millions	%	£ millions	%
Insurance companies	(835)	(42)	(305)	(24)	(1,140)	(35)	(70)	(43)
Pension funds	(485)	(24)	(95)	(8)	(580)	(18)	(20)	(12)
Investment trusts	19	1	79	6	98	3	4	2
Unit trusts	(2)	(—)	(13)	(1)	(15)	(—)	(2)	(1)
Total financial institutions	(1,341)	(67)	(492)	(39)	(1,833)	(56)	(96)	(59)
Other	(655)	(33)	(767)	(61)	(1,422)	(44)	(68)	(41)
Total market	1,996	100	1,259	100	3,255	100	164[1]	100

[1] Of which transactions on the London Stock Exchange £92 million, new issues plus redemptions £72 million. The total for The Stock Exchange includes, indistinguishably, transactions in overseas securities, but these are believed to be small. Such transactions are excluded from the turnover of the institutions.

Estimated figures are shown in parentheses.

Source: Bank of England.

The effect of corporation tax in enhancing the attractions to a company of issues of loan capital may indicate that this form of financing will be more popular in the future. (The total market value of quoted debenture and loan stocks in issue at 31 March 1964 was only £1,996 million against preference issues of £1,259 million and ordinary share issues of £27,508 million.) Each new issue must be examined in considerable detail, particularly as regards the security both of capital and of income, and the return to funds suffering from a variety of rates of tax. In the United States, Standard and Poor, one of the statistical service companies, provides a rating for each issue of loan capital. The ability of the computer to carry out a large number of comparative calculations in a short space of time should make it possible for one of the statistical service companies in the City, or an enterprising firm of stockbrokers specialising in this field, to produce a table of ratings for all debenture issues. New issues of loan capital and lines of existing stock could be compared against the stock rating to establish whether they appeared attractive investments.

RESEARCH DEPARTMENT

The past fifteen years, as has been mentioned earlier, have been the age of the analyst in stockbroking. The actuary, in particular, has moved out of the purely life side of insurance companies into investment. At first only in gilt-edged and then on a broader field covering all securities, the qualifications of the actuary have been appreciated. On the other side of the fence, stockbrokers have realised the importance of serving their institutional clients with the type of material which they will appreciate and of having individuals who talk the same technical language. As a result actuaries and accountants have found ready employment in the research departments of stockbroking offices.

The type of analysis on which the greatest concentration has been placed has therefore been largely a study of the published figures of industries and companies. Projections of future profits and share prices have been made, many of which, while they may well prove to be highly satisfactory in the long term, have been discouragingly inaccurate so far.

In my own view the emphasis placed on this type of statistical analysis is now on the decline, while, following the American pattern, we are beginning to see the emergence of the 'industry specialist'. Firms of stockbrokers will tend to become less and less general practitioners to their institutional clients and more and more specialists in one or two industrial sectors in which they will gain a particular reputation. This should open to the qualified engineer, chemist or quantity surveyor a new role in the City. The evidence of the published figures will be backed (or perhaps contradicted on occasion) by the evidence of someone who has experience of an industry and knows where to obtain the information about it.

The use of the computer in searching through the mass of published statistics and selecting critical figures is only in its infancy. The majority of stockbroking firms are looking to the computer primarily to save time and effort on the valuation of securities, followed by a small number who are gradually programming the full accounting procedures of their general offices. Only one or two use a computer as an indicator of industrial or economic trends, although American stockbrokers, who have been using computer methods for a longer period and who have an even greater weight of published evidence to sift, have made considerable headway in this respect.

It seems likely that the larger firms, with their own computers or sharing them on a co-operative basis, will devote more of their research effort towards improving computer techniques. Trained programmers will become more and more in demand for work in stockbroking research departments, although programming itself will become simplified as new advances are made in computer design.

NEW ISSUES

Two interesting developments have taken place in the new-issues business. The first is the sponsorship of issues by firms of stockbrokers without recourse to an issuing house. In the past this has been undertaken by one or two firms only, but recently the names of others, who have been primarily associated with handling the issues of one or two issuing houses with whom they have very close connections, have appeared as sole sponsors.

In the past it had been thought that, if they put their name to an issue on their own, it might put their connection with the issuing houses in jeopardy.

The second development occurred in the autumn of 1965, when the Westminister Bank appeared as sponsor for the issue of a debenture, the first time that one of the clearing banks had accepted this role. Although the Issuing Houses Association made no official comment on the matter, this step aroused considerable Press comment. Criticism was based largely on two counts: that, if the other clearing banks followed the Westminster's lead, far from increasing the competition and thus keeping down the charges for new issues, the new-issue business would become centred in very few hands; and secondly, that a conflict of interest must arise between the conventional banking side, which was lending money to a customer in the normal course of business and which might be under pressure from the Bank of England for national reasons, and the issuing side, whose task must be to fund the debt. The comparison with the West German situation was cited, where the raising of capital is mainly in the hands of the big banks, and it was pointed out that, if the clearing bank turned down a customer since it might not wish its name associated with the issue, this virtually precluded the company concerned from raising the money it required, since other issuing houses would be unlikely to touch it.

In my own view the entry of the clearing banks into the new-issue market will be unlikely to affect the established issuing houses, whose expertise in this connection is well-founded. The question of the clearing banks undertaking the role of sponsor had been widely discussed for some considerable time, and in October 1964, almost a year before the Westminister Bank's first issue, I concluded a talk to a banking group with the following words:

> . . . in my view the clearing bank has four separate roles to play as far as stock exchange investment is concerned. . . .
>
> (d) *As an Issuing House.* The clearing banks have New Issue departments which carry out much of the detailed work of sorting application forms, examining multiple applications, preparing allotments and despatching renounceable certificates, and so on, for new issues of stock and shares. In many cases the

banks actually introduce the company concerned either to a firm of brokers or to an issuing house, who will ultimately sponsor the issue. It may not be looking too far into the future to see the day when the bank itself acts as an issuing house and sponsors the issue of its clients' shares.

THE FOREIGN DEPARTMENT

The future development of trading in foreign securities in London covers an immense field, but can be divided broadly into two areas: the expansion of security dealing in the industrialised countries, which already possess established capital markets; and the provision of new capital markets in the developing countries.

(a) THE EXPANSION OF DEALING IN EXISTING CAPITAL MARKETS

Traditionally British investors have always been among the leaders in spreading their portfolios geographically as well as industrially, particularly as far as equity investments are concerned. The tradition of the merchant adventurers was carried on by the investment-trust movement, whose portfolios have for many years contained a relatively high proportion of foreign securities, with the greatest emphasis on U.S. common stocks. At market value on 31 December 1964, 336 investment trusts held foreign securities of no less than £1,035 million by market value, while unit trusts contributed a further £36 million. During the calendar year 1964 these two groups of institutions had added no less than £56 million and £7 million respectively to their overseas holdings.

The greatest emphasis in both institutional and private individuals' foreign holdings has been placed on U.S. common stocks. The American economy is one of the strongest in the world, with a vast supply of indigenous raw materials. The concentration of industry on increased productivity has kept the cost of living in check for a number of years. The reasons are fairly obvious: the markets in such securities are normally fairly free and considerable quantities of shares can be bought or sold; reports are published in English, or at least in a fairly intelligible language; but above all the accounting procedures and the quality of the information available is of the highest standard.

In the long-term future I can see a gradual reversal of this pattern, with a growing emphasis on European industrial securities. The absorption of the U.K. and the other E.F.T.A. countries into the Common Market as a matter of economic necessity should increase the competition between the small (by American size) national units in the various fields of industry and cause a series of widespread international mergers and amalgamations. The imagination of the investing public will therefore be impelled towards a more international outlook.

Side by side with the political advance towards European integration, two bodies are working towards the standardisation of accounting procedures and the dissemination of company information — the Fédération Internationale des Bourses de Valeurs and The European Federation of Financial Analysts' Societies.

In the report published by the Fédération Internationale des Bourses de Valeurs in December 1964 ('Information for the Public about the Operations and Assets of Companies whose Securities are Admitted to Quotation'), the four objects agreed at the Federation's General Assembly in 1963 were quoted:

> to improve the accuracy and standardise the presentation of the trading documents published by companies (balance-sheet, management accounts, trading results); to encourage the preparation of consolidated accounts by companies with holdings in the capital of subsidiaries; to instigate the publication of information apart from the accounting details of an economic and financial nature, giving in particular useful details as to the nature and composition of the assets and the progress of commercial activities; to accelerate the time of distribution of such information and encourage undertakings to publish interim results between the normal dates for the closing of annual accounts.

The Council of the London Stock Exchange was already acting on the lines of these recommendations, and had introduced a new Supplemental Undertaking in 1964 to be signed by all companies requesting the quotation of stock or shares. This was extended to a new General Undertaking in 1966, details of which are given in Appendix 6. Existing companies requiring the quotation of any additional securities, as well as new companies coming to the market for the first time, give the following additional undertakings:

(i) To circulate with the annual report a description of the operations carried on by the group, showing the contributions made by the different operations and a geographical analysis of trading operations.

(ii) To include a list of subsidiaries, giving both the name and country of operation and the company's interest in the subsidiary.

(iii) To give the same particulars as in (ii) for associated companies where the parent company in the group holds more than 25% of the equity.

(iv) To provide half-yearly interim reports.

A number of problems arise in the analysis of accounts currently published by European concerns. Of these the two most serious are possibly the lack of consolidation of accounts and the value which can be attached to the profit figures.

Consolidation

Consolidation of accounts, that is the incorporation of profits and assets of subsidiaries as though they were branches of the parent company and not separate entities, has never appealed in certain countries because company law in these areas is based primarily on the protection of the creditors rather than the shareholders. If the position is better than that revealed in the accounts, therefore, the creditor's position is not prejudiced. The tendency to amass hidden reserves and not to consolidate accounts is also accentuated by the attitude of the fiscal authorities. In some countries where traditionally accounts have been prepared largely with the fiscal authorities in mind, the consolidation of accounts, or the publication of profits before transfers to reserves, may actually incur additional liability to taxation. Gradually, however, the movement towards some standard practice in accounting procedures is gathering weight and it seems likely that more stock exchanges will make the consolidation of accounts a requirement for listing in the future.

Hand in hand with the move towards standardised accounting, steps are being taken towards the simplification of the transfer of securities. In February 1966, when Australia adopted decimal currency, the American system of share transfer was also introduced. The Fédération Internationale des Bourses de Valeurs has been concerned for some time about the possibility of an international Siccovam, the central register of securities operated in France. A trial run for such an organisation may be possible through an agreement between Siccovam in France and the Kassenverein in West Germany, under which the physical delivery of securities between the two organisations would be considerably reduced. The pace of international cooperation on all matters regarding international portfolio investment is quickening.

It is not looking too far ahead, therefore, to see the time when the Foreign Department of a stockbroker's office will account for more than just the fringe of sophisticated investment, and the industry specialist in the Research Department may spend almost as much of his time on the continent of Europe as he does in the United Kingdom.

(b) THE NEW CAPITAL MARKETS

The development and industrialisation of a country carries with it, as a necessary aftermath, the requirement for a capital market through which the savings of the public can be channelled into the maintenance and expansion of the economy.

In many countries the concept of joint-stock companies is virtually unknown. Wealth rests in the hands of ruling houses or the great families, and even partnerships are considered with suspicion. (In the words of a Persian banker: 'If God approved of partnerships, why has God not taken a partner?') But as more and more of the individuals who take over executive positions receive a Western education, and the standard of living at the lower levels improves, the power of the great houses diminishes.

To quote only two examples, the future economic plans of Turkey and Iran include the formation of capital markets. In the 'First Five-Year Development Plan, 1963–1967' for Turkey, one of the measures designed to encourage savings is given as:

Measures will be taken to help the formation of a capital market, the primary purpose of which is to facilitate the channelling of savings to the most productive areas. In this way, the lower income groups, who do not save for lack of opportunity to enhance their savings, will be encouraged to do so. Institutions operating on the capital market will be encouraged to give consideration to such measures as the issue of stocks with assured dividends or guarantee of profit, which will tend to channel savings to the capital market.

This programme makes a fascinating comparison with the doctrine of a Socialist Government in the United Kingdom, applying long- and short-term capital-gains taxes, designed to penalise the thrifty.

A second country taking the first steps towards the foundation of a capital market is Iran, where the policy of the Government is to offer land to the peasant farmer, and who must therefore find some method of compensating the existing landowners. Compensation might be offered either in Government stock or in shares in some of the nationalised industries.

The chief problem faced by developing countries in the formation of a capital market is one of confidence. Governments, even of the most highly developed countries, by their very nature fail to inspire confidence in investors. No one much cares for the management. With the developing countries the suspicion is often considerably greater.

In my own view there is no easy short-cut to the creation of a capital market where the free exchange of securities can be established. The steps must almost invariably be the same: the establishment of a well-managed Government debt, so that the public is confident of the ability of the State both to service its loans and to redeem them; the creation of a strong and independent organisation of auditors on whose accuracy and impartiality the public can rely; and a clear legislative system governing the conduct of companies and the prevention of fraud.

I find it fascinating that the foundation of the London Stock Exchange in the seventeenth century has an almost exact parallel in the present day.

To quote from a book written in 1954 at the request of the Council of the London Stock Exchange:

It was in the reign of William III that stock-dealing first became important — through the same circumstances that gave birth to the Bank of England. The Government was pressed for money. The Stuarts had been needy, too. But they had borrowed haphazardly and defaulted brazenly. William was better advised. He discovered that it was actually easier to borrow money steadily for long periods than casually for short — provided only that the interest payments were promptly met and the securities easily transferable from one person to another. That discovery started the National Debt. But State credit was so shaky that the first loans could not be raised direct from the public. Instead they were raised indirectly, through a corporation specially chartered for the purpose. That was in 1694, and the Corporation was the Bank of England.'[1]

This brings us back to where we came in. With the increased industrialisation of the underdeveloped countries, the growing level of individual wealth among the lower-paid sectors of all developed countries and the continuing demands for capital in expanding and re-equipping industrial organisations, there can be no lack of opportunity for the stockbroker in the years ahead.

[1] W. T. C. King, *The Stock Exchange* (Allen & Unwin, 1954).

APPENDICES

INSTITUTIONAL ASSETS
AND SHARE OF THE MARKET

ASSETS HELD, END-1963
(£ millions)

Values	Insurance companies Life funds book[3]	Non-life funds book[3]	Pension funds[1] book or market[4]	Building societies book	Investment trusts market	Hire-purchase finance companies book[3]	Trustee savings banks (special investment departments) market	Unit trusts market	Special finance agencies[3] book	Total	%
Cash and short-term assets (partly net)[5]	55	65	70	186	7	9	18	6	8	424	2
Gilt-edged stocks:											
0–5 years	38[6]	22[6]	} 1,055	130[7]	7	—	47[7]	1	} 4	3,655	16
Over 5 years	1,844[6]	180[6]		164[7]	31	—	131[7]	1			
U.K. local authority securities:											
Quoted	} 347[6]	} 41[6]	170	7	2	—	100	—	—	} 1,466	7
Unquoted			109	241	—	—	449	—	—		

										Total	
Overseas, Government, provincial and municipal securities	76	38	83	6	3	—	10	—	—	216	1
Company securities:											
Debenture and loan	1,057	72	532	—	36	—	—	3	50	1,750	8
Preference	357	37	104	—	85	—	—	12	15	610	3
Ordinary	1,538	194	1,759	3,578	2,664	—	—	327	12	6,494	29
Loans and mortgages	1,243	54	32	—	—	77	—	—	126	5,110	23
Land, property and ground rents	729	66	125[8]	—	—	—	—	—	—	920	4
Hire-purchase debt	—	—	—	—	—	659	—	—	—	659	3
Other	141[9]	203[9]	613[10]	47	13	51[11]	—	—	—	1,068	5
TOTAL	7,425	972	4,652	4,359	2,848	796	755	350	215	22,372	100

[1] Figures for some funds are for dates near to 31 December 1963.

[2] At end-March 1964.

[3] Except as shown.

[4] About half of the total is at book value, and half at market value.

[5] Includes local authority temporary money. The figure of 9 shown for hire-purchase finance companies is incomplete.

[6] Nominal values.

[7] Partly estimated.

[8] Information on holdings of 'land, property and ground rents' by local authorities' funds is not available; any figure (which will not exceed 3) is included in 'other'.

[9] Includes the working capital of the companies' agents.

[10] Of which 603 represents loans to parent bodies.

[11] Probably mostly ordinary shares, partly at market value.

Source: Bank of England.

ACQUISITION OF ASSETS DURING 1963
(£ millions)

	Insurance companies		Pension funds	Building societies	Investment trusts	Hire-purchase finance companies	Trustee savings banks (special investment departments)	Unit trusts	Special finance agencies[1]	Total	%
	Life funds	Non-life funds									
Cash and short-term assets (partly net)[2]	1	6	3	14	—20	8	3	2	1	18	1
Gilt-edged stocks:											
0–5 years	22	-4	-14	-23[3]	-6	-6	-3	-1	—	108	6
Over 5 years	88	-9		58[3]	-20		27	-1	—		
U.K. local authority securities:											
Quoted	25	3	20	—	-1	—	35	—	—	194	11
Unquoted			1	39	—		72				
Overseas Government, provincial and municipal securities	2	3	-1	2	—	—	-1	—	—	5	—

Company securities:											
Debenture and loan	146	1	76	—	2	—	—	1	6	232	13
Preference	21	1	5	—	-5	—	—	7	1	30	2
Ordinary	119	—	221	—	116	—	—	46	2	504	28
Loans and mortgages	93	—	4	422	—	19	—	—	13	551	30
Land, property and ground rents	60	2	26	—	—	—	—	—	—	88	5
Hire-purchase debt	—	—	—	—	—	37	—	—	—	37	2
Other	—[4]	—[4]	21[5]	6	2	13[6]	—	—	—	42	2
TOTAL	577[4]	3[4]	362	518	68	71	133	54	23	1,809	100
Rate of growth % during 1963[7]	8½	½	9	13½	3	10	21½	21	12		

[1] Year ended March 1964.
[2] Includes local authority temporary money.
[3] Partly estimated.
[4] Not including changes in the working capital of the companies' agents.
[5] Includes loans to parent bodies.
[6] Unclassified but probably mostly ordinary shares.
[7] Calculated on assets held at the beginning of the year. If the change in market values during the year was taken, the investment trusts and the unit trusts would have a much larger rate of growth than is shown here.
Source: Bank of England.

INSTITUTIONAL SHARE OF MARKET IN
U.K. QUOTED ORDINARY SHARES

	Holdings (*31 March 1964*) market value (£ millions)	%	Turnover (*4th quarter 1964*) (£ millions)	%[1]
Insurance companies	(2,410)	(9)	(75)	(8)
Pension funds	(2,290)	(8)	(75)	(8)
Investment trusts	1,756	6	49	5
Unit trusts	(310)	(1)	(21)	(2)
Total institutions	(6,766)	(25)	(220)	(23)
Other	(20,742)	(75)	(753)	(77)
Total market	27,508	100	973[2]	100

[1] The percentages for the institutions may be underestimated.

[2] Of which transactions on the London Stock Exchange £957 million, new issues £16 million. The total for The Stock Exchange includes, indistinguishably, transactions in overseas equities.

Estimated figures are shown in brackets.

Source: Bank of England.

SCALE OF
MINIMUM COMMISSIONS

GENERAL NOTE

The rates of commission on transactions effected in overseas currencies are chargeable as follows:

(a) Where the transaction is to be settled by the clients in sterling the rate of Commission is to be calculated on the sterling equivalent of the overseas currency price at the effective rate of exchange, any premium paid or received being included.

(b) Where the transaction is to be settled by the client otherwise than in sterling the rate of Commission is to be calculated on the sterling equivalent of the overseas currency price at the spot rate of exchange ruling on the day of the bargain.

A. (1) Securities quoted under the following headings in the Official List:

British Funds, etc. Securities issued by the International Bank for Reconstruction and Development Securities issued by the Inter-American Development Bank Corporation and County Stocks — Great Britain and Northern Ireland Public Boards, etc. — Great Britain and Northern Ireland Commonwealth Government and Provincial Securities† Commonwealth Corporation Stocks†	$\frac{3}{8}$ per cent on Stock up to £10,000 Stock. $\frac{1}{4}$ per cent on Stock on any balance in excess of £10,000 Stock.

†See also A. (2) below.

A. (2)   (i) Securities of or guaranteed by Commonwealth Governments, Provinces or Corporations:
Bonds to Bearer either expressed in a currency other than Sterling

or carrying an option for payment at a fixed rate in a currency
other than Sterling, where the
price is over 100.

(ii) Annuities (dealt in per unit of Annuity) issued by any of the Bodies
mentioned in A. (1) above $\tfrac{3}{8}$ per cent on
consideration.

(iii) Bank of Ireland Stock

B.   Debentures and Bonds and any other
securities representing loans (Debenture
Stocks, Loan Stocks, Notes, Annuities,
etc.) other than those included in Section A above:
Registered $\tfrac{3}{4}$ per cent on
consideration.

Loans quoted in London expressed or
optionally payable in a foreign currency
other than that of a Scheduled Territory $\tfrac{1}{4}$ per cent on
consideration.*

Other Bearer Securities $\tfrac{1}{2}$ per cent on
consideration.

* The concession allowed by Rule 197 (1) or 197D shall not be
applied.

C.   Registered Stocks (quoted
per cent) other than those
included in Section A or B $1\tfrac{1}{4}$ per cent on consideration

D.   Shares or Units of Stock,
Registered or Bearer
(other than Shares in-
cluded in Section E) $1\tfrac{1}{4}$ per cent on consideration.

E.   Shares of Companies incorporated in the United
States of America or
Canada (whether dealt
in in London on a Dollar
or Sterling basis), with
the exception of Shares
which are deliverable by
Transfer $\tfrac{3}{4}$ per cent on consideration.

See the General Note at the beginning of this Appendix.

F. Securities of New Issues passing by delivery in scrip form or by letters of Renunciation:

(*a*) Sales and purchases of Shares and Units of Stock included in Section D and Registered Stocks (quoted per cent) included in Section C $1\frac{1}{4}$ per cent on consideration.

(*b*) Sales and purchases of Debentures and Bonds, etc., included in Section B where these in their final form will be:

Registered $\frac{3}{4}$ per cent on consideration.

Bearer $\frac{1}{2}$ per cent on consideration.

(*c*) Sales and purchases of Securities included in Section A   At discretion until Security is fully paid and then at the rate laid down in Section A.

G. 'Givers' of option money for more than one Account   As on bargains.

'Takers' of option money for more than one Account   Half* the above scale.

Options for one Account or less

Securities Made-up or Made-down

Short-dated Securities (having Five Years or less to run)†   } At discretion.

†*Note*—Not applicable in the case of securities in default.

Unquoted units of Unit Trusts

*When a 'Taker' is charged at less than the scale as on bargains the concessions referred to earlier shall not be applied,

Small Bargains:

No lower Commission than £2 may be charged except in the case of:

(*a*) Transactions on which the Commission may be at discretion.

(b) Transactions amounting to less than £100 in value
on which a Commission of not less than £1 must be
charged.

(c) Transactions amounting to less than £10 in value
on which the Commission may be at discretion.

H.   (a) Powers of Attorney for Inscribed
          Stock   At discretion.

          (b) Transfers other than those in respect
          of bargains   At discretion.

          (c) Valuations:
              (i) Probate valuations
                  Under £5,000   At discretion.
                  £5,000 or over   1s.% on the
                                                   Probate value
                                                   up to £100,000
                                                   and 3d.% on
                                                   the balance,
                                                   subject to a
                                                   m i n i m u m
                                                   charge of 10s.
                                                   per item.

              (ii) Other valuations   At discretion.

QUOTATIONS ON THE
LONDON STOCK EXCHANGE

	All Securities Officially Quoted at 31 March 1967			*Applications for Quotation Granted in the year to 31 March 1967*		
	Number of Securities	*Nominal amount (£ million)*	*Market valuation (£ million)*	*Number*	*Nominal amount (£ million)*	*Proceeds received by issuing undertaking (£ million)*
1. British Government and Government-guaranteed	71	21,775	17,786	10	2,021	1,992
2. Local authority and public boards	572	1,654	1,464	208	330	324
3. Commonwealth Government, provincial and municipal	161	863	709	7	41	40
4. Foreign stocks, bonds and corporation stocks	333	1,728	851	22	101	90
5. Loan capital	2,084	3,693	3,186	} 1,090	1,778	586
6. Preference and preferred	2,382	1,646	1,272			
7. Ordinary and deferred	3,983	12,260	56,763			

Source: The Stock Exchange, London

APPENDIX 4

TABLE OF CHARGES
FOR QUOTATION

*To be made by the Council of The Stock Exchange,
London*

INITIAL CHARGES

(No fee is charged for conversion to stock units, unnumbering of
shares, or applications arising out of change of name, denomination,
dividend rights, or exercise of conversion or option rights.)

1. For all Quotations granted up to £100,000 money value other
   than those indicated above:

Up to £4,999	Nil
£5,000 to £19,999	10 ,,
£20,000 to £49,999	25 ,,
£50,000 to £100,000	50 ,,

2. Quotations involving a money value in excess of £100,000 are
   divided into two categories as under:
   Category I. Prospectuses, Offers for Sale, Placings and
   Introductions.
   Rights, Open offers, Reconstructions, and
   vendor consideration issues.
   Category II. Capitalisations, conversions and further issues
   of identical securities.

   For Category I Quotation charges are in accordance with
   the following scale:
   For Category II Quotation charges are at half the following
   scale:

SCALE OF CHARGES

Money value not exceeding	£200,000	100 guineas
,, ,, ,, ,,	£400,000	200 ,,
,, ,, ,, ,,	£600,000	300 ,,
,, ,, ,, ,,	£800,000	400 ,,

Money value not exceeding	£1,000,000	500 guineas
,, ,, ,, ,,	£2,500,000	750 ,,
,, ,, ,, ,,	£5,000,000	1,000 ,,
,, ,, ,, ,,	£10,000,000	1,500 ,,
,, ,, ,, ,,	£20,000,000	2,000 ,,
,, ,, ,, ,,	£30,000,000	2,500 ,,
,, ,, ,, ,,	£50,000,000	3,500 ,,
,, ,, ,, ,,	£75,000,000	4,500 ,,
,, ,, exceeding	£75,000,000	5,000 ,,

NOTES

1. No charge is made in the case of issues to be quoted in the following sections of the Official List:
   British Funds.
   Securities guaranteed under the Trade Facilities and other Acts.
   Corporation and County Stocks — Great Britain and Northern Ireland.
   Public Boards, etc. — Great Britain and Northern Ireland.
   Dominion, Provincial and Colonial Government Securities.
   Corporation Stocks — Dominion and Colonial.

2. In the case of a joint application for quotation in London and on one or more other Federated Exchanges, the initial London charge will be reduced by $12\frac{1}{2}\%$ or the total of the fees charged by the other Federated Exchanges whichever is the less.

3. Where the money value of an issue is in doubt it will be fixed by the Committee for the purposes of this Schedule.

ANNUAL CHARGES

A quotation charge for each company of 100 guineas per annum.

CONTENTS OF A PROSPECTUS

SUMMARY OF INFORMATION — OFFER FOR SALE OF SHARE CAPITAL

	Reference Companies Act, 1948	Reference Appendix 34*
1. Statement that permission has been obtained from the Capital Issues Committee, where applicable.		
2. Statement that a copy of prospectus and supporting documents has been sent to Registrar of Companies.	S 41	
3. Statement that application has been made to London (and/or other Federated) Stock Exchange for permission to deal in and for quotation for issue.		19
4. Date and time of opening of application lists.	Fourth Sch. 5	
5. Company's full name, date and country of incorporation and authority under which it was incorporated.		17 & 26
6. Authorised and issued or agreed to be issued share capital, amount paid up, description and nominal value of shares. Where 25% or more of capital is unissued a statement that no issue altering the control of the company will be made without shareholders' approval.		20
7. Loan capital and outstanding indebtedness of company and subsidiaries, including bank overdrafts,		21

* Rules and Regulations of The Stock Exchange, London.

	Reference Companies Act, 1948	*Reference Appendix 34*
guarantees, mortgages, hire purchase commitments and any material contingent liabilities.		
8. Voting rights of single-class capital, and, in cases where there is more than one class of share, voting rights of shareholders and rights to dividend, capital, redemption and issue of further shares, with consents to variation of rights.	Fourth Sch. 17	27
9. Terms of offer for sale, followed by instructions for application and conditions of allotment.	Fourth Sch. 6	
10. Full name, address and description of all directors.	Fourth Sch. 3	22
11. Name, address and professional qualification of auditors (and reporting accountants).	Fourth Sch. 15	25
12. Name and address of bankers, solicitors, brokers, registrars and trustees (if any).		24
13. Full name and qualification of secretary, and address of registered office and transfer office.		23
14. *History and Business* The general nature of the business, including the date business commenced, the relative importance of different activities (if applicable) and details of existing and projected subsidiaries. If the company or group trades outside the U.K., a geographical analysis of trading operations and names of principal products.	Fourth Sch. 18	31 & 32

	Reference Companies Act	*Reference Appendix 34*

15. *Management and Labour*
Statement usually including age and length of service of directors, service contracts, number of employees and other details covering continuity of management and labour relations, including pension arrangements.

16. *Plant and Premises*
Situation, area of factories and other main buildings, with details of tenure, freeholds, leaseholds, etc. (in the case of property companies a special layout is required).

31

17. *Working Capital*
A statement that, in the opinion of the directors, working capital is sufficient, and if not, proposals to provide for same. Where new money is being raised by this issue of ordinary shares, or has been so raised during the past two years, an estimate of the proceeds of the issue and an indication of their application.

Fourth Sch. 4 & S. 45

35 & 36

18. *Turnover*
A statement showing sales, turnover or gross trading income during the preceding three financial years, incorporating a breakdown between major trading activities.

33

19. *Accountants' Report*
A report signed by the auditors, including:

(a) *Profits.* Five-year profits record (or less if incorporated more recently), both for parent company and (if applicable) group; notes to this paragraph usually include: (i) the aggregate direc-

Fourth Sch. 19

S.E. requires ten-year record 37

	Reference Companies Act	Reference Appendix 34
tors' emoluments during the last year and the amount payable under the arrangements in force at the date of the prospectus; (ii) details of overseas interests (where material) with the basis on which foreign currencies and taxation have been dealt with, and any restrictions on remittance of funds.		
(b) *Assets and Liabilities*. Figures at the date of last balance-sheet for both parent company and group, including an explanation of the bases used for the valuations of fixed assets and a reasonably detailed indication of the nature of the tangible assets.	Fourth Sch. 19	37
(c) *Intended Purchase*. If proceeds of issue to be used in purchase of business or shares in a company, a separate report on the profits of the business or company for the last five years, and of its assets and liabilities.	Fourth Sch. 20–21	S.E. requires ten years 38
(d) *Dividends*. Dividend record for five years (or less as in (a) above).	Fourth Sch. 19	37
(e) *Accounts*. If date of last accounts earlier than three months before the date of the prospectus, a statement that no subsequent accounts have been made up.		

20. *Profits, Prospects and Dividends*

A statement of current trading with an indication, in the absence of unforeseen circumstances, of the outlook for profits and dividends.	Fourth Sch. 19	34

	Reference Companies Act	Reference Appendix 34
21. *General Information*		
(*a*) Particulars of any issue or change of capital of the company or its subsidiaries within past two years.		30 & 40
(*b*) Particulars of acquisitions within past two years by means of issuance of shares or for cash, with details of directors' interest and goodwill element.		39
(*c*) Names and shareholdings of substantial or controlling shareholders. Details of holdings of directors and their families distinguishing between beneficial and other interests.		30
(*d*) Particulars of present promotion, with consideration of any benefit paid to promoter currently and within past two years.		45 & 47
(*e*) Particulars of preliminary expenses and expenses of issue.		42
(*f*) Statement that no part of proceeds of issue is payable to company, if applicable.		
(*g*) Particulars of capital under option and any commissions, discounts, brokerages or other special terms granted.		41 & 43
(*h*) Statement of surtax clearance and indemnity as to surtax and estate duties, where applicable.		49 & 50
(*i*) *Articles of Association* Details of relevant provisions including those governing:		28
(i) Power of directors to vote remuneration to themselves.		

		Reference Companies Act	*Reference Appendix 34*

(ii) Retirement of directors under an age-limit.

(iii) Borrowing powers.

(iv) Directors' qualifying shareholdings.

(*j*) *Contracts* (not being contracts entered into in the ordinary course of business). All material contracts entered into during the past two years, by company and subsidiaries. Particulars of any consideration (concerning these contracts passing to and from the company.　　Fourth Sch. 14　　51

(*k*) Statement that a Certificate of Exemption has been given by Stock Exchange, where applicable. (This allows certain variations from the full provisions of the Fourth Schedule of the Act where it may prove unduly burdensome owing to the size of the issue, number of possible applicants, etc.)　　S. 39

(*l*) Details of any claim or litigation pending, or a statement that there is none.　　46

(*m*) Statement that no long-service agreements will prevent disposal of management.

(*n*) Declaration that no other capital issues have been made; options granted; commissions, brokerages, or other special terms granted within past two years.　　41 & 43

(*o*) Statement that any experts contributing to the prospectus (normally accountants and surveyors)　　S. 40　　48

	Reference Companies Act	*Reference Appendix 34*
have given and have not withdrawn their consent to the issue of the prospectus and to the inclusion of their report.		
(*p*) A statement that copies of all relevant documents supporting the prospectus may be examined for a period of not less than fourteen days at a place within the City of London (or other place, where quotation limited to other Federated Exchanges).		52
(*q*) The address(es) at which copies of the prospectus may be obtained.	S. 37	

22. The date.

ADVERTISEMENT — PLACING OR INTRODUCTION

The principal difference from the prospectus issued with an offer for sale is that, in place of Paragraph 3 of the prospectus mentioned above, a statement is made that the advertisement is issued in compliance with the regulations of The Stock Exchange, and that the directors accept full responsibility for the accuracy of the information given and also confirm that nothing relevant has been omitted (App. 34 (18)).

PROSPECTUS — ISSUE OF LOAN CAPITAL

In addition to the details included where applicable in the issue of ordinary shares, a prospectus covering the issue of loan capital will normally include, prior to the paragraph dealing with Future Prospects in the main body of the prospectus, paragraphs describing the use to which the proceeds of the issue will be placed; the asset cover; and the interest cover of the stock.

A complete section will also be devoted to particulars of the stock, quoting the provisions of the trust deed and giving the date of the resolution by which the directors created the stock (App. 34 (29)).

The main provisions which are quoted will normally include the following:

1. *Definitions*
   Definitions of the principal terms in the deed, of which the 'Adjusted Total of Capital and Reserves' and the 'Borrowings' may be the two most important.

2. *Security*
   A description of the charge on the assets (floating or specific).

3. *Redemption*
   The terms of redemption with details of sinking fund, if any.

4. *Security for Temporary Borrowings*
   Details of floating charges which the company may create on their undertakings for securing temporary borrowings (normally bank overdrafts).

5. *Further Issues of Stock*
   Details of the provisions under which the company may issue stock ranking *pari passu* in point of security.

6. *Undertakings by the Company*
   Details of action which cannot be taken by the company without the sanction either of the trustees or of an extraordinary resolution, usually a series of negative pledges by the company in respect of the size of aggregate borrowings, and prior or *pari passu* borrowings, the disposal of all or a substantial part of the undertaking, and the borrowing and issuance of shares by the subsidiaries.

APPENDIX 6

GENERAL UNDERTAKING
FOR COMPANIES

.... (name of company)

The following is an Extract from the Minutes of a Meeting of the Board of Directors held the..............day of..............

19......

In compliance with the requirements of the Council of The Stock Exchange, London, it was resolved:

1. To notify the Department[1] without delay of the date of the Board Meeting at which the declaration or recommendation of a dividend will be considered.

2. To notify the Department[1] by telex, telegram, telephone or letter immediately after the relevant Board Meeting has been held:

    (a) of all dividends and/or cash bonuses recommended or declared or the decision to pass any dividend or interest payment;

    (b) of the preliminary profits announcements for the year and half-year required by Schedule VII, Part C, of Appendix 34 to the Rules and Regulations of The Stock Exchange;

    (c) of short particulars of any proposed issue of new capital or any other proposed change in the capital structure; (*Note:* Announcement of a new issue may be delayed to avoid prejudicing underwriting.)

    (d) of any other information necessary to enable the shareholders to appraise the position of the company and to avoid the establishment of a false market in the securities.

3. To notify the Department[1] without delay:

    (a) of such particulars of any acquisitions or realisations of assets as are prescribed in the Memorandum of Guidance Regarding Acquisitions, etc., issued in June 1966;

    (b) of any changes in the Directorate; (*Note:* In the case of the appointment of a Director (other than a Director of another Company part of whose share or loan capital is already quoted), that Director must submit a Declaration in conformity with the Rules and Regulations of The Stock Exchange.)

(*c*) of any proposed change in the general character or nature of the business of the Company or of the Group or any change in voting control or in beneficial ownership of the securities carrying voting control;

(*d*) of an extension of time granted for the currency of temporary documents;

(*e*) of intention to make a drawing of any redeemable securities, intimating at the same time the amount and date of the drawing and, in the case of a registered security, the period of the closing of the transfer books (or the date of the striking of the balance) for the drawing;

(*f*) of the amount of the security outstanding after any purchase or drawing has been made.

4. To forward to the Department[1] four copies of:

(*a*) Proofs for approval (through the Company's Brokers) of all circulars to holders of securities, notices of meetings (other than those relating to routine business of the Annual General Meeting), forms of proxy and notices by advertisement to holders of bearer securities.

(*b*) All circulars, notices, reports or other documents at the same time as they are issued to holders of securities.

(*c*) All Resolutions passed by the Company other than Resolutions passed at an Annual General Meeting for the purpose of adopting the Report and Accounts, declaring dividends and re-electing Directors and Auditors.

5. To circularise to the holders of securities, not later than six months from the date of the notice calling the Annual General Meeting of the Company, a half-yearly interim report containing similar information to that required in Schedule VII, Part C (see Note (iv)) of Appendix 34 to the Rules and Regulations of The Stock Exchange.

6. To include in or circulate with each annual Directors' Report and Audited Accounts or Chairman's statement:

(*a*) (1) A description of the operations carried on by the Company or, if the Company has subsidiaries, the Group.

(2) If the Company or, as the case may be, the Group carries on widely differing operations, a statement showing the contributions[2] of such respective differing operations to its trading results.

(3) If the Company or, as the case may be, the Group trades outside the United Kingdom, a statement showing a geographical analysis[2] of its trading operations.

(b) If the Company has subsidiaries (see Notes (ii) and (iii)), a list giving for each:

(1) its name and country of operations;

(2) the percentage of its equity capital attributable to the Company's interest (direct and/or indirect).

(c) If the Company or, as the case may be, the Group has interests in associated Companies (see Notes (i) and (ii)), a list giving for each:

(1) its name and country of operations;

(2) particulars of its issued share and loan capital and the total amount of its reserves;

(3) the percentage of each class of share and loan capital attributable to the Company's interest (direct and/or indirect).

(d) A statement of persons holding or beneficially interested in any substantial part of the share capital of the Company and the amounts of the holdings in question together with particulars of the interests of each director (and also, so far as he is aware of or can by reasonable inquiry ascertain the same, of his family interests) in the share capital of the Company and, otherwise than through the Company, any of its subsidiaries, distinguishing between beneficial and other interests; the expression 'family interests' includes, in relation to a director, spouse, children under 21 years of age, trusts of which the director or spouse is a settlor or trustee and in which the director or spouse or any of such children are beneficiaries or discretionary objects and Companies known to him to be controlled by him and/or spouse and/or such children and/or the trustees of any such trusts as aforesaid in their capacity as such trustees. Subject to the necessity to distinguish between beneficial and other interests, between the Company and each subsidiary and between each class of capital, each director's interests may be aggregated with those of his family interests.

7. (a) To prepare and make available for inspection at the regis-

tered office or transfer office during the usual business hours on any weekday (Saturdays and public holidays excluded) from the date of the notice convening the Annual General Meeting until the date of the meeting and to make available for inspection at the place of meeting for at least 15 minutes prior to the meeting and during the meeting:

(1) A statement, made up to a date not more than one month prior to the date on which it is made available for inspection, for the period from the end of that covered by the last previous statement (or, in the case of the first such statement, for not less than 12 months) of all transactions (including put or call options, whether or not exercised) of each director (and also, so far as he is aware of or can by reasonable inquiry ascertain the same, of his family interests) in each class of the equity share capital of the Company and any of its subsidiaries since the end of the period covered by the last published statement of such transactions, or during the previous twelve months if no such published statement has been issued; the expression 'family interests' includes, in relation to a director, spouse, children under 21 years of age, trusts of which the director or spouse is a settlor or trustee and in which the director or spouse or any of such children are beneficiaries or discretionary objects and Companies known to him to be controlled by him and/or spouse and/or such children and/or the trustees of any such trusts as aforesaid in their capacity as such trustees. The word 'director' includes a person who was a director at any time during the relevant period but the information required shall not extend to transactions at a time when he was not a director.

(2) Copies of all contracts of service unless expiring, or determinable by the employing Company without payment of compensation, within one year, of any director of the Company with the Company or any of its subsidiaries and, where any such contract is not reduced to writing, a memorandum of the terms thereof.

(b) To state in or by way of note to the notice convening the annual general meeting or any accompanying circular letter, that the said statement or summary of transactions and copies or, as the case may be, memoranda of the said contracts of service will be available for inspection as aforesaid.

8. To insert in the Press a notice showing the basis of allotment in prospectus and other offers, and, if applicable, excess shares, such notice to appear not later than the morning after the allotment letters were posted.

9. To certify transfers against definitive certificates or temporary documents and to return them on the day of receipt or (should that not be a business day) on the first business day following their receipt and to split and return renounceable documents within the same period (see Note (v)).

10. To register transfers and other documents without payment of any fee (see Note (v)).

11. To issue, without charge, definitive certificates within:
    (a) one month of the date of expiration of any right of renunciation;
    (b) 21 days[3] of the lodgment of transfers (see Note (v)).

12. If requested by holders of securities, to arrange for designated accounts (see Note (v)).

13. Where power has been taken under the Articles to issue Share Warrants to Bearer: (i) to issue such Warrants in exchange for registered shares within fourteen days of the deposit of the Share Certificates; and (ii) to certify transfers against the deposit of Share Warrants to Bearer.

14. To send out with the notice convening a meeting to all shareholders and debenture holders entitled to vote thereat proxy forms with provision for two-way voting on all resolutions intended to be proposed (other than resolutions relating to the procedure of the meeting or to the remuneration of the Auditors).

15. In the absence of circumstances which have been agreed by the Committee to be exceptional, to obtain the consent of equity shareholders in General Meeting prior to issuing for cash to other than the equity shareholders of the company:
    (i) equity capital or capital having an equity element,
    (ii) securities convertible into equity capital, and
    (iii) warrants or options to subscribe for equity capital.

16. In the event of a circular being issued to the holders of any particular class of security, to issue a copy or summary of such circular to the holders of all other quoted securities unless the contents of such circular are irrelevant to such other holders.

NOTES

(i) For the purpose of this Undertaking 'associated company' means a company which is not a subsidiary but in which 25 per cent or more of the equity is held by the Company or, if the Company has subsidiaries, by the Group companies collectively (i.e. before excluding any proportion attributable to interests of outside shareholders in the subsidiaries).

(ii) The particulars required in paragraphs 6 (*b*) and 6 (*c*) in relation to subsidiaries and associated companies need not be given for any such company which is dormant or is not material. For this purpose a subsidiary or associated company should be considered material if

(*a*) the total investment in it normally represents more than 5 per cent of the assets of the Company or, as the case may be, of the Group;

or

(*b*) the interest in its profit or loss normally represents an amount which is more than 5 per cent of the profit or loss shown by the accounts of the Company or, as the case may be, of the Group.

(iii) Under circumstances to be adjudicated by the Committee the particulars required in paragraph 6 (*b*) in relation to subsidiaries may be omitted for non-trading subsidiary holding companies.

(iv) As an alternative to circularisation, interim reports may be inserted as paid advertisements in at least two leading daily newspapers.

(v) If the company does not maintain its own registration department, appropriate arrangements must be made with the registrars to ensure compliance with the provisions of paragraphs 9, 10, 11 and 12.

[1] 'The Department' means the Quotations Department of The Stock Exchange, London.

[2] Figures or percentages.

[3] 14 days on or after 1 January 1969.

I hereby certify that the above is a true and correct Extract from the Minutes of the Board.

Secretary

DEALING IN
THE UNITED STATES

STOCK EXCHANGES

New York Stock Exchange; American Stock Exchange, New York; National Stock Exchange, New York (limited trading).

Regional exchanges at Boston; Chicago Board of Trade; Cincinnati; Detroit; Midwest at Chicago; Pacific Coast at Los Angeles and San Francisco; Philadelphia–Baltimore–Washington; Pittsburgh; Salt Lake City; San Francisco Mining; Spokane; Colorado Springs; Honolulu; Richmond.

PRINCIPAL STOCK EXCHANGE

New York Stock Exchange

SECURITIES LISTED AT 31 DECEMBER 1966

	No. of issues	Nominal value ($ million)	Market value ($ million)
Government securities and N.Y. City Bonds	41	99,609	93,887
Foreign Government	210	2,180	1,879
Other bond issues	1,021	38,253	32,376
Common and other stock issues	1,639	—	474,214
Foreign company stock issues	26	—	8,327

SYSTEM

Trading-post.

HOURS OF BUSINESS

10 a.m.–3.30 p.m.

TRANSACTIONS

Normally in lots of 100 (round lots). Amounts less than 100 (odd lots) command wider prices.

EXPENSES

(a) *New York State Tax* (paid by the seller)

Price of stock less than $5   1c. per share
     ,,   ,, over $5 and under $10   2c.   ,,
     ,,   ,,   ,, $10   ,, $20   3c.   ,,
     ,,   ,,   ,, $20   4c.   ,,

(b) *Commission Rates* (paid by both seller and buyer)

Round Lots:

Consideration	Commission rate
$100 to $399	2% plus $3
$400 to $2,399	1% plus $7
$2,400 to $4,999	$\frac{1}{2}$% plus $19
$5,000 and over	$\frac{1}{10}$% plus $39

Odd lots as above with deduction of $2 per transaction.
Minimum commission per transaction $6 and maximum of $1.50 per share or $75 per 100 shares if smaller number.

SETTLEMENT

Most bonds are in bearer form.

Most stock is registered, but transferred by means of renounceable certificates. Foreign holders should register in 'good marking names' to avoid probate problems.

SAFE KEEPING

Securities may be kept either in an American bank (subject to charges for safe custody and for receipt and delivery) or in a U.K. authorised depositary (subject to insurance charges on transport to and from America).

DEALING IN CANADA

STOCK EXCHANGES
Calgary; Montreal (2); Toronto; Vancouver; Winnipeg.

PRINCIPAL STOCK EXCHANGE
Toronto.

SECURITIES LISTED AT 30 DECEMBER 1966

	No. of issues	Market value ($ billion)
Common and other stock issues (including foreign issues)	1,098	95·1

SYSTEM
Trading-post.

HOURS OF BUSINESS
10. a.m.–3.30 p.m.

TRANSACTIONS
Normal units (board lots) are as follows:

	Share price	Unit
Mining shares	Under $1	500 shares
	$1 and over	100 ,,
Others	Under $25	100 ,,
	$25 but under $100	25 shares
	Over $100	10 ,,

MARGIN TRADING
Margin trading permitted for shares with price of $1 or over. 50% margin must be maintained at all times.

EXPENSES
(a) *Ontario Security Transfer Tax* (paid by the seller)
    Bonds: 3c. per $100 or fraction thereof on face, except Government and other State securities.

Shares:

Price	Tax
Under $1	0·1% of price
$1 to $5	¼c. per share
Over $5 to $25	1c. ,,
,, $25 to $50	2c. ,,
,, $50 to $75	3c. ,,
,, $75 to $100	4c. ,,
,, $150	4c. plus 0·1% of value over $150 per share.

(*b*) *Commission Rates* (paid by both seller and buyer)
Bonds: Rate at discretion for Government of Canada issues, Treasury Bills, or bonds.

Shares:

Price	Commission per share
Under $ .05	3/20c. or $1.50 per 1,000
At $ .05 and under $ .10	3/10c. or $3.00 per ,,
,, $ .10 ,, ,, $ .25	½ or $5.00 per ,,
,, $ .25 ,, ,, $ .50	¾ or $7.50 per ,,
,, $ .50 ,, ,, $ .75	.01 or $10.00 per ,,
,, $ .75 ,, ,, $ 1.00	.01½ or $15.00 per ,,
,, $ 1.00 ,, ,, $ 2.00	.02½ or $2.50 per 100
,, $ 2.00 ,, ,, $ 3.00	.04½ or $4.50 per ,,
,, $ 3.00 ,, ,, $ 4.00	.07 or $7.00 per ,,
,, $ 4.00 ,, ,, $ 5.00	.10 or $10.00 per ,,
,, $ 5.00 ,, ,, $ 7.50	.15 or $15.00 per ,,
,, $ 7.50 ,, ,, $ 10.00	.20 or $20.00 per ,,
,, $ 10.00 ,, ,, $ 15.00	.25 or $25.00 per ,,
,, $ 15.00 ,, ,, $ 25.00	.30 or $30.00 per ,,
,, $ 25.00 ,, ,, $ 40.00	.35 or $35.00 per ,,
,, $ 40.00 ,, ,, $ 60.00	.40 or $40.00 per ,,
,, $ 60.00 ,, ,, $ 80.00	.45 or $45.00 per ,,
,, $ 80.00 ,, ,, $100.00	.50 or $50.00 per ,,
,, $100.00 ,, ,, $110.00	.55 or $55.00 per ,,
,, $110.00 ,, ,, $120.00	.60 or $60.00 per ,,
,, $120.00 and over	½ of 1%

Minimun

Total considerations less than $10, commission at discretion.
       „   „ $10 but less than $50, minimum commission $2.
       „   „ $50 or more, minimum commission $5.

Rights, warrants and fractional shares under different basis with minimum commission $1 even on considerations of over $50.

SETTLEMENT

Settlement date three days after transaction.

TRANSFER

Most bonds are in bearer form.

Most shares are registered, but transferred by means of transferable certificates. Foreign holders should register these in good marking names to avoid probate problems. In Canada private shareholders can have stocks in their own names, thus the term 'good marking names' is not used in Canada.

SAFE CUSTODY

Securities may be kept either in Canadian banks (subject to safe-custody charges and charges for receipt and delivery) or in U.K. authorised depositaries (subject to insurance charges on transport to and from Canada).

DEALING IN AUSTRALIA

STOCK EXCHANGES
Australian Associated Stock Exchanges
Adelaide; Brisbane; Hobart; Melbourne; Perth; Sydney.

Recognised Stock Exchanges
Ballarat, Vic.; Bendigo, Vic.; Cairns, Q'ld.; Launceston, Tas.; Newcastle, N.S.W.

PRINCIPAL STOCK EXCHANGES
The Stock Exchange of Melbourne; the Sydney Stock Exchange Ltd.

SECURITIES LISTED
Melbourne at 30 September 1966.

	No of issues	*Nominal value* ($A million)	*Market value* ($A million)
Commonwealth Government securities	50	7,358	7,350
Semi-Government and public authorities	798	783	790
Fixed-interest securities	900	933	876
Common and other stock issues	1,216	3,699	9,350
Foreign issues	14	18	18
	2,978	12,791	18,384

Sydney at 31 December 1966.

	No. of issues	Nominal value ($A million)	Market value ($A million)
Commonwealth Government securities	50	7,522	7,558
Semi-Government and public authorities	666	653	659
Fixed-interest securities	843	1,023	960
Common and other stock issues	1,246	3,873	10,321
Foreign issues	7	9	9
	2,812	13,080	19,507

SYSTEM

Trading-post.

HOURS OF TRADING

10 a.m.–3.30 p.m.

TRANSACTIONS

Marketable parcels are designated by the Australian Associated Stock Exchanges as follows:

    100 shares if price does not exceed $A5
     50   ,,   if price exceeds $A5 up to $A10
     25   ,,   ,,   ,, $A10 ,, $A20
     10   ,,   ,,   ,, $A20 ,, $A40
      5   ,,   ,,   ,, $A40 ,, $A100
      2   ,,   ,,   ,, $A100 ,, $A200
      1   ,,   ,,   ,, $A200

Odd lots are traded through the odd-lot specialist.

EXPENSES

(a) *Stamp Duties*

Stamp duties are levied on all securities, with the exception of Commonwealth loans, and certain mining, chartered and oil company shares. Transfer stamp duties are levied according to the rate payable in the State where the company's register is located (registers in Canberra being exempt). Contract stamp duties also vary from State to State.

(i) *Transfer Stamp Duties*

New South Wales	4c. per $A10 of purchase consideration
Queensland	10c. per $A25 or part of consideration
South Australia	30c. per $A80 of purchase consideration
Tasmania	10c. per $A20 or part of purchase consideration
Victoria	$\frac{3}{8}\%$ of purchase consideration with minimum of 8c.
Western Australia	10c. per $A25 or part of purchase consideration.

(ii) *Contract Stamps*

New South Wales	4c. per $A100 consideration or part thereof on purchase or sale
Queensland	3c. per $A100 ,, ,, ,,
South Australia	10c. per $A400 consideration on purchase or sale.
Tasmania	Nil
Victoria	Nil
Western Australia	5c. below $A200 purchase or sale consideration
	10c. on $A200 and below $A1,000
	20c. on $A1,000 and above.

(b) *Commission Rates*

(i) *Commonwealth Loans*

Loans maturing within three years	$\frac{1}{4}\%$ on first $A10,000
	$\frac{1}{8}\%$ on next $A40,000
	$\frac{1}{16}\%$,, $A50,000
	$\frac{1}{40}\%$,, $A100,000
	$\frac{1}{80}\%$ on over $A200,000.
Loans maturing after three years	$\frac{1}{4}\%$ up to $A50,000
	$\frac{1}{8}\%$ on next $A50,000
	$\frac{1}{20}\%$,, $A100,000
	$\frac{1}{40}\%$ on over $A200,000.

(ii) *Debentures*

Over one year	25c. per $A100 on the paid-up value
Under one year	25c. on first $A10,000
	50c. on amount over $A10,000.

(iii) *Shares*

Listed Companies

(1) On the first $A10,000 of consideration	2%
(2) On the next $A40,000 of consideration	$1\frac{1}{2}\%$
(3) On that amount exceeding $A50,000	1%.

Concessional rates in (2) and (3) above apply to a single instruction given at one time to buy or sell on behalf of one beneficial interest an issue of securities by a company of the same class and paid-up value on that part of the order completed within one month from the date of the order.

Unlisted Companies
Double the above rates.

Minimum Commission
 (i) When the value of order for one security placed on one day is less than $A10, a minimum commission of $A1 is charged.
(ii) When the value of order for one security on one day is over $A10 but less than $A100, a minimum commission of $A2 is charged.
(*c*) *Bank Charges*
Charges for receiving securities into a bank's nominee company or delivering them out of it amount to $\frac{3}{8}$%, with a minimum charge of $A1.50.
A deduction of 1 % is made on interest and dividend payments, with a minimum of 10c.

SETTLEMENT

Transactions for cash. For foreign clients, however, 'overseas delivery' can be specified giving up to six weeks' delay in delivery.

DELIVERY

With the exception of Government and semi-Government bonds, all securities are registered. There are advantages in utilising an Australian nominee company, since rights issues are frequent and often made at par.

SAFE KEEPING

Safe-deposit boxes available at city branches and large suburban branches of all banks. Annual rental up to $A20.
Safe custody of sealed envelopes and small packages available to customers only — no fee.

DEALING IN NEW ZEALAND

STOCK EXCHANGES
Auckland; Christchurch; Dunedin; Invercargill; Wellington.

PRINCIPAL STOCK EXCHANGE
Wellington.

SECURITIES LISTED 1 NOVEMBER 1966

(on all stock exchanges)	No. of issues	Nominal value	Market value
Government securities	37	n.a.	n.a.
Municipal and public boards	n.a.	n.a.	n.a.
Bond issues	40	n.a.	n.a.
Common and other stock issues (no. of companies)	279	n.a.	n.a.
Foreign issues (no. of companies)	63	n.a.	n.a.

SYSTEM
Trading-post.

HOURS OF BUSINESS
9 a.m.–5 p.m., Monday to Friday.

TRANSACTIONS
Transactions are in 'marketable parcels', viz:

Government securities	£200 face value
Local body stocks	£100 ,, ,,
Bonds	£100 ,, ,,
Shares	
Up to £2 per share	100
Over £2 and up to £5 per share	50
,, £5 ,, ,, £10 ,,	25
,, £10 ,, ,, £25 ,,	10
,, £25 ,, ,, £50 ,,	5
,, £50	2

Odd lots are dealt with through brokers appointed for each specific company.

EXPENSES

(a) *Stamp Duty*
3s. 6d. per £NZ50 or part thereof.

(b) *Commission*

(i) *Government and Municipal Stocks*

Up to £NZ25,000 nominal	$\frac{1}{2}$%
Over £NZ25,000 and up to £NZ50,000	$\frac{1}{4}$%
Over £NZ50,000	$\frac{1}{8}$%

(ii) *Debentures*

Debentures	1% on nominal value
Convertible debentures	$1\frac{1}{2}$% ,, ,,

(iii) *Listed Shares*
$1\frac{1}{2}$% of sale price (plus, where unit price is 10s. or less, 5s. per 100 or part of 100 units).

(iv) *Unlisted Shares*
As for listed shares plus 50%.
Minimum commission 10s.

(c) *Bank Charges*
Charges for receiving securities into a bank's nominee company or for delivering them out of it amount to $\frac{3}{8}$%, with a minimum charge of 15s.
A deduction of 1% is made on interest and dividend payments, with a minimum of 1s.

SETTLEMENT

Transactions are for cash settlement. Seller may deliver and demand payment on the first day the exchange is open after the date of sale.

TRANSFER

Almost all securities are registered. There are advantages in utilising New Zealand nominee companies, to preserve the shareholder's interest in rights issues, etc.

DEALING IN BELGIUM

STOCK EXCHANGES
Brussels; Antwerp; Ghent; Liège.

PRINCIPAL STOCK EXCHANGE
Brussels.

SECURITIES LISTED AT 30 DECEMBER 1966

	No. of issues	Nominal value (milliard francs)	Market value
Government securities	128	n.a.	n.a.
Municipal and public boards	119	—	—
Bond issues	49	—	—
Common and other stock issues*	414	—	184·5
Foreign issues	144	—	n.a.

* The total number of stock issues is 424, but the market value is known for 414 only.

SYSTEM
Call-over.

HOURS OF BUSINESS
11.30 a.m.–2.30 p.m.

TRANSACTIONS
For future delivery contracts the Stock Exchange Committee fixes the minimum amounts to be traded for each security; these vary from 5 to 100 securities according to their market value. There are no minimum amounts for cash transactions.

EXPENSES
(a) *Commission*
   (i) *Cash Settlement*
     Government securities   0·3% on market value including accrued interest

Securities redeemable by drawings	0·4% on market value
Belgian Railways preferred stocks	0·6% „ „
All other listed stocks	0·75% „ „
Minimum commission	15 francs.

(ii) *Account Settlement*

All shares quoted for the account	0·6%
Minimum commission	1 franc per share
Carry-overs for the following account	0·3%

(iii) *Monthly Public Sales*

Unlisted shares	0·75% on market value
Minimum commission	1 franc per share or 10 francs per transaction.

(b) *Listing Fee*

(i) *Cash Settlement*

Government Stock	Nil
Bonds and shares	0·05%

(ii) *Account Settlement*

On all shares	0·02%

The listing fees are payable by both buyers and sellers, but only half the fee for both bonds and shares is payable by the client, the other half being paid by the broker.

(c) *Contract Stamps*

Contract stamps are payable both on sale and purchase of securities, and on subscription for new issues, at the following rates:

(i) *Cash Settlement*

Government securities	0·06% of total cost or proceeds including other expenses
All other bonds	0·12% „ „
Shares	0·3% „ „

(ii) *Account Settlement*

Shares	0·15%.

SETTLEMENT

(a) *Cash Settlement*

Dealing in all bonds and listed stocks can be for cash settlement. Fluctuations in prices of securities for cash dealings are restricted from one day to the next, the maximum being 2% for fixed-interest stocks, 5% for stocks listed on the 'parquet market' (shares with a small market and with only one daily price) and 10% for stocks listed on the 'corbeille market' (shares with a very wide market having several prices during the market session), with exceptions for the 72 shares listed at the Account Settlement for which the fluctuations in prices are free.

(*b*) *Account Settlement*
Dealings for settlement in fortnightly accounting periods is permitted for 72 shares, generally those of the largest companies quoted.
The fluctuations in prices are free.

(*c*) *Unlisted Shares*
Auctions in unlisted securities take place at intervals through public sales, organised by the Committee of the Stock Exchange. Alternatively these securities may be traded over the counter. Public sales provide for certain delays in delivery and settlement, but over-the-counter transactions must be settled for cash on the following day.

TRANSFER

All securities quoted on Belgian stock exchanges are bearer.
Registered shares are traded in the special monthly public sales.

SAFE KEEPING

Belgian banks charge a fee of 0·15% on the nominal value for Government securities and on the market value for other issues.

DEALING IN FRANCE

STOCK EXCHANGES

Bordeaux; Lille; Lyons; Marseilles; Nancy; Nantes; Paris; Toulouse.

PRINCIPAL STOCK EXCHANGE

Paris.

SECURITIES LISTED AT 30 DECEMBER 1966

	No. of issues	Nominal value	Market value
		(thousand francs)	
Government securities	21	14,847,282	17,037,061
Municipal and public boards	320	49,855,980	53,011,140
Bond issues	862	11,773,533	11,812,182
Common and other stock issues	963	37,091,165	85,569,520
Foreign issues	144	—	—

SYSTEM

Combination of call-over on the 'open market' and a form of specialist on the 'closed market'.

HOURS OF BUSINESS

11.30 a.m.–noon for bonds enjoying a small market.
12.30 p.m.–2.30 p.m. for all other securities.

TRANSACTIONS

259 stocks, the largest and most representative foreign and domestic securities, are dealt in for both cash and account settlement. All other issues are dealt in for cash settlement.

EXPENSES

(a) *Cash Transactions*
  (i) *Brokerage*
  Government stocks $\frac{8}{10}\%$
  Commercial bonds $\frac{1}{2}\%$
  Shares $\frac{7}{10}\%$

(ii) *Tax*
Commercial bonds $\frac{3}{10}\%$
Shares $\frac{3}{5}\%$

(b) *Account Transactions*
  (i) *Brokerage*
Government stocks $\frac{1}{5}\%$
Commercial bonds $\frac{2}{5}\%$
Shares $\frac{1}{2}\%$

  (ii) *Tax*
Commercial bonds $\frac{3}{20}\%$
Shares $\frac{3}{10}\%$

SETTLEMENT

Transactions can be carried out for cash settlement or account settlement. The account is settled at the end of each month and the market in shares for this settlement is both larger and the expenses lower than for cash settlement.

TRANSFER

Shares can be issued in bearer or registered form, at the option of the shareholder. Partly-paid shares must be in registered form.

Unless otherwise instructed, shares purchased will be deposited with the central clearing agency, Siccovam.

DEALING IN ITALY

STOCK EXCHANGES
Bologna; Florence; Genoa; Milan; Naples; Parma; Rome; Turin; Trieste; Venice.

PRINCIPAL STOCK EXCHANGE
Milan.

SECURITIES LISTED AT 30 DECEMBER 1966

	No. of issues	Nominal value	Market value
		(million lire)	
Government securities	14	2,055,326	2,055,072
Municipal and public boards } Bond issues	372	9,301,794	8,947,780
Common and other stock issues	139	3,377,947	6,636,079
Foreign issues	1	$15.0 m.	$14.8 m.

SYSTEM
Call-over.

HOURS OF BUSINESS
10 a.m.–1 p.m.

EXPENSES
(a) *Contract Stamp Tax*
0·5 lire per 1,000 lire consideration.

(b) *Commission*
Official Commission Rates
(i) Government Securities   0·15% of nominal value.
(ii) Commercial Bonds
Up to a price of 600 lire   2 lire per bond
Over   ,,   ,,   ,,   4   ,,   ,,

(iii) Shares

Up to a price of 100 lire			1 lira per share		
from 101 lire to 250 lire			2 lire ,,		
,, 201 ,, 500 ,,			5	,,	,,
,, 501 ,, 1,000 ,,			6	,,	,,
,, 1,001 ,, 1,500 ,,			10	,,	,,
,, 1,501 ,, 2,000 ,,			14	,,	,,
,, 2,001 ,, 2,500 ,,			18	,,	,,
,, 2,501 ,, 3,000 ,,			20	,,	,,
,, 3,001 ,, 3,500 ,,			24	,,	,,
,, 3,501 ,, 4,000 ,,			27	,,	,,
,, 4,001 ,, 4,500 ,,			30	,,	,,
,, 4,501 ,, 5,000 ,,			34	,,	,,
,, 5,001 ,, 5,500 ,,			38	,,	,,
,, 5,501 ,, 6,000 ,,			42	,,	,,
,, 6,001 ,, 6,500 ,,			46	,,	,,
,, 6,501 ,, 7,000 ,,			48	,,	,,
,, 7,001 ,, 8,000 ,,			50	,,	,,
,, 8,001 ,, 9,000 ,,			60	,,	,,
,, 9,001 ,, 10,000 ,,			70	,,	,,
Over 10,000 lire			0·7% of value		

SETTLEMENT

Monthly accounting periods.

TRANSFER

The great majority of bonds are bearer.

The great majority of shares are registered, although a few are in bearer form.

DEALING IN WEST GERMANY

STOCK EXCHANGES

West Berlin; Düsseldorf; Frankfurt am Main; Hamburg; Munich; Bremen; Hanover; Stuttgart.

PRINCIPAL STOCK EXCHANGES

Düsseldorf; Frankfurt am Main.

SECURITIES LISTED AT 1 JANUARY 1966

Düsseldorf

	No. of issues	Nominal value	Market value
		(million DM)	
Common and other stock issues	219	19,400	n.a.
Foreign issues	18	13,800	n.a.
Foreign bonds	31	2,500	n.a.

Frankfurt am Main

SYSTEM

Trading-post.

HOURS OF BUSINESS

Noon–2 p.m.

TRANSACTIONS

Minimum of DM 3,000 for securities admitted to a consecutive quotation.

MARKETS

(a) *Official Market.* Bonds and shares in the Official List. Quote must be fixed by an official quotation-broker.

(b) *Semi-official Market.* A free market in other shares, controlled by a committee for this purpose. Dealings take place in the stock exchange and marks are printed on the last page of the Official List.

(c) *Over the Counter*. Trading in securities between banks and securities dealers, outside the stock exchange, is unregulated.

EXPENSES

(a) *Securities Turnover Tax*
Public loans	1‰
Bonds	2‰
Shares or promissory notes	2·5‰

(b) *Specialist Fees*
Bonds
Amounts up to DM 50,000	0·075% of nominal value
Over DM 50,000 and up to DM 100,000	0·05% ,, ,,
Over DM 100,000	0·0375% ,, ,,
Shares	0·7% on consideration.

(c) *Commission* (based on normal charges made by banks, but special terms are often made)
  (i) *Foreign Individuals*
Government stocks	0·4%[1]
Bonds	0·4%[1]
Shares	0·8% of consideration

 (ii) *Foreign Authorised Dealers*
Government stocks	0·2%[1]
Bonds	0·2%[1]
Shares	0·4% of consideration

[1] Commission based on percentage of bond price or nominal value, whichever is larger.

SETTLEMENT

Settlement is for cash. Dealings in shares are by nominal value and not by number of shares. For example, a purchase would not be made of twenty Deutsche Bank shares of DM 100 nominal, but of a nominal value of DM 2,000 of Deutsche Bank. Shares are also quoted as a percentage of their nominal value.

TRANSFER

The majority of shares, with the exception of those of a few large companies, mostly insurance firms, are bearer. A centralised clearing system, Girosammelverwahrung, is employed, and where shares are held in safe keeping in the centralised clearing system a warrant will be issued as a note of title.

DEALING IN
THE NETHERLANDS

STOCK EXCHANGES
Amsterdam; Rotterdam; The Hague.

PRINCIPAL STOCK EXCHANGE
Amsterdam.

SECURITIES LISTED AT 30 DECEMBER 1966

(a) *Dutch Common and Preferred Shares*

	Nominal value	Market value
	(million guilders)	
1. International concerns[1]	3,998·9	18,945·9
2. Trade, industry	2,769·1	7,058·9
3. Bank and insurance	919·7	1,897·9
4. Investment companies	816·2	2,952·8
5. Transport	801·1	1,516·1
6. Miscellaneous	249·9	565·0
	9,554·9	32,936·6

[1] i.e. A.K.U., Blast Furnaces and Iron Works, Royal Dutch, Philips, Unilever N.V.

(b) *Dutch Bonds*

Government	10,752	9,558
Local government	1,277	983
Banks and financial institutions	4,239	3,837
Trade, industry, transport, etc.	1,328	1,123
	17,596	15,501

(c) *Number of Securities Listed*

		Domestic	Foreign
Shares	953	602	351
Bonds	1,286	1,025	261
Total	2,239	1,627	612

SYSTEM

Auction market with specialised dealers (*hoekman*).

HOURS OF BUSINESS

1 p.m.–2.15 p.m., Monday to Friday.

EXPENSES

Commissions charged to the public for both shares and bonds are as follows:

(*a*) *Securities quoted as % of par value*   *Commission rate*

Price of up to 10% of par value	2·4% of real value
„ above 10% and up to 30%	0·3% of par value
„ „ 30% „ „ 105%	0·6% „ „ „
„ over 105%	0·6% of real value
Minimum commission per transaction	0·60 guilders

(*b*) *Securities quoted in guilders*

Standard rate for all prices	0·60% of real value
Minimum commission per transaction	0·60% guilders

(*c*) *Securities listed in dollars*

Price of up to $1	0·60 guilders per 10 shares
„ above $1 and up to $2.50	1.20 „ „ „
„ „ $2.50 „ „ $5	2.40 „ „ „
„ „ $5 „ „ $7.50	3.60 „ „ „
„ „ $7.50 „ „ $10	6 „ „ „
„ „ $10 „ „ $30	7.20 „ „ „
„ „ $30 „ „ $45	12 „ „ „
„ „ $45 „ „ $60	13.80 „ „ „
„ „ $60	13.80 (+2.40 for each $10 or part of $10 in excess of $60) per 10 shares.

SETTLEMENT

Cash settlement (four days' delivery).

TRANSFER

The great majority of stocks are in bearer form.

SAFE KEEPING

Brokers and banks are free to charge for safe custody. Charge of an average portfolio is 0·05–0·1% of the real value.

DEALING IN DENMARK

STOCK EXCHANGE
Copenhagen.

SECURITIES LISTED AT 30 DECEMBER 1966

	No. of issues	*Nominal value* (*million Danish kroner*)	
Bonds	912	45,216,102	in the
Shares	155	2,766,130	Official List

SYSTEM
Call-over.

HOURS OF BUSINESS
Each day (except Saturday) from 12.30 p.m. (no closing time is fixed).

TRANSACTIONS
Normal units are as follows:

Bonds	10,000 kr.
Shares	4,000 ,,

MARKETS
(*a*) *Official Market.* Bonds and shares in the Official List.
(*b*) *Semi-Official Market.* Shares in other companies.

EXPENSES
(*a*) *Stock Exchange Turnover Tax*
   Shares   ½% of market value (¼% paid by buyer and seller)
   Bonds   Nil
(*b*) *Commission*

	On consideration	*Minimum*
(i) *Bonds*		
Quoted stocks	0·15%	1 kr.
Unquoted stocks	¼%	1 kr. on Danish bonds
		2 kr. on foreign bonds

(ii) *Danish Shares*
    Quoted   ½%   2 kr.
    Unquoted   1%   2 kr.
(iii) *Foreign Shares*
                    1%   5 kr.

Reduced commission may be given to other firms of stock-brokers, not members of the Copenhagen Exchange, and to banks.

SETTLEMENT

Settlement date one day after transaction.

TRANSFER

Bonds and most shares in bearer form.

DEALING IN SWEDEN

STOCK EXCHANGE
Stockholm.

SECURITIES LISTED AT 30 DECEMBER 1966

	No. of issues	Nominal value	Market value
		(million Swedish kronor)	
Government securities	58	16,198	13,994
Municipal loans	106	2,981	2,594
Bond issues	536	23,354	20,361
Common and other stock issues	112	—	20,015
Foreign issues (only bonds)	16	436	428

SYSTEM
Call-over and afterwards free negotiations.

HOURS OF BUSINESS
10 a.m.–2.30 p.m. (shares 11 a.m.–2.30 p.m.).

TRANSACTIONS
Both 'round lots' and 'odd lots' are dealt in the market-place, but only 'round lots' are published in the official lists.

EXPENSES
(a) *Federal Tax*
  (i) Domestic and foreign shares: 0·3% payable on all transactions, normally charged between seller and buyer.
  (ii) Government and public bonds: tax-free.
  (iii) Other bonds: 0·05% on all transactions, normally charged between buyer and seller.
(b) *Commissions* (payed by both seller and buyer)
  Securities listed

	% on consideration	Kronor per unit
Swedish shares	0·35	—
Swedish bonds with fixed interest	0·10	—
Foreign bonds	0·25	—
Swedish premium bonds	0·20	0.10–0.20

Minimum commission at least 2.50 kr. when consideration does not amount to 500 kr., otherwise 5 kr.

Unlisted securities	% *on consideration*
Shares	0·50
Swedish bonds	0·20
Swedish unsecured debentures	0·25
Foreign bonds and unsecured debentures	0·375

Minimum commissions as for listed securities.

SETTLEMENT

Two days after the date of the transaction.

TRANSFER

Virtually all bonds in bearer form. Shares dealt in are generally endorsed in blank by the registered owner. Bearer shares can be issued only after exemption given by the Government.

SAFE KEEPING

From 1966 banks charge their customers 2.20 kr. per 1,000 kr. of the market value at the end of the year.

DEALING IN NORWAY

STOCK EXCHANGES
Oslo; Bergen; Trondheim.

PRINCIPAL STOCK EXCHANGE
Oslo.

SECURITIES LISTED AT 30 DECEMBER 1966

	No. of issues	Nominal value	Market value
		(million Norw. kroner)	
Government securities	38	2,625	—
Municipal and Public Boards	44	910	—
Bond issues	152	3,600	—
Common and other stock issues	177	830	3,550

SYSTEM
Call-over.

HOURS OF BUSINESS
Official quotation takes place Monday to Friday at 11.30 a.m.

EXPENSES
(a) *Treasury Stamp Duty*
   Shares
   For every 100 kr. or part thereof of the amount on the
   contract note   1 kr.
   Bonds
   For every 1,000 kr. or part thereof of the amount on the
   contract note   1 kr.
   Norwegian Government, municipality and county bonds,
   bonds guaranteed by the Norwegian Government or by
   municipalities and counties, and bonds issued by Norwegian
   authorised credit and mortgage associations are exempt from
   stamp duty.
(b) *Commissions*
   Norwegian Government and other bonds exempt from stamp
   duty   0·15%

All other bonds, debentures and shares guaranteed by the
Government $\frac{1}{4}$%
All other shares $\frac{1}{2}$%
Commission is charged to both buyer and seller.
Minimum commission on any transaction shall not be less
than 3 kr. and not less than 0.30 kr. per share.

TRANSFER

Shares are issued in registered form only.

OVERSEAS HOLDERS

Investment in Norwegian shares by non-residents, and also the
repatriation of proceeds from sales, is subject to licence from the
Bank of Norway.

The Norwegian Companies Act limits non-resident participation
to 10% of paid-up capital of banks and insurance companies, 40%
of paid-up capital of shipping and whaling companies. The majority
of other Norwegian companies, either because of concession laws
or Articles of Association, may bar non-residents from being accepted
as shareholders.

DEALING IN SWITZERLAND

STOCK EXCHANGES
Basle; Berne; Geneva; Lausanne; Neuchâtel; St. Gall; Zürich.

PRINCIPAL STOCK EXCHANGE
Zürich.

SECURITIES LISTED AT 30 DECEMBER 1966

	No. of issues	Nominal value	Market value
		(million francs)	
Government securities	—	—	—
Municipal and public boards	—	—	—
Bond issues	720	—	—
Common and other stock issues	112	—	19,813
Foreign bond issues	202	—	—
Foreign stock issues	76	—	—

SYSTEM
Call-over.

HOURS OF BUSINESS
10 a.m. to noon, Monday to Friday.

EXPENSES
(a) *Federal Tax*
Tax at the rate of 0·03% payable on all transactions in domestic securities normally charged equally between seller and buyer.

(b) *Canton Tax*
Tax of 0·01% on both domestic and foreign securities.

(c) *Commissions*

	Rate per share
Price per share below 1 fr.	At discretion
„ above 1 fr. and up to 5 fr.	0.10 fr.
„ „ 5 „ 10	0.15 „
„ „ 10 „ 15	0.25 „

	Rate per share
Price above 15 fr. and up to 25 fr.	0.30 ,,
,, ,, 25 ,, 50	0.35 ,,
,, ,, 50 ,, 100	0.60 ,,
,, ,, 100 ,, 250	1.0 ,,
,, ,, 250 ,, 350	1.25 ,,
,, ,, 350	⅜% of share price

Minimum Commissions

On amount of less than 5 fr. invested, at discretion; of less than 20 fr., minimum 1 fr.; of 20 fr. or above, 2.50 fr.

SETTLEMENT

Primarily cash transactions, delivery being effected five working days later.

TRANSFER

Virtually all bonds are in bearer form.

Approximately two-thirds of share issues are in bearer form, others registered. Some company articles forbid foreign holders, except through the medium of a Swiss-domiciled bank, in which case voting rights are forfeited.

SAFE KEEPING

(a) *Bonds*

A fee of 1 fr. per 1,000 fr. face value per year.

(b) *Shares*

A fee of 1 fr. per 1,000 fr. market value per year.
Minimum fee per account usually 5 fr.

DEALING IN AUSTRIA

STOCK EXCHANGE

Vienna.

SECURITIES LISTED AT 30 DECEMBER 1966

	No. of issues	Nominal value	Market value
		(million schillings)	
Government securities	70 ⎫		
Municipal and public boards	18 ⎬	47,500	46,800
Bond issues	455 ⎭		
Common and other stock issues	95	4,600	15,000
Foreign issues	11	n.a.	n.a.

SYSTEM

Transactions are arranged by 'Sensale' as intermediaries.

HOURS OF BUSINESS

11.30 a.m.–1 p.m., Monday to Friday.

EXPENSES

	National and foreign	
	Non-banker %	Banker %
(a) Bonds		
Sensal's commission	0·1	0·1
Banker's commission	0·5	0·25
	0·6	0·35
(b) Shares		
Sensal's commission	0·175	0·175
Banker's commission	0·775	0·375
	0·95	0·55

(c) *Unit Trust Certificates* issued by Österreichische Investment-gesellschaft m.b.H., if listed.

Sensal's commission	0·175	0·175
Banker's commission	0·425	0·125
	0·6	0·3

(a)–(c) Minimum commission for small orders

(*schillings*)

7.00   5.00

(However, the commission may not amount to more than 5% of the total amount.)

(d) *Stock Exchange Turnover Tax*

	Dealer's transactions %	Other than dealer's transactions %
National Government, county and municipality bonds	0·02	0·04
Bank and railway bonds	0·03	0·06
Other bonds	0·05	0·1
Unit-trust certificates	0·06	0·12
Shares	0·075	0·15

SETTLEMENT

Settlement by means of a special stock-clearing office (Arrangementbüro).

TRANSFER

All bonds and nearly all stocks are bearer securities.

DEALING IN SOUTH AFRICA

STOCK EXCHANGE
Johannesburg.

SECURITIES LISTED AT 31 MARCH 1967

	No. of issues	Nominal value	Market value
		(thousand rands)	
Government stocks	72	2,732,137	2,593,894
Municipal stocks	178	595,984	527,240
Statutory corporation loans	80	925,327	795,328
Debentures and notes	37	92,686	91,312
Preference shares	264	153,005	148,804
Ordinary shares	649	2,123,540	10,552,245

SYSTEM
Initial call-over followed by two-way open auction.

HOURS OF BUSINESS
9.15 a.m.–3.30 p.m.

TRANSACTIONS
100 shares. Odd-lot dealing in lesser amounts is permitted.

EXPENSES
(a) *Transfer Stamp Duty*
    Government Securities   nil
    All other securities   10 c. per R200 if registered within twelve months from the date of the transferor's signature on the transfer form.

                    Consideration   *Rate*

(b) *Marketable Securities Tax*
    Applied on all purchases and sales.
    (i) Government, Municipal and Debentures

                    Over R10 to R50   10c.
                    „   R50 „ R100   20c.
                    „   R100 „ R200   50c.
                    Over R200 at the rate of
                    50% for R200 or part thereof.

    (ii) All other securities: $\frac{1}{2}$% on consideration.

(c) *Contract Stamp*
    All contract notes bear a duty of 5c.

(d) *Commission*
    (i) Government, Municipal and Debenture Stocks
        On the first R20,000 of the consideration $\frac{1}{4}$%
        On the excess of R20,000 up to R100,000 $\frac{1}{8}$%
        On any excess above R100,000 $\frac{1}{12}$%
    (ii) On short-dated stocks within three years of redemption
        dates, the above commissions are reduced by half.
    (iii) On shares (including options):
        Basic charge $\frac{1}{2}$% per share (maximum R25).
        Brokerage: $\frac{3}{4}$% on consideration.

SETTLEMENT

Cash settlement twenty-four hours after transaction.

TRANSFER

All securities are registered.

SAFE KEEPING

The minimum bank charge is R1.50 per year. Additional charges
depend on the size of the account and are at the discretion of the
banks.

DEALING IN JAPAN

STOCK EXCHANGES

Fukuoka; Hiroshima; Kobe; Kyoto; Nagoya; Niigata; Osaka; Sapporo; Tokyo.

PRINCIPAL STOCK EXCHANGE

Tokyo.

SECURITIES LISTED AT 30 DECEMBER 1966

	No. of issues	Nominal value	Market value
		(million yen)	
Government securities	1	200,000	196,900
Municipal and public boards	38	622,500	501,572
Bond issues	22	27,910	26,664
Common and other stock issues	1,296	4,730,994	9,867,865
Foreign issues	0	—	—

SYSTEM

Trading-post.

HOURS OF BUSINESS

9 a.m.–11 a.m., 1 p.m. to 3 p.m.

For special designated stocks opening trading begins ten minutes before the official hour and closing trading begins after the official hour for each session.

MARKETS

(a) *Listed Stocks*

(i) *First Section*

All listed stocks satisfying certain requirements, including: paid-up capital of at least 1,000 million yen; minimum of 3,000 shareholders; at least 20% of outstanding shares in holdings of less than 5,000 shares (or in case of the company with outstanding shares of 5 million, at least 10%).

(ii) *Second Section*
Listed stocks in smaller companies satisfying certain conditions, including: paid-up capital of at least 100 million yen; minimum of 400 shareholders.

(b) *Special Designated Stocks*
Eight leading stocks, while traded normally during the sessions, have their opening and closing prices determined on a special auction system.

(c) *Margin Stocks*
Only certain stocks in the first section, and none in the second section, are eligible for margin trading. Margin trading is not authorised for foreign investors, but represents as much as 20% to 25% of domestic turnover.

TRANSACTIONS

The unit of transaction for shares with nominal value of 500 yen (mostly utilities) is 100 shares. For those of nominal value of 100 yen or less in the first section it is 1,000 shares, and for others in the second section, 500 shares.

EXPENSES

(a) *Commission rates*
    (i) *Shares* (single transaction)

Price per share	less than 5,000 shares (*yen per share*)	5,000 to 9,999 shares (*yen per share*)
50 yen or under	1·30	1·20
Over 50 yen and not exceeding 75 yen	1·50	1·30
„ 75 „ „ „ „ 100 „	1·70	1·50
„ 100 „ „ „ „ 150 „	1·90	1·70
„ 150 „ „ „ „ 200 „	2·00	1·80
„ 200 „ „ „ „ 250 „	2·20	2·00
„ 250 „ „ „ „ 300 „	2·40	2·20
„ 300 „ „ „ „ 350 „	2·60	2·30
„ 350 „ „ „ „ 400 „	2.70	2·40
„ 400 „ „ „ „ 450 „	2·90	2·60
„ 450 „ „ „ „ 500 „	3·10	2·80
„ 500 „ „ „ „ 600 „	3·40	3·10
„ 600 „ „ „ „ 800 „	4·00	3·60
„ 800 „ „ „ „ 1,000 „	5·00	4·50
For every 200 yen or less exceeding 1,000 yen	1·00	0·90

Price per share						10,000 to 29,999 shares (yen per share)	30,000 shares or more (yen per share)
50 yen or under						1·00	0·90
Over 50 yen and not exceeding 75 yen						1·20	1·00
,, 75 ,,	,,	,,	,,	,,	100 ,,	1·40	1·20
,, 100 ,,	,,	,,	,,	,,	150 ,,	1·50	1·30
,, 150 ,,	,,	,,	,,	,,	200 ,,	1·60	1·40
,, 200 ,,	,,	,,	,,	,,	250 ,,	1·80	1·50
,, 250 ,,	,,	,,	,,	,,	300 ,,	1·90	1·70
,, 300 ,,	,,	,,	,,	,,	350 ,,	2·10	1·80
,, 350 ,,	,,	,,	,,	,,	400 ,,	2·20	1·90
,, 400 ,,	,,	,,	,,	,,	450 ,,	2·30	2·00
,, 450 ,,	,,	,,	,,	,,	500 ,,	2·50	2·20
,, 500 ,,	,,	,,	,,	,,	600 ,,	2·70	2·40
,, 600 ,,	,,	,,	,,	,,	800 ,,	3·20	2·80
,, 800 ,,	,,	,,	,,	,,	1,000 ,,	4·00	3·50
For every 200 yen or less exceeding 1,000 yen						0·80	0·70

(ii) *Bonds*
(1) Government Bonds and Public Board Bonds

Nominal value of a purchase or sale	*Rate per 100 yen of nominal value*
100,000 yen and above but under 1,000,000 yen	0.15 yen
1,000,000 yen and above	0.10 yen

(2) Municipal Bonds and Special Financial Institution Bonds

Nominal value of a purchase or sale	*Rate per 100 yen of nominal value*
100,000 yen and above but under 1,000,000 yen	0.20 yen
1,000,000 yen and above	0.15 yen

(3) Corporate Bonds

Nominal value of a purchase or sale	*Rate per 100 yen of nominal value*
100,000 yen and above but under 1,000,000 yen	0.25 yen
1,000,000 yen and above	0.20 yen

(b) *Other Charges*
The securities transaction tax is levied on all sales at a rate of 0.15 yen per 100 yen of market value of securities sold.

SETTLEMENT

Settlement on the third business day following the date of the transaction. Penalties paid for late delivery.

DELIVERY

Renounceable stock certificates normally in amounts of 500 and 1,000 shares. Power of attorney in favour of a Japanese bank or securities house should be given to protect shareholders' interests in the case of rights, etc., and securities should be held in Japan to effect sales easily.

SAFE KEEPING

Service fee is chargeable by securities companies on foreigners' account for safe keeping of securities and other services. Annual fee is at least 5,000 yen but not over 50,000 yen.

DEALING IN ISRAEL

STOCK EXCHANGE
Tel-Aviv.

SECURITIES LISTED AT 31 DECEMBER 1964

	No. of issues	Nominal value	Market value
		($£I$ million)	
Government debentures	118	254	334
Other debentures (companies, municipalities, etc.)	233	634	776
Ordinary and other share issues	149	584	975

Note: Most debentures are linked as to principal and interest to the official exchange rate of foreign currency or to the cost-of-living index.

SYSTEM
Call-over.

HOURS OF BUSINESS

	Opening time	
Debentures	11.15 a.m.	No fixed closing time.
Shares	11.30 a.m.	

TRANSACTIONS

	Nominal value
Shares	
Round lot in 'opening price session'	I$£$100
,, ,, variable ,, ,,	I$£$1,000
Debentures: no fixed trading unit.	

EXPENSES
Commissions

	Rate on consideration of less than I$£$5,000	of I$£$5,000 or more
Debentures redeemable within twelve months	0·25%	0·25%
Premium bonds	1·0%	0·7%
All other debentures	0·7%	0·5%
Shares and rights	1·0%	0·7%

SETTLEMENT

Cash settlement, through clearing-house, twenty-four hours after transaction.

TRANSFER

Securities are both registered and to bearer, in approximately equal proportion. A considerable amount of securities are deposited with the clearing-house, which, in turn, deposits them for safe keeping at commercial banks or registers them in the name of nominee companies. Most registered securities are registered in the names of nominee companies. There are no transfer fees as long as the security remains in the name of a nominee company. There are small charges, to cover costs, in case of the necessity to transfer in the company's books.

SAFE KEEPING

Safe-keeping charges are not uniform, and amount annually to about $0\cdot3\%$ of market value.

GLOSSARY

ABOVE THE MARKET   At a price in excess of the normal market quotation.

ACCOUNT   (i) The Stock Exchange year is divided into periods, normally of two weeks' duration but over Bank holidays of three weeks, and these are termed accounts. Purchases and sales made during one of these periods are settled on Account Day.

(ii) The ledger entries of a client, jobber, etc.

(iii) The term can be used in reference to clients — 'He introduced several new accounts'.

(iv) Dealing for the new account ('new time') refers to transactions carried out for settlement on the next Account Day but one. Such transactions are permitted in the last two days of the existing account.

ACCRUED INTEREST   The amount of interest which would be due to the holder of the security if interest were paid on a day-to-day basis. In the case of short-dated Government securities, the accrued interest on a daily basis is paid to the seller by the buyer. When yields are calculated on other fixed-interest securities, it is normal to make an allowance for the accrued interest in these calculations.

ACTIVE, ACTIVITY   Used to describe securities in which a comparatively large number of bargains have been transacted.

AD VALOREM   *Ad valorem* is Latin for 'according to value'. The Stamp Act requires that a buyer of most registered securities shall pay a duty based on the value of the purchase.

AGENT   A Register of Agents is maintained by The Stock Exchange. They include chartered accountants, solicitors and others professionally engaged in investment to whom a return of commission can be granted.

ALLOTMENT   (i) The amount of stock or shares allocated to an applicant at the time of an issue.

(ii) 'Allotment letter' is the document of title representing an allotment.

ANOMALY SWITCH   Normally used in reference to the gilt-edged market, an anomaly indicates that the prices of two stocks have moved out of their normal relationship. An 'anomaly switch' is often carried out when this situation occurs, selling one stock and buying the other, with the object of reversing the process when the price relationship returns to normal.

APPRECIATION   Improvement in capital value.

ARBITRAGE   Transactions in securities quoted in two centres, buying in one and selling in the other.

ASSET COVER   Normally used in reference to fixed-interest capital, particularly loan capital, asset cover is the multiple by which the net tangible assets of the company cover the total amount of loan capital in question, i.e. 'asset cover five times'.

ASSET VALUE (per share)   The balance-sheet figure for the net assets available for each ordinary share, calculated by ascertaining the net assets available for the ordinary and dividing it by the number of ordinary shares in issue.

ASSOCIATE MEMBER   A member of a stock exchange who is not a partner in his firm.

ASSOCIATED STOCK EXCHANGES   Stock exchanges operating in provincial areas in England, Scotland, Ireland and Wales, other than London or the Provincial Brokers Stock Exchange.

AUTHORISED CAPITAL   The nominal capital of a company which is authorised by the Memorandum of Association.

AUTHORISED CLERK   An employee of a member firm who is permitted to deal in securities on the floor of The Stock Exchange.

BALANCE   (i) When referring to an uncompleted transaction, the amount still to be bought or sold.

(ii) When referring to a certificate, the amount due to a seller who has disposed of only part of his holding.

(iii) When referring to accounts, the process of ensuring that all entries have been properly completed in the books of account is known as 'finding the balance'.

BARGAIN   Any deal on The Stock Exchange.

BEAR   (i) Anyone who anticipates a fall in prices.

(ii) An individual who, in this anticipation, has sold securities in the hope of repurchasing them at lower levels.

BEARER   Securities that are transferable without the need for registration.

BELOW THE MARKET   At a price beneath the normal market quotation.

BEST   At the most advantageous price obtainable at the time of dealing.

BETTER   In reference to share prices, at an improved level.

BID   (i) Price at which a jobber will agree to buy stock or shares in the market.

(ii) Also short for 'take-over bid', when one company offers to purchase a controlling interest or the whole of another company's shares.

BLUE BUTTON An unauthorised clerk, so called because of the circular blue badge which used to be worn in the buttonhole and which has now been replaced by a blue badge showing the name of the firm.

BOND (i) A term used widely in America and elsewhere to denote a fixed-interest security, such as a debenture.

(ii) In connection with local authority issues, short-dated securities, issued normally in units of £1,000.

BONUS (i) A capitalisation issue.

(ii) An increment to the salaries of stock-exchange employees, normally based on the profits of the firm.

BOOK The operation of a jobber dealing in a specific security is termed 'making a book'.

BOX (i) A small room adjacent to the floor of The Stock Exchange, used by the dealing staff of broker firms.

(ii) A container in the Settlement Room where tickets may be placed for collection.

(iii) A compartment in the security vaults beneath The Stock Exchange building.

BULL (i) Anyone who anticipates a rise in prices.

(ii) Anyone who, in anticipation of this, purchases securities in the hope of selling them at a higher level.

BUYING IN Procedure used in order to obtain the delivery of securities which have not been forthcoming after a reasonable time.

CALL (i) The right to demand payment of additional money due on 'partly paid' securities.

(ii) The option to buy a security at an agreed price at a future date.

CALL-OVER The procedure of fixing opening and closing prices in stock exchanges where auction markets are operated.

CAPITALISATION ISSUE An issue of shares to existing shareholders, without payment, normally created by the capitalisation of reserves (also known as a bonus issue).

CARRY-OVER See Contango.

CASH (i) With reference to company accounts, the item indicating the total credits at the bank.

(ii) 'Cash bargains' or 'dealing for cash' refers to transactions in securities where the settlement is normally on the first business day after the transaction is done, i.e. gilt-edged securities, new issues transferable on allotment letters, etc.

CASH FLOW The amount of money generated by a company each year from its own trading operations.

CERTIFICATE The document of title to a holding of stocks or shares.

CERTIFIED, CERTIFICATION Transfers so stamped, either at the office of the company's registrar or at The Stock Exchange, indicate that the certificate representing the shares transferred has been duly exhibited.

CHARTIST An individual who studies the movement of share prices or indices over periods of time, usually by means of graphs.

CHECKING (i) The agreement between broker and jobber, normally on the first business day after a deal, of the details of the transaction.

(ii) 'Checking the market' is enquiring of more than one jobber the price and amount of shares in a given security.

CHOICE When it is possible to sell or to buy shares at the same price with different jobbers, this is called 'having the choice'.

CLEAN The price of a security (normally fixed-interest) after the deduction of any accrued interest.

CLEARING The name for the Settlement Department to which brokers and jobbers submit a daily list of transactions in certain stocks.

CLEARING STOCKS Those securities which are handled by the Settlement Department.

CLOSE (i) To reverse an open position by either buying a security which has been sold short or selling one which has been previously purchased.

(ii) A small fraction (usually $\frac{1}{64}$ or $\frac{3}{4}$d.) used in quoting securities, i.e. '96 close to close' means $95\frac{63}{64}$–$96\frac{1}{64}$. '10s. close to close' means 9s. $11\frac{1}{4}$d.–10s. $0\frac{3}{4}$d.

(iii) Close company status was introduced in the Finance Act, 1965, to define certain companies. The principal criterion for it is that the company should be controlled by five or fewer persons.

CLOSED END In America and other overseas areas, a 'closed-end trust' indicates an investment trust with a fixed capital, as opposed to an 'open-end trust', indicating a unit trust whose issue of units can expand or contract.

CLOSER When a broker asks a jobber, 'Have you anything closer?', he is enquiring whether the jobber will narrow the margin between the buying and selling prices.

CLOSING THE BOOKS The procedure carried out by the registrar of a company at the time of a dividend or other distribution. Only shareholders on the register at the date of closing the books will receive a distribution.

COMMISSION The brokerage fee charged by member firms, normally based on the minimum scale shown in Appendix 2.

COMMON STOCK The term used in America and other countries to denote equity capital.

CONCESSION Normally used in reference to the minimum scales of commissions where certain bargains attract a reduced scale.

CONSIDERATION The cost of a purchase before adding expenses, calculated by multiplying the amount of stock or number of shares by the price per unit.

CONSOLIDATED ACCOUNTS Accounts which include not only those of the parent company but also the subsidiaries.

CONTANGO Continuation of an open position for a consideration. Securities which have been bought or sold for settlement during one account can be 'carried over' to another account so that settlement is deferred.

CONTINGENT An order which depends upon another order, normally in the opposite direction, being executed at the same time.

CONTINUATION Normally used to explain the commission charge on a bargain where part of the initial order has already been transacted previously.

CONTRACT The invoice signed by the firm of stockbrokers confirming a sale or a purchase.

CONTRACT STAMP The Government stamp affixed to the contract note and paid at the scale shown in Table 5 (pp. 66–7).

CONVERTIBLE Used to describe a security which, normally at the option of the holder, can be converted into another class of security. In particular this refers to loan stocks which may be converted into ordinary shares.

CORPORATE MEMBER A member firm which is constituted as an unlimited company, rather than as a partnership.

COUPON (i) The rate of interest payable on a fixed-interest security, i.e. 'a 5% coupon'.

(ii) On a bearer document, a warrant which is detachable from the certificate and which entitles the owner to some distribution, normally a dividend.

COVER See Asset Cover and Dividend Cover.

CROSS Purchase and sale transactions in the same amount of the same security which are matched within the broker's office, so that the delivery can be undertaken without recourse either to the Settlement Department or the jobbers.

CUM This phrase is used in connection with dividends, rights, etc., and indicates that shares are entitled to the distribution concerned. It is the Latin for 'with'.

CUMULATIVE Normally descriptive of preference shares to indicate that, if the dividend is not paid out of current earnings, it ranks for payment out of future earnings.

DEAL A bargain or transaction.

DEALER One who carries out a bargain. Members of either broking or jobbing firms whose occupation is to buy and sell shares in The Stock Exchange are normally entitled 'dealers'.

DEBENTURE A stock issued by a company, in exchange for the loan of money, normally secured by the pledging of certain assets.

DEED (i) The form of document by means of which securities are transferred from seller to buyer.

(ii) The trust deed securing the issue of loan capital.

DELIVERY The transfer of securities between seller and buyer, or the documents concerned in the transfer. 'Good delivery' indicates that the documents are in order; 'bad delivery' indicates that the documents do not conform with the regulations.

DIFFERENCES The balances due to clients and other member firms at the end of each account.

DISCOUNT (i) The margin by which a stock or share stands below either its issue price or parity value.

(ii) Make allowance for future developments, i.e. 'the price fully discounts an increase in dividend'.

(iii) To quantify the present value of a sum of money at the end of a certain number of years at a given rate of interest.

DISCRETION Orders 'at discretion' are those where the broker is required to use his own judgement in the execution of a transaction.

DIVIDEND COVER The ratio of the available earnings to the dividend distribution, which can be quoted either as a multiple, i.e. 'dividend cover five times', or as a priority percentage, i.e. 'dividend cover 0–20%'.

DRAWINGS Selection of securities for redemption, usually by means of a ballot.

EASIER Descriptive of the market where share prices are lower.

EQUITY Ordinary shares. These are the shares which have the right to participate in all the profits and assets of a company after the rights of the prior fixed charges have been satisfied.

EX The opposite of 'cum': shares quoted 'ex dividend' or 'ex rights' are not entitled to participate in the forthcoming distribution. The word is the Latin prefix meaning 'without'.

EXCESS SHARES   At the time of a rights issue, shareholders are entitled to apply for their proportion of the issue. Any shares for which application has not been received, or which are available through fractions of a share which cannot be allocated, are often available to shareholders as 'excess shares' and rationed between those who apply for them.

EXECUTE   To carry out an order.

FEE   (i) The charge payable for the performance of a service.

(ii) The charge made by companies for the registration of transfers (in the U.K. usually 2s. 6d. per deed). Many companies now dispense with this charge.

FIRM   (i) Descriptive of the market where prices are steady.

(ii) A 'firm' offer or bid is one which is not conditional, as opposed to 'subject' offers and bids (i.e. subject to their being available).

(iii) 'In firm hands' is descriptive of holders of securities who are not short-term operators.

FIXED ASSETS   The assets which are continually employed in a business and which are not intended for conversion into cash in the course of normal trading, e.g. buildings, plant and machinery.

FIXED-INTEREST   Where the interest or dividend payable per annum is not variable.

FLOATING CHARGE   A charge on assets not specifically secured on such assets.

FLOOR   The trading area of The Stock Exchange.

FRACTIONS   (i) In Stock Exchange quotations, particularly those securities quoted per cent, fractions of a £ are used down to $\frac{1}{64}$ ($=3\frac{3}{4}$d.).

(ii) In rights or capitalisation issues, the amount issued may not exactly divide proportionately among shareholders. Since only whole numbers of shares can be issued, the 'fractions' will be sold in the market and the proceeds either distributed in cash to the shareholders or retained by the company.

FRANKED INCOME   Income which has already suffered corporation tax. When received by another corporation, this income does not attract a further liability to corporation tax.

FREE   (i) Referring to securities, particularly new issues, where a purchase does not attract *ad valorem* stamp duty or the company's fee.

(ii) Sales of very small amounts of securities are uneconomical to jobbers owing to the high cost of paperwork involved. They may therefore require the seller to pay the normal *ad valorem* stamp duty and company's fee in order to compensate for these costs. Such sales would be done at the normal bid price in the market, but 'free'.

FREE MARKET A market where it is possible to deal in reasonably large amounts at all times.

FREE OF TAX Usually descriptive of dividend or interest payments where income tax is not payable by the recipient, e.g. building society interest.

FUNDING Raising long-term or permanent capital to repay a debt.

FUNDS (i) Cash.

     (ii) A common term for Government securities.

     (iii) Investment portfolios.

GEARING The relationship between fixed-interest capital and equity. An ordinary share which is 'highly geared' is one where the fixed-interest capital is high compared with the equity capital. The opposite is one which is 'low geared'.

GILT-EDGED A term generally applied to issues of British Government, Dominion and colonial Government, U.K. corporation and certain public authority stocks, originally indicating a first-class security.

GIVER Someone who has purchased shares and wishes to delay delivery until the following account, effecting a contango. The giver normally has to pay a rate of interest to the deliverer of the security to compensate for the delay in payment.

GOVERNMENT BROKER The individual member of The Stock Exchange, London, who acts on behalf of the Bank of England and the Government.

GROSS In connection with yields, the return on an investment before the deduction of tax.

HALF COMMISSION The Stock Exchange rules permit the return of commission to employees in member firms. The maximum which has traditionally been allowed to Stock Exchange members employed by firms is 50%.

HAMMERED When a member or member firm is unable to comply with his liabilities, he is declared a defaulter. The term is derived from the use of a wooden mallet which is struck to command the attention of members to the announcement in The Stock Exchange.

HOUSE The colloquial expression for either the premises of The Stock Exchange or the trading floor.

INDEX, INDICES   Indicators, often constructed from a series of share prices, which are used to illustrate market movement.

INSTITUTION   A term used to indicate a class of corporate investors, particularly the insurance companies, investment trusts, unit trusts, merchant banks and pension funds.

INTEREST COVER   See Dividend Cover.

INTRODUCTION   (i) Since stockbrokers are not permitted by the rules of The Stock Exchange to approach members of the public direct with a view to carrying out business, a formal 'introduction' is required from an existing friend or client.

(ii) Securities which do not enjoy a quotation in a particular stock exchange may obtain this by means of an 'introduction' under certain circumstances, provided that the capital is already widely held and that no part of it requires to be sold immediately.

INVESTMENT COUNSELLOR   An individual who specialises in investment advice and the management of portfolios.

INVESTMENT TRUST   A limited company whose assets are wholly or largely investments and whose operations are primarily the management of those investments. The Finance Act, 1965, lays down certain criteria for these companies as far as taxation is concerned.

IRREDEEMABLE   Having no final date of redemption.

ISSUE   Although to be exact this term should refer to the creation of additional stock or shares, it is generally used to indicate any quotation of a previously unquoted security.

ISSUING HOUSE   An organisation which sponsors issues of stock and shares, often a merchant bank.

JOBBERS   Members and member firms who maintain the market in securities, buying and selling from fellow member firms but without contact with members of the general public.

KAFFIRS   The colloquial term applied to shares of South African gold-mining companies.

LIMIT   A restriction applied to the price at which an order may be executed.

LIMITED MARKET   Descriptive of the fact that dealings in a particular stock or share may be restricted.

LINE   A large amount, i.e. 'line of shares'.

LIQUID   Having cash.

LIQUID ASSETS   Generally, as opposed to fixed assets, cash or assets held for the purpose of conversion into cash during the normal course of trading.

LIQUIDATION   (i) In connection with a company, the fact that it has been or is in the process of being wound up.

(ii) In connection with a line of shares, the fact that it has been or is being sold.

LIST BOOK   Journal used in a stockbroker's office showing, in stock classification, purchases and sales of individual securities during an account.

LISTED   A security 'listed' on a stock exchange is one which is included in the Official List of securities quoted on that exchange.

LISTS CLOSED   At the time of making an issue, the sponsoring organisation closes the application list at a time after which no further applications will be considered. The advertised particulars or prospectus must state the time at which lists will open and, if the issue has been fully subscribed, it is normal to close them shortly after the opening time.

LONG   (i) Having a 'bull' position. Particularly used of a jobber who has purchased more stock than he has sold.

(ii) In reference to a Government stock, having a life of more than about fifteen years.

MADE UP (MADE DOWN)   Refers to the process of settling bargains following the 'hammering' of a member firm.

MAKING-UP PRICE   Price supplied by the jobbers in the Settlement Department for the purpose of settling payment of transactions between member firms in clearing stocks.

MARGIN   An amount payable on a speculative order by a client, the broker financing the balance. Should the price of a security bought 'on margin' fall to such an extent that, if the purchase were reversed the loss would use up all the margin payment, the broker is normally at liberty to close the transaction to avoid involving his own capital in risk.

MARK   The price at which a bargain has been executed, recorded for publication in the Official List and in certain daily newspapers.

MARKET   (i) The trading floor of The Stock Exchange.

(ii) A section of that floor, i.e. the 'oil market', the securities comprising that section, or the jobbers dealing in those securities.

(iii) The freedom of dealing in a particular security, i.e. 'enjoys a free market'.

MARKET PRICE   The price of a security quoted in the market.

MARKET VALUE   The amount of stock or shares multiplied by market price.

MARKETABILITY   Freedom of dealing in a security.

MATCH (or MARRY)   A broker who receives orders from different clients both to buy and sell the same security is permitted to match one against the other. In order to ensure, however, that the price is fair to both sides, he must first offer the business to the market. Usually the business is 'put through' a jobber at a very small price difference.

MEDIUM-DATED   Normally used for fixed-interest securities with final redemption dates of between ten and fifteen years.

MERCHANT BANK   A City banking house which engages in some or all of many activities such as acceptance credits, export finance, issue of securities, etc.

MIDDLE PRICE   A price mid-way between the bid and offered price.

MONEY STOCKS   Short-dated securities used as alternatives to deposits, i.e. short-dated Government securities, etc.

NAMES   (i) Names and addresses of clients used in registration of securities.

(ii) The department concerned with passing tickets, which used to carry this information.

NAMES DAY   The day on which tickets for purchases are passed.

NEGOTIATION   Dealings in securities which do not enjoy a free market are carried out 'by negotiation', which means that some delay will probably ensue before a jobber can find a buyer either to take the security or to make a bid for it.

NET   (i) In dealing with country brokers, contracts for relatively small amounts may be rendered at a 'net' price, i.e. a price which takes account of the London broker's commission.

(ii) In connection with yields, the return after deducting tax.

NEW   (i) In connection with stock or shares, this usually applies to a recent issue, particularly where securities are transferable on allotment letters or renounceable certificates free of *ad valorem* stamp duty and the company's fee.

(ii) In connection with the account (or 'new time'), this refers to the account just about to commence, not the current account.

NO PAR VALUE (N.P.V.)   Shares having no nominal value.

NOMINAL   (i) When referring to a share, the value printed on the share certificate, i.e. 'shares of 5s. each'. This must not be confused with the market price.

(ii) When referring to a quotation in the market, this indicates that it is impossible to deal in this security except by negotiation.

NOMINATION   Applicants for admission to membership of The Stock Exchange, London, must obtain the right of nomination. This can be purchased from retiring members at the normal price ruling in the market.

NOT TO PRESS (N.T.P.) Where a security enjoys only a restricted market, a jobber may sell shares which he has not got on the understanding that the buying broker will not press for delivery.

ODD LOTS A broken or small number of shares, or amount of stock, which, in American markets, necessitates a wider price than 'round amounts'.

OFFER FOR SALE A public issue where securities are offered to the public for purchase.

OFFERED (i) Where shares are easily obtainable in the market they are said to be 'freely offered'.

(ii) 'Offered, not bid' indicates that there are only sellers, not buyers, of this particular security.

OFFICE (i) 'General office' applies to the departments in a stock-broking firm which are concerned with the accounts and the transfer of securities.

(ii) 'In the office' indicates that an initiating order has been given by one of the brokers' own clients and is not a market bid or offer.

OFFICIAL LIST The Stock Exchange Daily Official List of securities, closing prices and prices at which transactions have taken place (marks), published daily by The Stock Exchange, London.

OPEN-ENDED (i) An expression used in the U.S.A. to indicate that a fund is based on the unit-trust principle where its capital can fluctuate by the variation in the number of units in issue.

(ii) In referring to loan-stock issues, the trust deed provides for further issues of similar stock subject to certain carefully defined limits.

OPENING PRICE (i) The price at the opening of the market each day.

(ii) The first price quoted in dealings in a new issue.

OPTION The right to deal in a security at a fixed price over a specified period. A 'call option' gives the right to purchase a security at the 'striking price' over a period normally up to three months. A 'put option' gives a similar right to sell the security. A 'double option' gives the right up to the end of the period to buy or sell.

ORDER An instruction to buy or sell a security.

ORDINARY The most common title for the equity or capital of a company which is entitled to the residue of both profits and assets after the rights of the prior-charge capital have been satisfied.

OVERSUBSCRIBED   In the case of a new issue, where applications are received for a total in excess of the amount available, the issue is said to be 'oversubscribed'.

PAR   The nominal or face value.

PARI PASSU   Having equal rights.

PARTICIPATING   (i) In connection with capital, usually preference shares, holders are entitled not only to the fixed-interest dividend, but also to an additional distribution as described in the particulars of the issue.

(ii) Participating partners in stockbroking firms are those who derive their remunerations solely from a share in the residual profits after the fixed charges have been met. It should be pointed out, however, that all partners whether participating or not are at risk as to the whole of their resources on behalf of the firm.

PARTLY PAID   Securities on which a liability still exists which may be called in due course.

P/E RATIO   The ratio of price as to earnings which is used in assessing relative values of shares in the market, since it indicates the number of years' purchase of latest earnings represented by the price.

PLACING   Direct sale of securities by stockbrokers to their clients. This term is used either in the context of a new issue or in disposing of other securities which they are instructed to sell.

PORTFOLIO   A list of holdings in securities.

POSITION   The state of an operator's book, particularly a jobber's, showing whether he is 'long' or 'short' of a security.

POST TRADING   System of operating a stock market where buying and selling of securities takes place at fixed points, known as 'trading posts'.

PREFERENCE CAPITAL   Capital whose holders are entitled to prior rights as far as dividends and assets are concerned.

PREMIUM   (i) In the case of a new issue, the excess of the market price over the issue price.

(ii) This term is also used to indicate the excess over the nominal value of quoted stocks.

(iii) 'Dollar premium' is the excess over the official rate of exchange which must be paid for investment dollars required to purchase securities outside the Sterling Area.

PROBATE PRICE   The price of a security accepted by the Estate Duty Office, which is normally the bid quotation from the

Official List plus one-quarter of the difference between this and the offered quotation. It is also sometimes called the 'quarter up' price.

PROCEEDS The amount raised on a sale, having taken into account the expenses.

PROSPECTUS The document published in connection with the issue of securities, subject to both statutory requirements and the rules and regulations of The Stock Exchange.

PROTECT An offer, usually by a jobber, to maintain a 'firm' bid or offer while the stockbroker consults his principal or endeavours to obtain a better price elsewhere.

PROVINCIAL BROKERS STOCK EXCHANGE The association of stockbrokers operating in areas which do not have their own stock exchanges.

PUT OPTION The right to sell a security at the 'striking' price within some specified period.

PUT-THROUGH See Match.

QUOTATION (i) A dealing price in the market.
 (ii) The price taken from the Official List.
 (iii) In the case of securities previously unquoted, the Council of The Stock Exchange grants 'permission to deal' and 'official quotation' when they approve an application for quotation.

RED BUTTON Settlement Room clerks, who check their firm's bargains, wear a red button in their lapel and are termed 'red buttons'.

REDEEMABLE With reference to a stock, one which is repayable at some future date.

REDEMPTION YIELD Used in connection with a stock which is repayable, the yield is calculated to include both the interest receivable and an annual increment to allow for the increase or decrease in capital value to redemption. In calculating the 'net redemption yield', allowance is made for income tax and capital-gains tax at the relevant rates.

REGISTRATION The process of including a holding of securities in the company's books or other appropriate register.

RENOUNCEABLE CERTIFICATES Documents of title which bear, usually on the reverse, facilities for the original allottee to renounce his holding in favour of someone else.

RENUNCIATION FORM That part of a renounceable certificate or an allotment letter which is completed by the allottee in renouncing his allotment.

RETURN　(i) Income obtainable from an investment.

(ii) Return of commission is allowable by stockbrokers to certain agents on the relevant stock exchange register, namely banks and certain professional individuals such as chartered accountants, solicitors, etc.

RIGHTS　Any entitlement. In the case of issues to existing shareholders on a proportionate basis, this is generally known as a 'rights issue'.

RULING PRICE　The market price applicable at the time.

SCRIP　(i) Any form of security, particularly those in bearer form.

(ii) 'Scrip issue' is a term often applied to a capitalisation issue.

SECURITY　(i) A generic term used to describe all stock exchange investments.

(ii) A document of title.

(iii) Assets pledged as collateral for a loan.

SELLING-OUT DEPARTMENT　The Stock Exchange department to which a seller resorts if he is unable to obtain the ticket from the buyer so that he may deliver a security.

SERVICE COMPANY　A company owned by a stock exchange partnership which carries out the essential servicing of the firm. Utilisation of a service company may have tax advantages.

SETTLEMENT　(i) The seven-day period during which accounts between member firms are settled.

(ii) The date of payment for securities bought and sold.

(iii) Short for the Settlement Department, that section of The Stock Exchange which 'clears' the most active stocks.

SHAPE　Where one purchase is satisfied by a number of sales, or vice versa, the part deliveries are known as 'shapes'.

SHORT　(i) Having a 'bear' position. Particularly used of a jobber who has sold more stock than he has bought.

(ii) In reference to a Government stock, having a life of less than five years.

SHUNTER　Brokers who transact business on an arbitrage basis with the provincial exchanges.

SINKING FUND　A fund, normally established in connection with an issue of loan capital, to extinguish all or part of the liability over a period.

SPECIALIST　A stock exchange member (especially in New York) who arranges the matching of transactions at the trading post.

SPLIT　The division of a ticket, or the loss involved in this division.

SPONSOR　The issuing house or stockbroker arranging the details of a new issue.

SPREAD　A diversity of interest, usually to describe the constitution of an investment portfolio between different classes of security and holdings in different geographical and industrial areas.

SQUEEZE   Application of pressure. This term is applied both to Government pressures on restricted credit and also to operations by jobbers to force bears to buy back their stock or bulls to liquidate.

STAG   A speculator who applies for a new issue with the object of selling his allotment when dealings commence and taking a profit.

STAMP   See Ad Valorem and Contract.

STAND   The communication system on the floor of The Stock Exchange is controlled by 'waiters' who occupy raised seats, somewhat like open pulpits, which are known as 'stands'. Each member firm is allotted one or more stands, depending on the nature of the business, and contact may be obtained here with members of the firm.

STRIKING PRICE   See Option.

SUBJECT   An offer or bid from the market, which has been made to more than one broker, is designated 'subject' to denote that it is not 'firm' and may thus not be available unless accepted immediately.

SWITCH   An exchange from one security to another.

TAKE-OVER   A bid by one company to acquire another.

TAKE UP   To pay for a security, normally one allotted at the time of a new issue.

TAKER   (i) Someone who, in a contango transaction, having sold a security will accept a rate for not delivering it.

(ii) In an option transaction a 'taker' is one who acquires an option to sell.

TAP   An expression applied to a security where consistent sales are coming from one source, in particular a Government issue where the departments are gradually liquidating their holdings to the public.

TAPE   Two services supply information reproduced in subscribers' offices, the Exchange Telegraph Company and Reuters Ltd. Information received in this manner is known to be 'on the tape'.

TENDER   A method of selling securities, particularly new issues, whereby applicants submit bids independently and the issue is either allocated to bidders from the highest price downwards (e.g. issues of water stocks) or an issue price is selected at which subscriptions fully cover the offer and the required spread of shareholders is established.

TICKET   A slip, prepared by the buying broker, to identify a purchase and passed, either through the Settlement Department
or through the jobbers, to the selling broker.

TICKET DAY   The second day of the settlement and the day on
which tickets must be passed. This is also called Name Day.

TITLE   Short for entitlement, denoting ownership.

TRACE   The act of identifying, or the record of, the intermediaries between the seller of a security and the buyer. When
a ticket is given by the buying broker to the market it may pass
through several hands before it finally reaches the selling broker
who will deliver the security. The names of the firms through
which it passes are recorded on the back of a ticket in the case
of registered securities.

TRADE   To deal or do business.

TRANSACTION   The name applied to any completed purchase or
sale of securities.

TRANSFER   (i) The act of exchanging a security from one owner
to another.

(ii) The document recording the change of ownership which
is signed by the vendor is the 'transfer deed', abbreviated to
'transfer'.

TURN   This term generally refers to the difference between the bid
and offered price quoted by a jobber. The jobber's 'turn' is
only the same as the gross profit he makes on a transaction in
a security when he buys and sells equal quantities at the bid
and offered prices.

UNAUTHORISED CLERK   An employee of a member firm who is
admitted to the trading floor of The Stock Exchange but is not
allowed to deal in securities. See also Blue Button.

UNDATED   A security without final date of redemption is termed
'undated'.

UNDERWRITE   To insure. Offers of securities to the public are in
most cases underwritten as a form of insurance that the issue
is fully subscribed.

UNFRANKED INCOME   Revenue which has not already suffered
U.K. corporation tax.

UNIT   (i) A subdivision of capital quoted as 'stock', i.e. 5s. stock
unit.

(ii) Unit trust. An investment fund formed under the terms of a
trust deed. Unlike an investment trust, which is a company with
a fixed capital, the capital of a unit trust fluctuates with the
injection or withdrawal of funds by investors.

UNQUOTED   Having no quotation on a recognised stock exchange.

UNSECURED   Usually descriptive of loan capital having no specific assets earmarked as security.

VOTING RIGHTS   Rights attached to share capital which permit the owner to vote at general and other meetings of the company under circumstances laid down in the Memorandum of Association.

WAITER   The uniformed attendants in The Stock Exchange, London. The name is derived from the origins of the stock market, which first operated in a City coffee-house.

WALL STREET   The colloquial term used for the New York Stock Exchange.

WITHHOLDING TAX   Tax deducted at source from dividend payments, especially in the case of overseas companies, where tax is deducted before dividends are remitted to non-residents.

YIELD   The yield is the annual return from an investment. It is usually quoted per cent. In the case of dated securities see Redemption Yield.

RECOMMENDED READING

F. E. Armstrong, *The Book of the Stock Exchange* (Pitman, 5th ed., 1957). Now out of print.

H. D. Berman, *The Stock Exchange* (Pitman, 4th ed., 1963).

Investors Chronicle, *Beginners, Please* (Eyre & Spottiswoode, 2nd ed., 1960).

E. V. Morgan and W. A. Thomas, *The Stock Exchange* (Elek Books, 1962). A history.

'Nedlaw', *Stock Exchange Precedents for the Professional* (Straker Bros., 1961).

L. G. Whyte, *Principles of Finance and Investment* (Cambridge U.P., 2 vols., 1950).

INDEX

Capital-gains tax, 42, 146
Capitalisation issues:
  dividend rate, 169
  eligibility, 169–70
  marketability, 169–70
Cash flow, 111
Cash transactions, 59–60
Central Stock Payment Office, 63,
  75, 83, 94–5, 95–8
Certification Office, 94
Charts, 117
Checking of market in different
  exchanges, 7–8
City of London College, 202
Clearing banks, and new issues
  market, 232–3
Clearing House Splits Account, 83
Clerks:
  authorised, 10, 50
  unauthorised, 10, 50
Clients' ledgers, 70–1, 79
Closing transactions, 42, 68
Commission, 8, 34–5, 42, 45, 67
  scales of, 245–8
Companies, General Undertaking
  for, 259–64
Companies Act (1967), 10, 212
Company accounts:
  balance-sheet figures, 108–9
  cash flow, 111
  profit and loss account, 109–10
  profitability, 110
Company visits, 111–15
  organised, 115
Compensation funds, 120–1
Computers, 117–18, 134, 224–5
Concessions, 67–8
Consolidation of accounts (foreign
  markets), 235–6
Contangos, 43, 75
Continuation, 67
Contract Department, 63–5
Contract journals, bought and sold,
  69
Convertible stocks, 143, 172
Cork Stock Exchange, 14
Corporate memberships, 124
Corporation tax, 146

Costing, 129–32
Country brokers, sales and service,
  34

Daily Express, 39
Daily Mail, 39, 209
Daily Mirror, 209
Daily Telegraph, 39, 209
Day-to-day finance, 121–2
Dealing staff, 50–4
Debenture market, 143–6
  definition, 143
  future of, 228
  issue size, 144
  new issues, 172
  security, 144–5
  taxation, 146
  terms, 145
Declaration Day (options), 45
Delivery of securities:
  bought bargains, 83, 85
  general procedure, 60–3
  sold bargains, 90
Denmark, dealing in, 287–8
Dictum Meum Pactum (Stock Ex-
  change motto), 54
Disputes, 12
Dividend account, 98
Dividend Department, 97–8
Dividend ledger, 97–8
Dividend yield ratios, 117
Dividends, 28
  bought bargains, 97–8
  claiming period, 97
  foreign securities, 193–4
  sold bargains, 98
Dublin Stock Exchange, 14

Earnings, 28–9
Economist, 40
Equities, 26
Estate Duty Office, 32
  and new issues, 152
European Common Market, 234
Examinations, Stock Exchange,
  203–4
Exchange Telegraph Co. Ltd., 40
Ex dividend list, 95